BIBLE
ARCHAEOLOGY

I dedicate this book to my children,
Carl and Cathe,
who walked with me
over a good portion of these biblical lands.
Al Hoerth

I dedicate this book to my grandchildren,
Melanie, Zachary, Jonathan, Michael, Anna,
Mitchel, Matthew, and Skyler,
with whom I am blessed to share my love
for the Holy Lands.
John McRay

BIBLE
ARCHAEOLOGY

An Exploration of the History
and Culture of Early Civilizations

ALFRED HOERTH
JOHN MCRAY

BakerBooks

Grand Rapids, Michigan

© 2005 Lion Hudson Ltd/
Tim Dowley & Peter Wyart trading
as Three's Company

Published in 2005 by
Baker Books
a division of Baker Book House
Company
P. O. Box 6287,
Grand Rapids,
MI 49516-6287

Library of Congress
Cataloging in Publication Data
is on file at the Library of
Congress,
Washington, D.C.

ISBN 0-8010-1287-2

Book Design: Peter Wyart

Except where noted otherwise, all
Scripture quotations in this book
are from the Holy Bible: New
International Version, © 1973,
1978, 1984 by the International
Bible Society. Used by permission
of Zondervan Bible Publishers.

Worldwide co-edition organized
and produced by
Lion Hudson plc
Mayfield House
256 Banbury Road
Oxford OX2 7DH
England
Tel: +44 (0) 1865 302750
Fax +44 (0) 1865 302757
email: coed@lionhudson.com
www.lionhudson.com

Printed in Singapore
1 2 3 4 5 6 05 04 03 02 01 00

Picture Acknowledgments

Photographs
akg-images, London, Erich,
Lessing: pp. 61, 81
Ashmolean Museum, Oxford: pp.
36 top, 43
Bildarchiv Preussischer
Kulturbesitz pp. 59, 64
The Bridgeman Collection: p. 84
bottom left
British Museum: pp. 42, 108
Tim Dowley: pp. 9, 26, 71, 118,
151, 158, 159 top, 161 top, 164,
165 bottom, 168, 170 bottom, 172
top, 180, 185, 191 top, 195, 197,
199, 200 top, 221 bottom, 224
bottom, 231, 245 top, 250, 251 top,
274, 275 top right
Werner Forman: pp. 68, 69, 90
Heritage Image Partnership:
p. 132
Al Hoerth: pp. 5, 7, 72, 75, 85 top,
89, 97, 100, 102, 103, 104, 109,
116, 118 inset, 122 top left, 126,
137, 139, 141, 142–143, 144, 145,
212, 213
James Hoffmeier: p. 80 bottom
Israel Government Tourist Office:
pp. 153, 157, 174–175, 178, 203
John McRay: pp. 10, 17, 136, 150,
155, 159 bottom, 161 bottom, 163,
165 top, 166 top, 167, 169, 170 top,
171, 172 bottom, 176, top, 177,
179, 181, 182, 184 top, 186 top,
187, 188, 190, 194, 196, 198, 200
bottom, 201, 202, 204, 206, 211,
216, 219, 220, 221 top, 222, 223,
224 top, 225, 226 top, 227, 228,
229, 230, 232, 233, 234, 235, 236,
238, 239, 240, 241, 242, 243, 244,
245 bottom, 249, 251 bottom, 252,
253, 254, 255, 256, 257, 258, 259,
260, 261, 262, 263, 264, 270, 271,
272, 273, 275 top left and bottom,
276, 277, 278, 279, 280
Oriental Institute of the University
of Chicago: p. 54
Zev Radovan: pp. 36 bottom, 40
bottom, 47 top, 98, 105, 110, 111,
121, 122 top right, 123, 124, 125,
133, 138–139, 146, 192
Jamie Simson: p. 63
Tiger Design: p. 217
Peter Wyart: pp. 27, 28, 40 top, 41
top, 48, 50, 51, 55, 120, 152, 156,
157 inset, 160, 162, 166 bottom,
176 bottom, 184 bottom, 186 bottom, 189, 191 bottom, 205, 226
bottom

Illustrations
Brian Bartles: p. 173,
Tony Cantale: p. 15
Jeremy Gower: pp. 56–57, 63, 77,
86, 103, 111, 113, 114–115
James MacDonald: pp. 15, 39, 41

Charts
Peter Wyart: pp. 20–25, 38, 60, 62,
183
Three's Company: p. 117

Maps
Tiger Design Ltd/Hardlines

Contents

Preface   6

1. Archaeology and the Bible   9

2. Mesopotamia and the Bible   31

3. Egypt and the Bible   67

4. Palestine and the Bible: Old Testament   95

5. Persia and the Bible   129

6. Palestine and the Bible: New Testament   149

7. Anatolia and the Bible   209

8. Greece and the Bible   247

9. Italy and the Bible   267

Recommended Reading   282

Index   284

PREFACE

This book is written with the intention of covering the most significant archaeological data relevant to the people and places named in the Old and New Testaments. The authors' aim is to provide historical, geographical, and literary material that will enrich the knowledge of everyone who is interested in a fuller understanding of the Bible in its cultural setting and thus provide a basis for deeper faith and appreciation for what God has done throughout history to bring about the fulfillment of his promises.

It is not the purpose of this volume to debate controversial topics with academicians but rather to provide information for the vast reading public who want to know what archaeology has to contribute to their understanding of, and confidence in, the Bible as the Word of God. For those who want to go a step further in their quest for a deeper understanding of the archaeological data available, each author has written a textbook on the academic level: Alfred Hoerth, *Archaeology and the Old Testament*, 1998, and John McRay, *Archaeology and the New Testament*, 1991, both published by Baker Book House. Both authors recently retired from Wheaton College, where undergraduate and graduate degrees in Biblical Archaeology are offered.

Hoerth taught Old Testament studies at the college for 29 years. Prior to that he was a Research Archaeologist with the University of Chicago's Oriental Institute. Hoerth has made nearly twenty trips to the Mediterranean and Near East, residing there as briefly as one week and for as long as two years. Besides excavating in the United States, he has participated in, or directed, ten excavations in Egypt, Israel, Jordan, Sudan, and Syria. He has also taught in seminaries and graduate schools in Costa Rica, Estonia, and Israel.

McRay taught New Testament studies at Wheaton College for 22 years. Prior to that he taught for 20 years in three other schools, which included serving as a professor of Bible at Harding University in Searcy, Arkansas, and David Lipscomb University in Nashville, Tennessee, and then as Professor of Religious Studies at Middle Tennessee State University in Murfreesboro, Tennessee. McRay has made twenty-six trips to the Holy Lands, and has been an area supervisor for eight seasons of excavation at the sites of Caesarea Maritima, Sepphoris, and Herodium in Israel. He has lectured internationally on archaeology and the New Testament in Croatia, England, Greece, Germany, Czechoslovakia, Israel, Russia, and Australia.

Thanks are due to Tim Dowley for his invitation to write this volume and for his dedicated and expert assistance in bringing

The king fights a bull: Hall of One Hundred Columns, Persepolis.

the project to fulfillment. Thanks are also due to Rhona Pipe for her expertise in editing the manuscript, to Peter Wyart for his care and attention in designing the book, and to Nick Jones for his enthusiasm in getting the project under way.

Readers will find B.C.E. (Before Common Era) and C.E. (Common Era) in some archaeological publications. The authors prefer to use the B.C. and A.D. time designations.

Alfred Hoerth
John McRay

1

ARCHAEOLOGY AND THE BIBLE

ARCHAEOLOGY AND THE BIBLE

Archaeology is by definition the "study of antiquity," and in its quest to recover and better understand earlier civilizations it embraces much more than excavation. Many relevant fields of study, such as language, geography, history, art, geology, biology, and chemistry, are utilized by archaeologists as they reach into the past.

Archaeology is especially valuable in supplying information about objects, places, and activities for which no historical data exist. Sometimes historical records are clarified, or even corrected, by archaeological discoveries.

The investigation of classical sites in the Mediterranean world is a field of inquiry

Archaeological excavations in progress at Tell Gezer, Israel. Note the carefully measured squares.

Heinrich Schliemann gives an account of his exploits at ancient Troy to a London meeting.

designated Classical Archaeology, while the exploration of sites farther east is called Near Eastern Archaeology. Biblical Archaeology focuses on those areas of both Classical and Near Eastern Archaeology that have biblical relevance.

THE ROLE OF BIBLICAL ARCHAEOLOGY

Biblical Archaeology is a scientific discipline, which, when properly employed, can contribute to the placement of the Old and New Testament narratives in their correct historical and cultural settings for more accurate interpretation of the biblical text. In this respect it can do for Abraham, Moses, Jesus, or Paul what Classical Archaeology does for Alexander the Great or Homer, and Near Eastern Archaeology for Hammurapi or Ramses II. The milieu in which different peoples of the Bible lived and worked has

been greatly illuminated by the discovery of a wide range of cultural evidence: homes, domestic utensils, coins, burials, temples, religious artifacts, public buildings, and weapons of warfare, to mention just a few.

As archaeology helps place biblical characters and events within the stream of extra-biblical history and geography, it answers those who would try to mythologize the Bible. But it must be recognized that it does not "prove" the truth of the Bible in its theological and spiritual statements. The excavation and identification of such biblical sites as Babylon, Caesarea, Corinth, Ephesus, Hazor, and Susa have greatly illuminated our understanding of these ancient cities and their historical settings, but this has not proved the Bible to be the Word of God. A similar, though non-biblical, parallel would be when Heinrich Schliemann's passion to demonstrate the historical accuracy of Homer's *Iliad* led him to search for Troy. He did excavate Troy, but he did not prove

11

that the *Iliad* is true, only that it is historically accurate in its geographical placement of the site.

The Bible does not need confirmation of its theological truths or its historical references in order to do that for which it was written and canonized, that is, to produce faith in the hearts and minds of its readers. The author of the Gospel of John stated his purpose for selecting which materials to include in his writing with these words: "These are written that you may believe that Jesus is the Christ, the Son of God, and that by believing you may have life in his name" (John 20:31).

Archaeology provides a means of looking beneath the soil of contemporary civilization and beyond the limits of twenty-first-century contexts to identify for a time with the world in which the activities of God occurred under his direction. Archaeology is an important tool that enables a person to put on twentieth-century B.C. glasses when reading the story of Abraham, fifteenth-century B.C. glasses when reading about the life and work of Moses, and first-century A.D. glasses when reading the stories of Jesus and his disciples. It is a thrill for the archaeologist to pause occasionally and reflect on the fact that he or she is in the actual place where a biblical event occurred, whether in a valley, on a mountain, by a river, or among the ruins of an ancient city.

ARCHAEOLOGICAL MILESTONES

Since early in the Christian era, people have been fascinated by the history of the eastern Mediterranean countries, regarded by Jews, Christians, and Moslems as the Holy Lands. Helena, mother of Constantine, the first Roman emperor to be a Christian, visited this part of the world in about A.D. 328, and built churches over some of the holiest places. Her visit is recorded by a contemporary historian and friend of the family,

Eusebius of Caesarea, and is discussed in church histories written within a century of her death. These records are confusing, some of them claiming that Helena alone constructed the churches, and others that they were built by both Helena and Constantine. But they all agree that the churches were built during the reign of Constantine, a view supported by the archaeological evidence.

Holy places

Eusebius himself made a careful search for the holy places, and left a record of more than one thousand place names in his book *Onomasticon*, which we have today. In the centuries that followed, pilgrims went to the Holy Lands largely for religious purposes, although occasionally study-visits were made, prompted largely by an interest in history, art, architecture, sculpture, or coins. Efforts to obtain antiquities of this kind amounted to little more than treasure-hunts, having very little scientific value for the archaeologist.

Probably the earliest recorded attempt at what we might properly call archaeological excavation was made on 1 October 1738 at Herculaneum in southern Italy by the Spanish engineer, Rocco Giocchino de Alcubierre, assisted by the Swiss architect, Karl Weber, and later by Francesco La Vega, although these were not excavations in the modern sense of the term.

Herculaneum, like Pompeii, which was first excavated on 23 March 1748 by Alcubierre and Giacopo Martorelli of Naples, was covered when Mount Vesuvius erupted in A.D. 79. The "excavations" consisted of tunneling operations into the hardened mud lava, which was more than fifteen meters (fifty feet) thick in some places. In this way the excavators gained access to underground streets, buildings, and passageways through which they removed many of the precious treasures of the buried city. There was none of the systematic, sci-

Excavated Sites in Palestine

Tell Dan
Tell Anafa

Hazor

Acre **GALILEE**

W. el-Mughara
Tiberias
Sea of Galilee

Tell Megadim Carmel Caves
Ubeidiya

Athlit Beth-Shearim

Megiddo *Jezreel Valley*
Beth Alpha

Caesarea
Wadi Ara Beth-Shean

Hadera *Mt. Gilboa* Gilead

Mt. Ebal Tell el-Fara'h

Shechem

*M E D I T E R R A N E A N
S E A*

Tell Qasile *Mt. Gerizim*

Jaffa

W. Natuf Bethel
Ekron Jericho
Gibeon
Beth- Gibeah
Shemesh Qumran

Tell Ashdod *Valley of Sorek*

Ashkelon Tell el-Hesi *W. Maraba'at*

Galli Mareshah Beth-
Hacchcrem
Gaza Lachish Beth-Zur
Tell es-Safi Hebron
En-Gedi

Jordan R.

Dead Sea

Mt. Casion

El-Arish

Arad Masada

Tell Beersheba

Judaean Desert

N E G E B

Har Yeroham

A R A B A H

▲ *Kadesh-barnea*

Jebel Helal ▲

S I N A I

● Major excavations

| | | | | | | |
| 0 | 10 | 20 | 30 | 40 | 50 | 60 miles |

| | | | | | |
| 0 | 20 | 40 | 60 | 80 | 100 km |

Timna

Ezion-geber

Workers remove a gigantic human-headed bull from the mound at Nineveh, directed by Sir Austen Layard.

entific removal of layers of earth, carefully recorded, measured, drawn, and reported, which characterizes modern archaeological excavations. Pompeii, unlike Herculaneum, rested beneath layers of soft pumice, ash, and earth.

Precious stones

The continuing search for ancient treasure was extended to the Near East in 1799 by the unexpected discovery, by an officer of Napoleon, of a stone with a trilingual inscription. This was the famous "Rosetta Stone" (see page 94). Throughout the nineteenth century, entrepreneurs filled the museums of Europe and the private collections of wealthy sponsors with antiquities taken from the Near East.

Expeditions were also sent to Mesopotamia. Paul Botta ravaged Khorsabad, ten miles north of Nineveh, in 1842, and filled the Louvre in Paris with antiquities from the reign of Sargon II, an Assyrian monarch. Sir Austen Layard, beginning in 1845, surpassed Botta, and filled the British Museum with still greater treasures from Nineveh,

from the reign of another Assyrian king, Ashurnasirpal II.

Reading the tablets

However a positive note amidst this plunder of the past was struck between 1846 and 1855 when Sir Henry Rawlinson deciphered the cuneiform script of the Old Persian language on the trilingual Behistun Relief, the "Rosetta Stone of the East" (see page 137). Soon the Elamite and Akkadian languages were also deciphered, and in this way the history of Assyria and Babylonia was opened to the world, through the translation of stone inscriptions and clay tablets, approximately 500,000 of which have now been discovered.

Since Palestine itself, the land comprising modern Israel, Jordan, and Syria, seemed to be largely devoid of valuable artifacts, the first scholars there undertook geographical surveys and the identification of ancient sites. Prominent among those who performed this vital work were the Germans Ulrich Seetzen and Johan Ludwig Burckhardt (1805), the Americans Edward Robinson and Eli Smith (1838), and the Britons

C. R. Conder and H. H. Kitchener (1872).

Palestinian excavation began in Jerusalem in 1850 with the Frenchman F. de Saulcy, but his work was unscientific; he mis-dated the tomb of Helen of Adiabene by 600 years. The British archaeologist Charles Warren worked in Jerusalem from 1867, as did the Frenchman Charles Clermont, but their work was no more scientific than that of de Saulcy.

In 1890, the English Egyptologist Sir Flinders Petrie worked briefly at Tell Hesi in Palestine and observed that each layer in the tell contained its own unique type of ceramic pottery. By carefully recording the pottery in each layer one could observe the changes in cultural occupation. He saw that some of the pottery had different forms, which he recognized from his work in Egypt. There he had found similar pottery in contexts which could be dated from inscriptions found at the levels in which the pottery was discovered. In this way originated "ceramic typology," the most important technique in modern Palestinian archaeology for dating stratigraphic levels which do not contain inscriptions or coins. More often than not the pottery had been broken, and the potsherds had to be carefully extracted from the debris and studied for identification and possible reconstruction.

POTS AND DATES

The importance of Petrie's discovery was almost immediately acknowledged as revolutionary. Since ancient people often made their own pottery, when they moved from one place to another they did not bother to take it with them because it was so inexpensive. Since pottery was virtually imperishable, every layer of a tell contains an abundance of potsherds. Once this was recognized, a chronology based on ceramic typology had to be established so that more precise dates could be given to the changes in pottery styles, which could be distin-

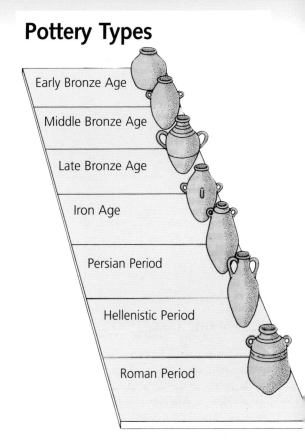

Pottery Types

Early Bronze Age

Middle Bronze Age

Late Bronze Age

Iron Age

Persian Period

Hellenistic Period

Roman Period

Diagrammatic explanation of ceramic typology, by which different pottery styles help date strata at a dig.

guished as precisely as changes in car models today.

The man who recognized and met this need was the pre-eminent Near Eastern archaeologist, William Foxwell Albright. Working at Tell Beit Mirsim in southern Palestine from 1926–1932, he was fortunate enough to excavate a well-stratified mound with enough pottery in each stratum to record scientifically the typological and chronological evolution of their major forms. His work remains the basis of all modern ceramic typology, which is constantly being refined by continuing excavation.

Some of the largest excavations in Palestine were carried out before this method of dating had matured, and were for this reason less effective than if they had been conducted later. This is true, for example, of the original excavations at Jerusalem, Samaria, Jericho, Tanaach, Megiddo, Gezer, Lachish, and Hazor. Most of these have been re-excavated since World War II by British, American, and Israeli archaeologists.

EXCAVATION

Most excavated sites in the Near East are tells (mounds) that were formed by the successive rebuilding of those sites on the same spot because fresh water was available and the hill on which they were founded was defendable, or perhaps because it was near a main road, or had some religious importance. Surprisingly, it was not until the nineteenth century that the scholarly world became convinced that these mounds were not just natural hills, but that ancient cities were buried within them. Some tells contain twenty or more rebuildings and a variety of reasons account for the successive "living levels": for example, earthquake, fire, war, urban renewal. Like layers of a cake, each new level added another stratigraphical layer to the site's history. When excavating, the archaeologist reads the history of the site from the surface down, from the most recent to the most ancient.

Many sites of classical antiquity, for example, Rome, Ostia, Pompeii, Herculaneum, Corinth, Philippi, Ephesus, Sardis, Pergamon, and Hierapolis, are not tells. The same is true for classical sites in Palestine, such as Caesarea, Jerash, Baalbek, and Petra. Some sites in Palestine, such as Capernaum, Magdala, and Chorazim, simply were not founded on hills or not occupied long enough to generate successive levels of occupation.

Archaeological excavation is not an exact science capable of producing irrefutable evidence for a given hypothesis. If properly conducted, however, it is a unique and comprehensive method of research that employs scientific technology in the exca-vation, investigation, and evaluation of cultural data. Methods of excavation vary to some degree depending on the size and nature of the site under investigation. However, a general outline of what is involved may be helpful.

One or more directors initiate an archaeological dig. An administrator handles such details as travel arrangements for the team, on-site transportation, housing, and meals. Normally a site will have several areas under excavation at the same time, and each area will have a supervisor. The supervisor directs the work of volunteers, who do much of the actual excavation. Field architects and photographers record the daily progress, while other specialists, such as botanists, geologists, linguists, and paleontologists, study the excavated materials. The funds necessary to mount an excavation are sometimes provided by interested individuals. On other occasions institutions such as schools, museums, and foundations underwrite the expenses.

ARCHAEOLOGISTS AND THEIR TOOLS

Tools used in excavation typically include picks (including a small hand-held pick called a *patish*), trowels, brushes, baskets, plumb bobs, and tape measures. Heavy equipment, such as front loaders, back hoes, and bulldozers, is sometimes used, but only when there is sufficient overburden to ensure that there is no danger of damaging important aspects of the site not yet uncovered. Computers and microfiche systems are frequently used on-site to record data and to make reference libraries available in the field.

In recent decades, archaeologists have made use of increasingly sophisticated tools. Both ground and aerial photogrammetry are now employed to produce better maps as well as extremely accurate three-dimensional drawings of balks, tomb

Tell Beth Shan. Beth Shan was an important Canaanite center in the Old Testament (see for example 1 Samuel 31). Archaeologists have found that the tell contains eighteen levels of occupation and despite years of excavation only a small portion of the site has been studied. By New Testament times occupation had shifted to the base of the tell where Scythopolis, in the foreground, spreads out around tell Beth Shan and would also take many years to excavate fully.

facades, and other structures. Laser guided and computerized transits allow faster and more accurate area surveys and architectural drawings to be made. Magnetometers and resistivity instruments locate underground features. Infrared photography can locate stone structures beneath the surface by measuring the different amounts of heat given off by the stones and the soil around them. Neutron activation analysis and "thin section petrographic analyses" of temper and clay content are two ways of determining if pottery was made locally or brought into the area from elsewhere.

Currently, some archaeologists prefer to do regional studies rather than excavate a specific site. Others choose to excavate sites that are small, and perhaps only one or two occupation levels in depth. These smaller sites are more likely to be completely excavated and published within the available time and resources. Some large sites, on the other hand, will probably never be fully, or perhaps even sufficiently, dug. The Israeli archaeologist Yigael Yadin once estimated that at the rate he was excavating the 200-acre (82-hectare) biblical site of Hazor it would take eight thousand years to finish. How long would it take to completely excavate the eight thousand acres of Caesarea Maritima!

OLD TESTAMENT CHRONOLOGY

There is a tendency to think of ancient history as little more than a stream of dates in which kings ruled or battles were fought. Some dates are, however, a necessary tool.

17

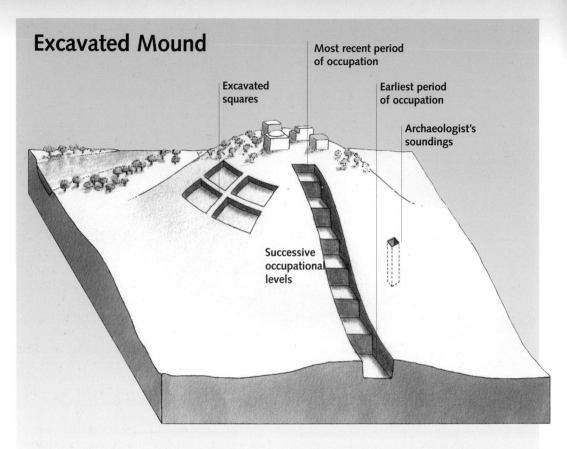

Excavated Mound

Most recent period of occupation

Excavated squares

Earliest period of occupation

Archaeologist's soundings

Successive occupational levels

Archaeologists' squares. Archaeologists generally excavate within 5 or 10 meter squares. (In the Near East archaeologists use the metric system for recording.) The undug perimeters of the squares are called balks. The stratigraphy in their vertical faces is studied to help determine when a new occupation level has been reached within the square. Measurements are taken, both horizontally and vertically, of important artifacts as they are uncovered so that the exact findspots within the square can be plotted on the drawing the field architect makes of each level. Artifacts are tagged with square and level information and placed in appropriate containers to be transported to the field house for cleaning and analysis. The area supervisors prepare detailed descriptions of each day's work.

Without them, for example, it would be impossible in the next chapters to mesh the Bible with extrabiblical history.

Beginning with Abraham, the Old Testament spans some 1,500 years of history. Abraham fits early in what archaeologists call the Middle Bronze Age (c. 2300–1550 B.C.), but conservative scholars are divided over whether he lived in the twenty-second or twentieth century B.C. To take a position on the matter, it is necessary to work back from the firm dates available in the first millennium B.C. Chapter 3 accepts the statement of 1 Kings 6:1 that 480 years elapsed between the Exodus from Egypt and the fourth year of King Solomon's reign, rather than that the time span is erroneous or only symbolic. Solomon's fourth year can be fixed at 967 B.C., and this then gives 1447 B.C. as the date of the Exodus.

The Hebrew of Exodus 12:40 is open to two interpretations, and chapter 4 follows those scholars who take its 430-year time-span to encompass both the Patriarchal period and the Egyptian sojourn, rather than only the Egyptian sojourn. This choice puts Joseph into the Hyksos period, when upward mobility in society was more possible than had previously been the case. Additionally, Joseph rode in a chariot (Genesis 41:43), and chariots were not introduced into Egypt until the time of the Hyksos. If 1 Kings 6:1 and Exodus 12:40 are understood this way, the beginning of Abraham's life (chapter 2) occurred during the chaotic years of the Isin-Larsa period. Terah would have had good reason to move his family out of southern Mesopotamia during that turbulence.

The exodus from Egypt and the conquest of Palestine both fall within the Late Bronze Age (c. 1550–1200 B.C.). The period of the Judges extends from Late Bronze into the Iron I period (c. 1200–1000 B.C.). Some scholars have faulted the Bible for not naming the pharaohs involved with Abraham, Joseph, and Moses, and have used this silence as evidence that the Bible's early history is suspect. Egyptologists have, however, established that until the tenth century B.C. the title "pharaoh" stood alone in Egyptian texts. It was only then that the title began to be followed by the name of the specific king. The biblical writers were simply following Egyptian precedent. Shishak is the first Egyptian pharaoh to be named in the Bible (1 Kings 11:40). In 925 B.C. his army marched into Palestine (1 Kings 14:25).

Until the first millennium B.C. (largely Iron II and III in archaeological terms), the Bible contains only a handful of date pegs. Then, by contrast, the books of Kings and Chronicles are very rich in chronological detail. The years of reign for all the kings of Judah and Israel are given, often with synchronisms between the two countries. Some events are placed within a specific year of a king's reign, and some are recorded in both the Bible and extrabiblical history. But when this wealth of information is carefully studied, various disharmonies seem to exist within the biblical text. Charges of "obvious error" were raised by liberal scholars, and "corrected" chronologies were proposed.

Then in the 1950s the scholar Edwin R. Thiele demonstrated that the Old Testament followed several chronological practices in use in the ancient Near East. For example, when a king died he was awarded full credit for the year of his death. Depending on the system then in vogue, his successor would either wait until the next full year to begin counting the years of his reign (the accession year system), or he would claim the partial year in which he took the throne as his first year (the non-accession system). In the non-accession system both the dead king and the new king were given credit for the same calendar year, thus creating an artificial year in the records. Thiele was able to identify when the non-accession system was in use in the Old Testament.

Kings in the ancient Near East sometimes had their sons join them on the throne so that the heir apparent could gain experience in how to govern. The king also hoped the "coregency" would lessen the likelihood of a struggle over the throne when he died. The problem this practice created for chronology is that in the official records both father and son were given full credit for the years of coregency. Thiele determined when coregencies occurred within the reigns of the kings of Israel and Judah and where overlaps in years of reign need to be recognized. Thiele's application of these and the other chronological principles to the reigns of kings of Israel and Judah, known as "Thiele's chronology," has been accepted by both conservative and liberal scholars.

The Kings and Prophets, based on Thiele's Chronology

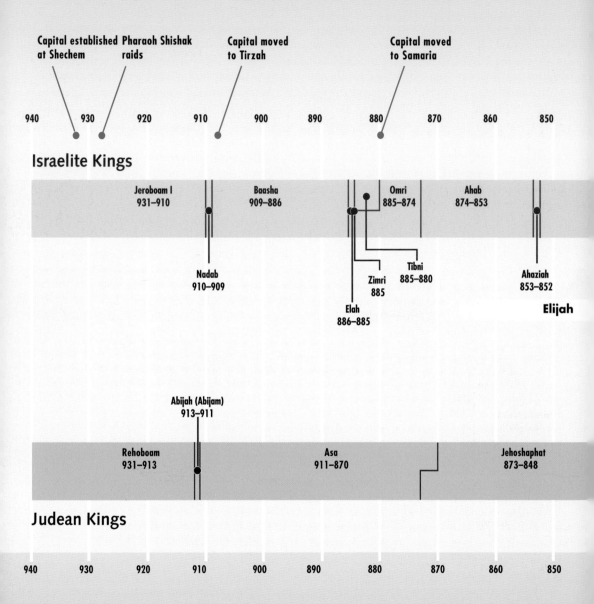

Capital established at Shechem

Pharaoh Shishak raids

Capital moved to Tirzah

Capital moved to Samaria

940   930   920   910   900   890   880   870   860   850

Israelite Kings

Jeroboam I
931–910

Baasha
909–886

Omri
885–874

Ahab
874–853

Nadab
910–909

Tibni
885–880

Zimri
885

Ahaziah
853–852

Elah
886–885

Elijah

Abijah (Abijam)
913–911

Rehoboam
931–913

Asa
911–870

Jehoshaphat
873–848

Judean Kings

940   930   920   910   900   890   880   870   860   850

Pays tribute to
Shalmaneser III

Amaziah defeated,
Jerusalem sacked.

| 850 | 840 | 830 | 820 | 810 | 800 | 790 | 780 | 770 | 760 |

| Joram (Jehoram)
852–841 | Jehu
842–814 | Jehoahaz
814–798 | Jehoash (Joash)
798–782 | Jeroboam II
793–753 |

Amos

Elisha

Jonah

Isaiah

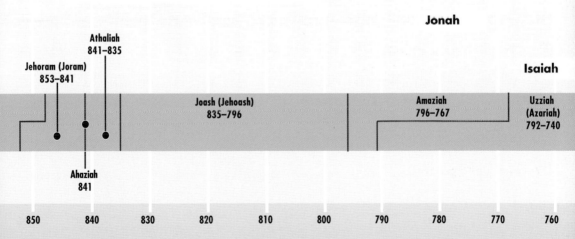

Athaliah
841–835

Jehoram (Joram)
853–841

Joash (Jehoash)
835–796

Amaziah
796–767

Uzziah
(Azariah)
792–740

Ahaziah
841

| 850 | 840 | 830 | 820 | 810 | 800 | 790 | 780 | 770 | 760 |

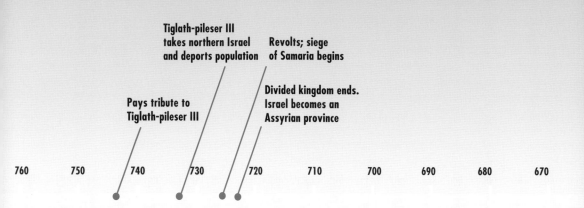

Tiglath-pileser III
takes northern Israel
and deports population

Revolts; siege
of Samaria begins

Pays tribute to
Tiglath-pileser III

Divided kingdom ends.
Israel becomes an
Assyrian province

| 760 | 750 | 740 | 730 | 720 | 710 | 700 | 690 | 680 | 670 |

Israelite Kings

| Jeroboam II 793–753 | Menahem 752–742 | Pekah 752–732 | Hoshea 732–722 |

ASSYRIA

Zechariah
753

Shallum
752

Amos

Hosea

Micah

Isaiah

| Uzziah (Azariah) 792–740 | Jotham 750–732 | Ahaz 735–716 | Hezekiah 716–687 |

Judean Kings

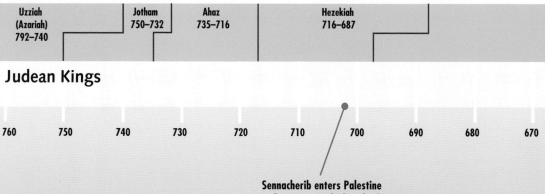

| 760 | 750 | 740 | 730 | 720 | 710 | 700 | 690 | 680 | 670 |

Sennacherib enters Palestine
and captures Lachish and other cities

22

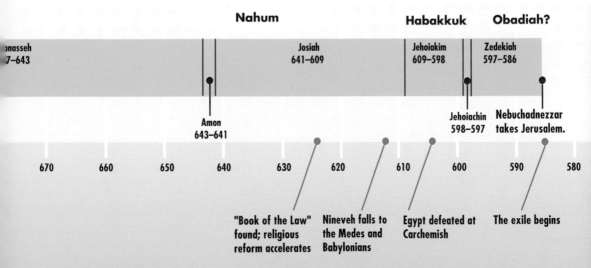

| 670 | 660 | 650 | 640 | 630 | 620 | 610 | 600 | 590 | 580 |

BABYLONIA

Ezekiel

Daniel

Zephaniah

Jeremiah

Nahum

Habakkuk

Obadiah?

| ınasseh 7–643 | | | | Josiah 641–609 | | Jehoiakim 609–598 | | Zedekiah 597–586 | |

Amon
643–641

Jehoiachin
598–597

Nebuchadnezzar
takes Jerusalem.

| 670 | 660 | 650 | 640 | 630 | 620 | 610 | 600 | 590 | 580 |

"Book of the Law"
found; religious
reform accelerates

Nineveh falls to
the Medes and
Babylonians

Egypt defeated at
Carchemish

The exile begins

23

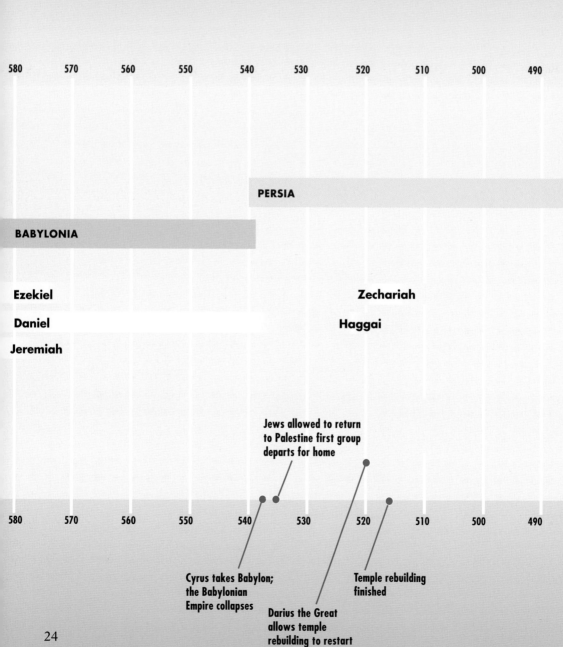

| 580 | 570 | 560 | 550 | 540 | 530 | 520 | 510 | 500 | 490 |

PERSIA

BABYLONIA

Ezekiel

Zechariah

Daniel

Haggai

Jeremiah

Jews allowed to return
to Palestine first group
departs for home

| 580 | 570 | 560 | 550 | 540 | 530 | 520 | 510 | 500 | 490 |

Cyrus takes Babylon;
the Babylonian
Empire collapses

Darius the Great
allows temple
rebuilding to restart

Temple rebuilding
finished

490	480	470	460	450	440	430	420	410	400

Malachi?

Joel?

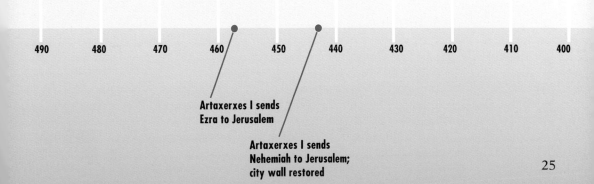

490	480	470	460	450	440	430	420	410	400

**Artaxerxes I sends
Ezra to Jerusalem**

**Artaxerxes I sends
Nehemiah to Jerusalem;
city wall restored**

NEW TESTAMENT CHRONOLOGY

Most of the time between the Old and New Testaments consisted of what has historically been designated the Hellenistic period and cover the years between the conquests of Alexander the Great (332 B.C.) and the emergence of the power and influence of Rome in the mid-first century B.C. The Republic of Rome, which was founded in 509 B.C., eventually became an empire under Augustus Caesar (Octavian), after he defeated Mark Antony and Cleopatra at the Battle of Actium in 31 B.C.

The Roman period lasted until the emergence of the Byzantine period in A.D. 325 under the emperor Constantine. Fourteen Roman emperors reigned during the approximately one hundred years of New Testament history.

The life and death of Jesus

Augustus reigned as emperor from 27 B.C. until A.D. 14, and Jesus Christ was born during that time: Luke writes that it was in the days of "Caesar Augustus" that Joseph and Mary went to Bethlehem from Nazareth to be enrolled in a census of the Roman empire (Luke 2:1-7). A study of the chronology of the life of Jesus as revealed in the first four books of the New Testament is limited by the fact that the first thirty years of his life are passed over in virtual silence (Luke 2:40, 52; 3:23), and only about forty days of his public career of three and a half years are identifiable. It can be known that he was born before 4 B.C., because Matthew writes that he was "born in Bethlehem of Judea in the days of Herod the king" (Matthew 2:1), and Herod (the Great) died in that year, having reigned from 37 B.C. Our modern designations of B.C. and A.D. are therefore somewhat inaccurate. Jesus was "about thirty years of age" when he began his ministry (Luke 3:23), and judging from the number of Passovers mentioned in the Gospel of John, he lived another three years before being crucified. This chronology thus places the date of his death as approximately A.D. 30.

Excavation at the site of Roman Caesarea, Israel. Digs like this illuminate our understanding of ancient cities.

Part of the site of biblical Hazor, Israel; archaeologist Yadin estimated that it would take 8,000 years to excavate completely.

Paul

The chronology of most of the New Testament is primarily based on a study of the life of the apostle Paul as recorded in the book of Acts and his letters. Four historical/archaeological pinpoints must be considered in working with Pauline chronology. These pinpoints provide a comparatively secure basis on which to build an understanding of Paul's movements:

1. The death of Aretas IV, king of Nabatea in A.D. 40 (2 Corinthians 11:32f; Acts 9:23-25).
2. The expulsion of Jews from Rome by Claudius in A.D. 49 (Acts 18:2).
3. Gallio's proconsulship in Achaia began in May/June, A.D. 51 (Acts 18:12).

4. Procuratorship of Festus in Judea began in May/June, A.D. 56 (Acts 24:27).

1. Paul's Visit to Jerusalem

Galatians 1:18 states that Paul visited Jerusalem three years after his conversion, which, according to Acts, took place during his mission of persecution to Damascus. This visit would not likely have happened before A.D. 38: Josephus states that the high priest in Jerusalem had authorized Paul's mission and was still in office at the time of the mission (this high priest will have been either Joseph Caiaphas or Jonathan), but in A.D. 37, during the feast of Passover, the Roman general Vitellius deposed Caiaphas, replacing him with Jonathan, the son of Ananus the high priest. A few weeks later, during Pentecost, general Vitellius deposed

27

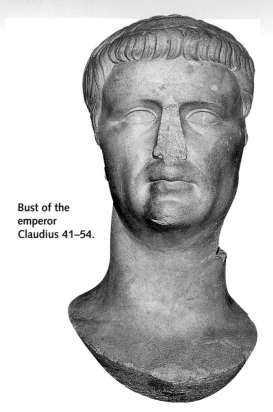

Bust of the emperor Claudius 41–54.

Roman Emperors of the New Testament period

Augustus	27 B.C.–A.D. 14
Tiberius	14–37
Gaius Caligula	37–41
Claudius	41–54
Nero	54–68
Galba	68–69
Otho	69
Vitellius	69
Vespasian	69–79
Titus	79–81
Domitian	81–96
Nerva	96–98
Trajan	98–117
Hadrian	117–138

Jonathan and replaced him with Jonathan's brother Theophilus. This would have allowed Paul to return to Jerusalem without having to confront the man who gave him letters of authority for his mission. *A terminus ad quem* for Paul's visit would be A.D. 40, because according to coins and inscriptions, Aretas IV died in that year. Paul had escaped from Damascus and gone to Jerusalem while Aretas was still alive (Acts 9:25; 2 Corinthians 11:32), thus before A.D. 40.

2. The Expulsion of Jews from Rome

The second important pinpoint in Pauline chronology is provided by Luke's statement in Acts 18:2 that when Paul arrived in Corinth on his second journey he found Aquila and Priscilla, Jews who had "recently" come from Rome "because Claudius had commanded all the Jews to leave Rome." This expulsion is also referred to by ancient Roman authors, such as Suetonius and Orosius, and can be dated to A.D. 49.

3. Gallio's Proconsulship

The third pinpoint of Pauline chronology relates to this same missionary journey, which included an eighteen-month stay in Corinth (Acts 18:11). At the end of that time, Paul's Jewish opponents brought him before Gallio, the proconsul of Achaia, presumably seeing Gallio's recent appointment as a fresh opportunity for a "united attack" on the apostle (Acts 18:12). Their charge had to do with Paul's supposed violations of Jewish law, a matter about which Gallio was little concerned (Acts 18:15).

The discovery at Delphi, across the Corinthian Gulf from Corinth, of four inscribed stone fragments, which contain information about the accession of Gallio, helps us to determine the date of his tenure in office. The fragments are from a copy of a letter sent from the Roman emperor Claudius to the city of Delphi, either to the people of Delphi or to Gallio's successor. These fragments contain the names of both

Gallio and Claudius with dates for the reign of Gallio.

The letter is dated to A.D. 52, and, since proconsuls normally held office for one year and were required to leave Rome for their posts not later than the middle of April, Gallio probably began his term of office in May of A.D. 51. And since Paul had arrived in Corinth eighteen months earlier than his appearance before Gallio (Acts 18:11), he would have entered Corinth in the winter of 49/50—perhaps in January of A.D. 50. This would coincide well with the "recent" arrival of Priscilla and Aquila from Claudius' expulsion in A.D. 49.

4. The Procuratorship of Festus
The fourth pinpoint of Pauline chronology is the date when Festus succeeded Felix as procurator of Palestine (Acts 24:27). A coin has been found with micrographic writing on it that gives the date of Festus' accession as A.D. 56. This would mean that Paul stood before Festus (Acts 24:27) in the spring (per-haps May) of A.D. 56, and that he had arrived in Jerusalem at the end of his third journey two years earlier. Some scholars, however, have placed the date a year later, in A.D. 57. This would mean that Paul's death in Rome a few years later would likely have been near the end of the reign of the emperor Nero, who died in A.D. 68.

The apostle John

The latest point of chronology related to the New Testament has to do with the life of the apostle John and his writings. Early Christian literature firmly places him on the island of Patmos during the reign of the Roman emperor Domitian (81–96) and in Ephesus during the reign of Nerva (96–98). Eusebius, who wrote his history of the early church in the fourth century, places John in Ephesus at the time of his death during the reign of Trajan (98–117; *Ecclesiastical History*, III 20.8-9; 23.1-4; 31.3).

2

MESOPOTAMIA AND THE BIBLE

MESOPOTAMIA AND THE BIBLE

The last seven verses of Genesis 11 introduce us to Abraham. Initially, they place him in southern Mesopotamia (Ur of the Chaldees) and later in the northwest corner (Haran) of that same region. He is married but childless.

Abraham was born approximately 2000 B.C. While most scholars put his birth year in the first half of the twentieth century B.C., some prefer a date in the twenty-second century B.C., their choice hinging on how they understand Exodus 12:40 (see pages 18–19). Either way, archaeology clearly demonstrates that, contrary to common perceptions, Abraham lived in a world that had advanced far beyond basic subsistence levels.

MESOPOTAMIA PRIOR TO ABRAHAM

The archaeological record begins thousands of years prior to the appearance of Abraham. A reader consulting books covering those centuries of ancient Mesopotamia (largely modern Iraq) will find that the timespan has been divided into several phases of development. The more formative phases have been labeled: Ubaid, Protoliterate, Early Dynastic, Akkad, Ur III. Prior to the earliest of those phases, the stamp seal, the prototype of our present day stamp seals, had come into use. In the field of art, the finest pottery ever produced in B.C. Mesopotamia had already been thrown.

During the Ubaid period (c. 5300–3750 B.C.), artistic skills expanded further as Mesopotamia became dotted with towns containing thousands of people. Temples were a necessary feature in the towns and, in the south, irrigation canals criss-crossed the surrounding landscape.

The Protoliterate period (c. 3750–2900 B.C., alternately divided into the Uruk and Jemdat Nasr periods) is so-named because the first writing was invented then. The writing, initially used for an early form of book-keeping, progressed from pictographs to the wedge-shaped form (cuneiform) that was still in use as late as the first century A.D. By about 3000 B.C. temple architecture had evolved into the "temple tower," the ziggurat, which became characteristic of Mesopotamian worship for centuries to come. Also within the Protoliterate period the cylinder seal was introduced, and the gravings on some of these seals have been called "little masterpieces."

The Early Dynastic period (c. 2900–2334 B.C.) saw the rise of city-states and the blossoming of the Sumerian culture, which first appeared in the Protoliterate period. A centralized economy was largely in the hands of

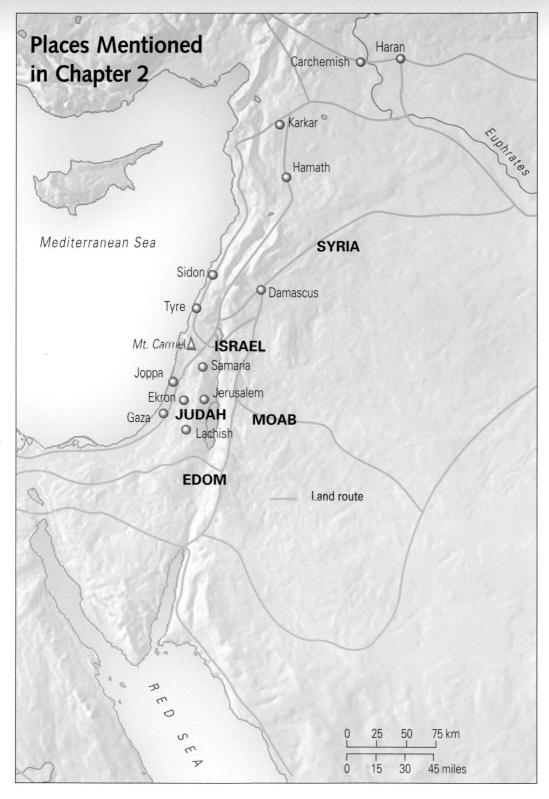

Places Mentioned
in Chapter 2

Haran

Carchemish

Karkar

Hamath

Euphrates

Mediterranean Sea

SYRIA

Sidon

Damascus

Tyre

Mt. Carmel △   ISRAEL

Joppa   Samaria

Ekron   Jerusalem

Gaza   JUDAH   MOAB

Lachish

EDOM

Land route

RED SEA

| 0 | 25 | 50 | 75 km |
| 0 | 15 | 30 | 45 miles |

Places Mentioned
in Chapter 2

B L A C K

Carchemish

TAURUS MOUNTAINS

AMANUS MOUNTAIN

CYPRUS

Mt. Lebanon △

MEDITERRANEAN SEA
(Upper / Great Sea)

Jordan

DEAD SEA

Nile

E G Y P T

RED
SEA

C A S P I A N   S E A

A

"Mt. Ararat"△

U R A R T U

Khorsabad

Nineveh

Nimrud

Haran

A S S Y R I A

P E R S I A

Tigris

Nuzi

M E S O P O T A M I A

Euphrates

Babylon

SHINAR

CHALDEA

E L A M

Isin

Larsa

Ur

(LOWER SEA)

A R A B I A

P E R S I A N   G U L F

0		250		500 km

0	100	200	300 miles

Fertile land

Desert

Above: A Protoliterate-period cylinder seal.
The photograph above shows the impression the seal would make when rolled over soft clay: a line of cattle and a row of reed huts containing pots and calves. Right: White magnesite with silver ram figure, 2 inches (5.3 centimeters) tall.

the king. He, and an increasingly visible priestly class, controlled much of life. The best evidence of continuing sophistication in the material realm comes from the Royal Tombs that were excavated at Ur (see below). The use of writing expanded during this time as scribal schools, dictionaries, love songs, and proverbs appeared. History began to be recorded as well. A king named Urukagina left "reform texts" in which he stated that earlier rulers had taken too much control and that he was going back to the good old days and ways. So even before Abraham's time people were talking of the "good old days!"

The Akkad period (c. 2334–2193 B.C.) marks a Semitic takeover of Mesopotamia. A Semite named Sargon (not the biblical Sargon) established himself in central Mesopotamia and, in time, ruled an empire

Above: A typical clay tablet from the Protoliterate period.

stretching from "the upper to the lower sea," that is, from the Mediterranean to the Persian Gulf. Future kings would feel they were entitled to the same boundaries, a conviction that eventually impacted biblical history. Akkadian replaced Sumerian as the official language, city-states gave way to a larger centralized government, and the economy began to shift from state monopoly to private enterprise.

IN THE TIME OF ABRAHAM

When the Akkad period collapsed into turmoil as a result of invasion from the east, the Ur III period (c. 2112–2004 B.C.) restored stability. For a third time the city of Ur was politically dominant. The earliest known collection of laws dates to this period and, for one last time, Sumerian was the official language. Most scholars would place Terah, Abraham's father, into this period of peace and prosperity, but some prefer to place Abraham here. In either case, the archaeological record makes it clear that Abraham entered a world that rested on a long and rich heritage.

When Ur III collapsed, southern Mesopotamia became politically fragmented. The cities of Isin and Larsa fought for control, and Ur was ruled first by one and then the other city. Scholars are not sure how far the economy had already progressed toward private enterprise, but the thousands of business documents that have been recovered from this Isin-Larsa period (c. 2004–1800 B.C.) make it clear that possession of private property was the norm. Archaeologists also found two additional collections of law that date to this period.

Right: This nearly lifesize bronze head is considered one of the most important works of art from the Akkad period. It represents either Sargon or, more likely, his grandson Naram-Sin.

©Photo SCALA, Florence

The City of Ur

The biblical account of Abraham begins while he was living in Ur. Ancient Ur grew from a small village in the Ubaid period to become one of the more important cities in southern Mesopotamia. Over time the Euphrates has shifted several miles from the city, but in ancient times Ur was both a port city and an important link in caravan routes. Under Ur-Nammu and his son, Shulgi, during the Ur III period, the city dominated Mesopotamia.

Thousands of deities were wor- shiped in Mesopotamia, but each city had a specific main god. At Ur, the moon god held that primary position. Ur's sacred precinct was situated in the northern part of the walled city. In that precinct Ur-Nammu built the ziggurat, which still stands to half of its original 120-foot (36.5-meter) height. This ziggurat is approximately 200 feet by 150 feet (60.9 meters by 45.7 meters) at its base, and its mud brick inner core is protected by a thick outer facing of baked bricks set in bitumen. Originally the ziggurat probably rose in three levels, and as many staircases gave access

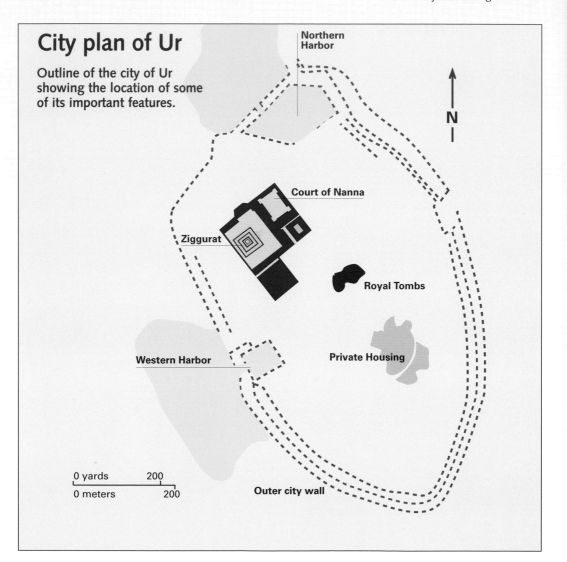

City plan of Ur

Outline of the city of Ur showing the location of some of its important features.

Northern Harbor

N

Court of Nanna

Ziggurat

Royal Tombs

Western Harbor

Private Housing

0 yards 200

0 meters 200

Outer city wall

to a shrine resting on its top. Additional religious structures clustered around the ziggurat's base.

Southeast of the sacred precinct the archaeologists found the "Royal Tombs." These sixteen tombs date to about 2500 B.C., centuries before Abraham, and the riches of their contents astonished the world. The objects crafted in gold and silver alone reveal high artistic skill. The long list of recovered tomb objects, including musical instruments and game boards, provides extensive insights into the pre-Abrahamic world. There is much that is impressive. Unfortunately, our appreciation is dampened by the evidences of human as well as animal sacrifice within these same tombs.

An area of private housing was also excavated. We are, therefore, able to say that houses in Ur were generally two-storied, and built around a central court. The whitewashed walls, and rooms filled with such items of furniture as tables, chairs, beds, and chests, likely provided a rather comfortable life. Further, the unbaked mudbrick construction of these houses acted both to cool the interior rooms in summer and to hold in the heat during colder weather.

It is most likely that Terah lived to see the political upheaval that followed the collapse of Ur III, and that the ensuing turbulent times of the Isin-Larsa period provided an incentive for him to move his extended family elsewhere.

Because of the rather static culture of that day, any reconstruction of Abraham's life in Mesopotamia would remain essentially the same whichever side of 2000 B.C. one chooses to place him.

Reconstruction of the era can go far beyond city plans and housing. Dress and hairstyles, for example,

Top: The partially restored ziggurat to the moon god as it exists today.

Bottom: The ziggurat as it is thought to have appeared during the Ur III period.

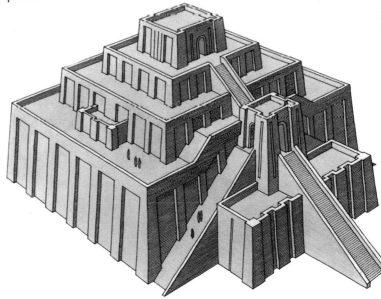

are known to us. From texts we learn a great deal concerning the daily fabric of life, including details such as the diet, the relative cost of certain commodities, and interest rates.

The collections of laws that have been found provide insight into how people interacted with one another. As an example, the marriage laws reveal that it was normal for a man to divorce a barren wife. That Abraham did not do what was normal indicates how great his love was for Sarah. Texts relating to religion allow us to recognize that, since Terah was a polytheist (Joshua 24:2), he would have believed in a world swarming with capricious gods and full of demons ready to do one harm.

Two daggers. The right-hand dagger has a sheath in gold and lapis lazuli.

Rampant he-goat in small tree.

One of the inlaid game boards discovered at Ur.

40

House

Restoration of one of the houses excavated at Ur. The central courtyard acted as a light well during the day, and a drain in its floor allowed rainwater to collect in a cistern for later use. First-floor windows were placed near the ceiling to allow the escape of hot air in the summer.

Solid gold and lapis lazuli bearded bull from the sounding box of a lyre.

1. Chapel
2. Bedroom
3. Kitchen
4. Guestroom
5. Bathroom

THE CITY OF HARAN

Genesis 11:31 records Terah's relocation, with his extended family, to Haran in the northwest corner of Mesopotamia. Excavation at the site has been very limited, but Haran's location on one of the more important routes of that day implies that it was a major trade center. The city figures briefly in later biblical, as well as extrabiblical, history but of interest here is the fact that, as in Ur, the moon god was the chief deity of Haran. This religious similarity could have been a factor in Terah's decision to stop there.

THE EARLY CHAPTERS OF GENESIS

The volume of writings that have been recovered from Ur and elsewhere in Mesopotamia allow us to identify more intimately than hitherto with the ancient Mesopotamians. These writings, together with other archaeological finds, also allow us to make observations concerning the first ten chapters of Genesis.

Archaeology cannot address the question of the date of creation. It can, however, show the uniqueness of the Genesis account by comparing it with the polytheistic conjectures of other ancient Near-Eastern cultures. The creation account called *Enumah Elish* was apparently first written close to the time Abraham lived in Mesopotamia. In this story the world was formed as the result of a cosmic war, and people were created so the gods would no longer have to cook their own meals, or sweep out their own temples. This story also argued for the primacy of a particular god and city (in the version of the story pictured below, Marduk and Babylon) to rule over Mesopotamia; thus the story was used for political ends.

Critical scholarship, which assumes that the early chapters of Genesis contain a collection of myths, has been unable to find a

Above: A tablet containing the *Enumah Elish*. No extant texts date earlier than the first millennium B.C., but, from internal evidence, most scholars would date the story's composition to early in the second millennium B.C.

Opposite: Clay prism containing the Sumerian king List, c. 2000 B.C. The pre-flood kings averaged reigns of 30,125 years. The post-flood kings are divided into three groups. The average reign in the first group is 1,065 years, then 192 years, and lastly, 44 years. This prism is eight inches (20.3 centimeters) high.

Mesopotamian source behind the biblical creation story. In fact, a comparison with the *Enumah Elish* shows that, while the Bible might not relate as much detail concerning creation as we would now like, the biblical account is unique. Not only that, but in comparison with other texts of the day, the Genesis account is full of detail.

Archaeology can say little concerning the Garden of Eden. Ancient texts seem to locate the four waterways of Genesis 2:10-14 in

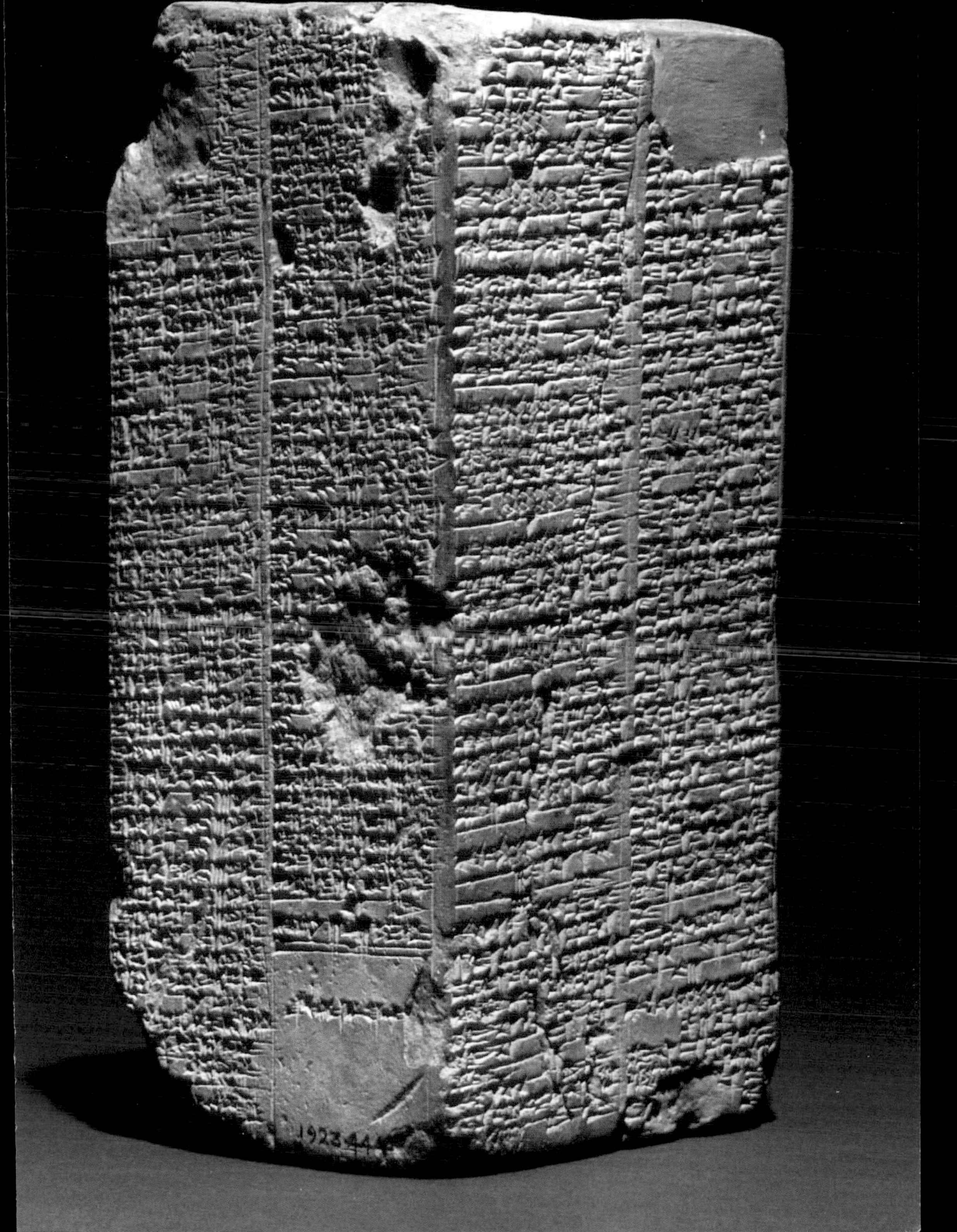

southern Mesopotamia, but other theories have also been put forward. Here, too, critical scholarship has attempted to prove the story a myth. A NASA spotting of an ancient river bed in Saudi Arabia, for example, led one scholar to suggest that the Pishon of Genesis 2:11 had been found. This scholar was not trying to give precision to the Eden story. Rather, he used the sighting to suggest how, in his view, such a story originated.

According to the list of generations in Genesis chapter 5, some early people lived hundreds of years. Likewise, in the Sumerian king list prism eight "great men" ruled thousands of years each before the flood. The time spans for the post-flood people, as in the Bible, are drastically reduced. It has been suggested that this king list reflects a memory of longer lifespans in early prehistoric times.

Decades ago, when Sir Leonard Woolley was excavating Ur, he reported finding conclusive evidence of the flood recorded in Genesis chapters 6–8—an eight-foot-thick (2.4 meter) deposit of what he took to be waterborne silt. Subsequently, Woolley admitted that this single "flood layer" was actually two layers close together in time, but sufficiently separate for people to have briefly reoccupied the site. Still, Woolley was not dissuaded from his conclusion because he was not seeking evidence that would harmonize with the biblical text. What Woolley sought was a flood layer sufficiently thick to account for the Mesopotamians to have invented a story from which, he believed, the biblical account derived. That Woolley's discovery has no relation to the biblical story is clear on several counts, one being that excavated sites no more than fifteen miles (24 kilometers) from Ur show no sign of a "flood" deposit. Therefore, whatever the cause of the layers found by Woolley, they were confined to the environs of Ur itself. Unfortunately, echoes of "Woolley's flood" still circulate.

In Genesis 6 Noah built a boat. Genesis 8:4 tells us that the ark came to rest on the mountains of Ararat or, more specifically, on the mountains of Urartu. Ancient Urartu stretched for hundreds of miles and over the centuries several suggestions have been made for the landing-place of the ark. Although Buyuk Aghri Dagh (the Turkish identification of the extinct volcano that is currently favored as Mount Ararat) did not become a candidate until the eleventh or twelfth centuries, many people have climbed this "Mount Ararat" in search of the ark. Some have claimed to have seen it, to have touched it, or to have brought back pieces of its remains. Invariably their claims have not withstood rigorous scrutiny. Even those who hope remains of the ark will be found have rejected the alleged sightings. As yet, "arkeology" has not abated.

The best extrabiblical evidence of the flood can be found in Mesopotamian literature. In a Sumerian "deluge" story, composed before Abraham was born, a man named Ziusudra escaped a flood by means of a boat:

> . . . a flood . . . to destroy the seed of mankind . . . is the decision, the word of the assembly [of the gods]. . . . All the windstorms, exceedingly powerful, attacked as one. At the same time, the flood sweeps over the cult-centers. . . . The flood had swept over the land, (and) the huge boat had been tossed about by the windstorms on the great waters . . . Ziusudra opened a window of the huge boat. . . .

Another story, known as the Gilgamesh Epic, was written somewhat later. This epic is essentially secular in theme and recounts how the priest-king Gilgamesh sought eternal life. The flood story was incorporated into his quest. A man, now named Utnapishtim, tells Gilgamesh how he survived the flood. Utnapishtim relates that, when the storm had subsided:

> I opened a hatch, and light fell upon my face . . . . On Mount Nisir the ship came to a halt . . . I sent forth and set free a dove. The dove went forth, but came back. . . . Then I sent forth and set free a swallow. The swallow went forth, but came back. Then I sent forth and set free a raven. The raven went forth and, seeing

that the water had diminished, he eats, circles, caws, and turns not round. Then I let out all to the four winds and offered a sacrifice.

The Gilgamesh Epic became so popular that copies of it have been found throughout the Near East. Some writers have concentrated on the numerous differences between the biblical story and the epic. For example, in the epic gods scurry about acting like cowards, and no clear reason is given for the flood. The boats are differently shaped and Utnapishtim had to launch his ark personally. But concentrating on the differences does not erase the fact that there are striking similarities. Most people are struck by the similar use of birds.

Tablet XI of the Babylonian version of the Gilgamesh Epic. This is dated c. 650 B.C., and is six inches (15.2 centimeters) high. It is a long story. Tablet XI, which contains the flood account, is more than 300 lines long.

When the epic was first translated, some scholars immediately reasoned that the similarities could only mean that the Genesis account was a myth borrowed from Mesopotamia, and was therefore plagiarized, not inspired. That conclusion continues among critical scholars.

A more conservative response is to argue for common inheritance, that is, that both accounts go back to a common source—that there was a flood, which both record. When the flood story was incorporated into the Gilgamesh Epic, much more than the boatman's name changed (in an intermediary version the man was named Atrahasis). The Gilgamesh Epic represents only one of many redactions as people tried to make the memory of the flood fit their changing religious beliefs. There are similarities because some points are necessary to write any flood story. Other points—for example the birds—are similar because they were not altered during the various Mesopotamian retellings.

Genesis chapter 10 summarizes the spread of Noah's descendants. Then Genesis 11:1-2 relates how, at one point, that spread came to a halt in the "plain of Shinar," which is a term for southern Mesopotamia. Since southern Mesopotamia lacks stone, it is not surprising that the Bible tells us that the people began making mud bricks to construct a tower. This "Tower of Babel" is often pictured as a ziggurat, but Mesopotamian religious architecture evolved over the centuries and, as noted above, no ziggurats were built before about 3000 B.C. This date is much too late if one takes Genesis 11:1 at face value. Genesis 11:1 states that the tower was constructed at a time when people spoke only one language and without doubt there were several language families by 3000 B.C.

What form, then, did the tower take? Everywhere else in the Bible the Hebrew word (*migdal*), which in Genesis 11 is trans- lated "tower," refers to a fortified tower built inside a city as a last line of defense. On that analogy, it is most probable that the people in Genesis 11 were building a tall, but probably simple, defensive structure.

POST-ABRAHAM IN MESOPOTAMIA

For several centuries after Abraham left Haran and moved into Palestine, Mesopotamian history is largely peripheral to the biblical story. Amorites had already appeared and now additional players entered and exited the stage: Hurrians/- Horites, Kassites, Sealanders, Mitannians, Elamites, Aramaeans. Even the Hittites played a bit part. Assyria briefly threatened to be a major power, but then sank back into a dark age.

Hammurapi (c. 1792–1750 B.C., alternatively, Hammurabi) ruled within those turbulent centuries. Although little can be said about his life or career, his "law code" has made him famous. As already noted, earlier collections of laws have been found, but none, including Hammurapi's, can accurately be called "codes." None try to cover all contingencies of life, and the bases for their compilations are not clear. Similarities can be found between Hammurapi's "code" and these earlier collections, but they are not extensive enough to require the hypothesis of direct borrowing. Rather, the similarities are explained as evidence that a "common law" existed in the ancient Near East.

During the excavation of a site called Nuzi in east central Mesopotamia, many clay tablets were found. The approximately 5,000 "Nuzi texts" date to the fifteenth century B.C., and provide evidence that "common law" remained largely static for several centuries. Of particular interest are the several insights into patriarchal life provided by the tablets (see pages 106–107).

Right: Popularly known as the Code of Hammurapi, this diorite stele stands over seven feet (2.1 meters) tall. Hammurapi is shown facing the seated god Marduk. Beneath the two figures were approximately 300 laws (some near the base were effaced). The reason for this specific collection of laws is unknown, but in its prologue Hammurapi states that the gods had chosen him to, "promote the welfare of the people . . . to cause justice to prevail in the land, to destroy the wicked and the evil, that the strong might not oppress the weak. . . ."

Left: Transcription of a Nuzi tablet. In this a man gave his wife full authority over her sons and divided the family inheritance so that the eldest son received a double share.

THE RISE AND FALL OF THE ASSYRIAN EMPIRE

Assyria, in northern Mesopotamia, played only a minor role in history until, beginning early in the first millennium B.C., the Assyrians began their rise toward becoming the greatest power the Near East had ever seen. In 876 B.C. Assurnasirpal II (883–859 B.C.) led the Assyrian army west into Syria. At that time Omri (885–874 B.C.) was king of Israel. The Assyrians did not advance beyond Syria, but they must have then learned of Omri because from that point on they repeatedly referred to the kings of Israel as being from the "house of Omri."

Assurnasirpal inflicted heavy damage before he reached the Great Sea (the Mediterranean), and he later had wall after wall in his palace at Kalhu (biblical Calah, modern Nimrud) filled with scenes of death and destruction. The beginning of Assyria's policy of cruelty toward other peoples was recorded in both words and reliefs.

I built a pillar over against his city gate, and I flayed all the chief men . . . and I covered the pillar with their skins; some I walled up within the pillar, some I impaled upon the pillar on stakes, and others I bound to stakes round about the pillar . . . and I cut off the limbs of the officers. . . . Many captives from among them I burned with fire, and many I took as living captives. From some I cut off their hands and from others I cut off their noses, their ears, and their fingers, of many I put out the eyes. I made one pillar of the living, and another of heads, and I bound their heads to posts round about the city. . . .

Shalmaneser III took the throne of Assyria in 858 B.C. when Ahab was in his last years as king of Israel, and he was on the battlefield nearly every year of his reign. The lives of these two kings intersected early in 853 B.C. when the Assyrian army moved into Syria.

Relief from Assurnasirpal's palace at Nimrud. This relief shows archers and slingers attacking an enemy.

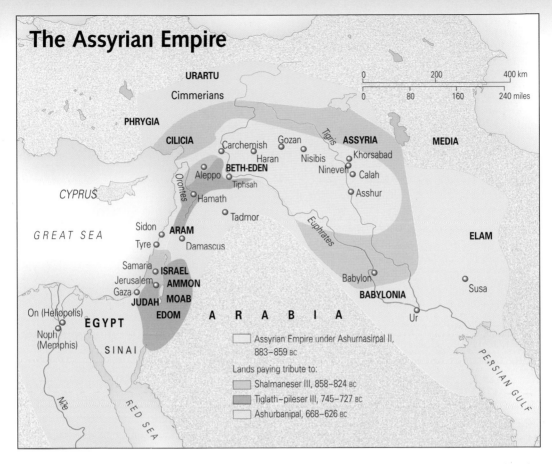

The Assyrian Empire

URARTU

Cimmerians

0   200   400 km
0   80   160   240 miles

PHRYGIA

CILICIA   Carchemish   Gozan   Tigris   ASSYRIA   MEDIA
Haran   Nisibis   Khorsabad
Aleppo   BETH-EDEN   Nineveh   Calah
Tiphsah
CYPRUS   Hamath   Asshur
Orontes
Tadmor
GREAT SEA   Sidon   ARAM   Euphrates   ELAM
Tyre   Damascus
Samaria   ISRAEL
Jerusalem   AMMON   Babylon   Susa
Gaza   BABYLONIA
JUDAH   MOAB
On (Heliopolis)   EDOM   A R A B I A   Ur
Noph   EGYPT   PERSIAN GULF
(Memphis)   SINAI

Assyrian Empire under Ashurnasirpal II,
883–859 BC

Lands paying tribute to:
Shalmaneser III, 858–824 BC
Tiglath-pileser III, 745–727 BC
Ashurbanipal, 668–626 BC

Nile   RED SEA

A coalition of twelve kings drawn from west of the Euphrates River confronted Shalmaneser III near Karkar (or Qarqar) in northern Syria. The Assyrian list of opposing troop strengths reports, "2,000 chariots, 10,000 foot soldiers of Ahab." Those figures represent over half the chariots said to have been fielded by the coalition, and only the Syrians contributed more foot soldiers.

Shalmaneser III boasts of a great triumph over the coalition: "I spread their corpses everywhere, filling the entire plain with their widely scattered fleeing soldiers. During the battle I made their blood flow." But scholars note that the Assyrian army withdrew, and that for several years thereafter Damascus needed no help to hold off Assyrian inroads. They credit Shalmaneser III with no more than a pyrrhic victory.

The number of men and chariots Ahab contributed to the coalition implies that he was one of the more powerful kings of that day. There is no mention, however, of this battle in the Bible: the biblical writer's focus was on Ahab's religious condition, not his military might. The battle of Karkar represents the first physical contact between Israel and Assyria. Assyria had heard about the "land of Omri," now their forces had met on the battlefield.

When, in 841 B.C., Shalmaneser III marched west again, Jehu had just begun his reign over Israel (841–814 B.C.). This time no coalition came out to meet the Assyrians. Although siege was laid to Damascus, the city did not fall. The Assyrian army moved southwest to Mount Carmel, where the annals say they received tribute from Tyre, Sidon, and Jehu, the "son of Omri." Here is another event in the reign of an Israelite king

Right: The Black Obelisk of Shalmaneser III.
This obelisk stands 6.5 feet (1.9 meters) tall.
Of the different campaigns featured on the stele our
interest here is in the portion showing Jehu
kneeling before the Assyrian king (bottom). On the
stele Shalmaneser III says: I received from him
silver, gold, a golden *saplu*—bowl, a golden vase
with pointed bottom, golden tumblers, golden
buckets, tin, a staff for a king, [and] wooden
puruhtu.

Top opposite: Relief of Tiglath-pileser III.
Bottom: Panel relief depicts his army conquering an
unidentified city. The men on the left carry spears
and shields as they use a scaling ladder to gain
entry into the city. On the right a battering ram is
breaking down the defensive walls. Behind the ram,
and in a greatly different scale, archers in mail shirts
shoot arrows from behind large wicker shields. The
inhabitants of the city are shown surrendering,
dead, and dying. Some have been impaled on poles.

which was only recorded extrabiblically.

Jehu's tribute is commemorated on what
we today call the Black Obelisk of
Shalmaneser. On this obelisk Jehu is shown
kneeling before Shalmaneser III, and the
accompanying text lists the gifts he paid to
placate the Assyrians. The Bible implies that
although Jehu had a respectably long reign,
he was never a particularly strong ruler. The
Black Obelisk supports that impression.

The obelisk also lets us mark another rise in Assyria's involvement with Israel's history. First Assyria heard of this "land of Omri," then it fought one of its kings. Now Assyria receives the first of several tributes.

There seems to be a surprising exception to Assyria's increasing pressure on Israel. Shalmaneser III's grandson, Adad-nirari III, reigned from 810 to 783 B.C. Jehoahaz was king of Israel from 814 to 798 B.C. During his reign Jehoahaz was so harrassed by Syria that he momentarily called on the Lord, and 2 Kings 13:5 cryptically states that God gave Israel a "deliverer" (in some translations, a "savior") who freed Israel from this Syrian threat. The verse does not name the deliverer. From an inscribed slab found at Nimrud we know that about 803 B.C. Adad-nirari marched into Syria: "I shut up the king of Damascus in Damascus, his royal residence. The terror-inspiring glamor of Ashur [the chief god of Assyria] overwhelmed him and he seized my feet, assuming the position of a slave of mine. Then I received . . . [a list of tribute follows]." Syrian forces were forced to withdraw from Israel to defend their own lands. It is tempting to see Adad-nirari III as the "deliverer" who freed Israel from Syrian pressure.

Tiglath-pileser III (sometimes called Pul) became king of Assyria in 744 B.C. (744–727 B.C.). The next year he moved west and reached south of Syria into Israel. In his annals Tiglath-pileser III boasts that, concerning Menahem (king of Israel 752–742), "I overwhelmed him like a snowstorm and imposed tribute upon him." According to 2 Kings 15:19-20, in raising this tribute Menahem required the wealthy men of his kingdom to contribute fifty shekels each. The Bible gives no hint of the significance of this amount, but ancient sources reveal that fifty to sixty shekels was then the going price on the slave market. In essence then, the rich men of Israel were told they could remain free by contributing the equivalent of their slave price.

Tiglath-pileser III marched west again in 734 B.C. In his annals for this campaign we read:

> Nineteen districts of the city of Hamath, together with the towns in their environs, situated on the shore of the sea of the setting sun [Mediterranean] . . . I restored to the territory of the land of Assyria, my officers as governors I placed over them.

Empire had definitely begun. As empire increasingly enveloped the Near East, Syria began to dream of a coalition that could once again stand up to the Assyrian army. Pekah of Israel (752–732 B.C.) agreed to ally himself with Syria, but the two nations were rebuffed when Judah declined to join them. In Judah, Ahaz (735–716 B.C.) had recently been put on the throne by a faction that thought it better to pay Assyria tribute than be destroyed. When Syria and Israel tried to take control of Judah (2 Kings 16:5), Ahaz quickly gathered tribute and rushed it to Tiglath-pileser III with a cry for help. Soon all of Syria fell to the Assyrians. Tiglath-pileser III occupied the northern half of Israel and deported its people (2 Kings 15:29).

Deportation has not been mentioned earlier in the Bible, and Tiglath-pileser III is credited with instituting the policy. Assurnasirpal had slaughtered those who resisted him; Tiglath-pileser III added the practice of moving captured populations within the expanding empire. Those who made these forced migrations were not badly treated—the Assyrians wanted them alive in order to continue their tribute—but Tiglath-pileser III hoped that people relocated to distant areas would be less inclined to revolt. For those groups who felt that the power of their gods did not extend beyond their homelands, this policy could have been quite effective.

Hoshea (732–722 B.C.) murdered his way to the throne of Israel (2 Kings 15:30). If Tiglath-pileser III's annals are to be believed, he had a hand in this assassination: he took

Tiglath-pileser III of Assyria depicted in his chariot.

the credit for Hoshea's accession. Hoshea withheld tribute when Shalmaneser V (726–722 B.C.) succeeded his father as king of Assyria. Shalmaneser V forced Hoshea back into line, but then he revolted a second time. This second defiance of Assyria resulted in Samaria coming under siege. Three years later, in 722 B.C., "The king of Assyria captured Samaria and carried Israel away into exile to Assyria" (2 Kings 17:6).

The identity of this "king of Assyria" is not fully clear. Perhaps Shalmaneser V died just before Samaria fell. In any event, in one of his annalistic reports Sargon II (722–705 B.C.) claimed credit for the victory:

> I besieged and conquered Samaria, led away as booty 27,290 inhabitants of it. I formed from among them a contingent of 50 chariots and made [the] remaining inhabitants assume their social positions. I installed over them an officer of mine and imposed upon them the tribute of the former king.

Judah had now lost the northern buffer between it and the Assyrian army; the empire was advancing closer. And 2 Kings 17:24 names cities elsewhere in the empire from which Sargon II drew people to repopulate Israel.

Sargon II ordered that a new capital, Dur-Sharrukin, be built. In one text he claims, "Day and night I planned the building of that city." When Khorsabad, as the city is now called, was excavated, the archaeologists found that it was never fully completed. Sargon's son abandoned the project and no future king had anything to do with it. As one scholar puts it, the "sudden rise and decline apparently reflect only the whim of a single monarch." Still, Khorsabad is a beautiful capsule in time, and provides evidence of how powerful Assyria, the destroyer of Israel, had become.

Sargon II went back into Palestine in 720 B.C. and then again in 712 B.C. This second campaign is mentioned in Isaiah 20:1, the only direct reference to Sargon in the Bible. Concerning this second campaign Sargon says in his annals:

> Philistia, Judah, Edom, Moab, who had paid tribute and gifts to Ashur my lord [the chief god of Assyria], planned rebellion and evil against me; they brought gifts of friendship to Pharaoh king of Egypt, a prince who could not save them, and endeavored to form with him an alliance.

Ahab's participation in the battle of Karkar and Jehu's tribute to Shalmaneser III are only known to us extrabiblically. More of this extrabiblical amplification occurs within the reign of Hezekiah (716–687 B.C.). Trouble broke out when Sargon II died and Sennacherib (704–680 B.C.) took the throne. Sennacherib's Prism relates that only three kings in Palestine, including Padi king of Ekron, remained loyal to Assyria:

> The officials, the patricians, and the common people of Ekron [threw] Padi, their king, into fetters because he was loyal [to me] and handed him over to Hezekiah . . . and Hezekiah held him in prison. . . .

Sennacherib had other problems to deal with but by 701 B.C. he was able to lead his armies west. One by one the revolting cities were brought back into line. Again Sennacherib's Prism:

> I assaulted Ekron and killed the officials and patricians who had committed the crime and hung their bodies on poles surrounding the city. . . . I made Padi, their king, come from Jerusalem and set him as their lord on the throne . . .

The mural reconstructed, found in "residence K" shows Sargon II, perhaps followed by the owner of the residence, standing in front of a statue of the god Ashur. Two men were added by the modern artist to provide scale to the mural.

The twenty-five-ton human-headed bull is one of several that guarded the entrance to the throne room of the palace. See also illustration on p.14, which depicts similar bull figures found at Nineveh.

Reconstruction of the Citadel of Khorsabad

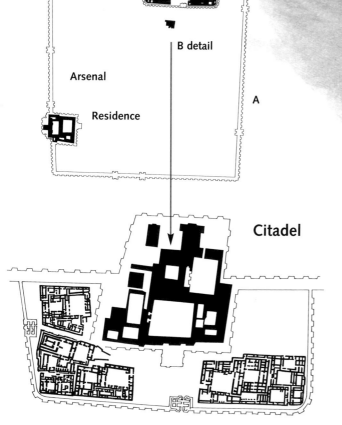

Gate

Town gate

Temple of Nabu

B

B detail

Arsenal

A

Residence

Citadel

Plan of Dur-Sharrukin (Khorsabad) built by Sargon II but then abandoned by all future kings.

A. The outer walls of Khorsabad form a near perfect square just over a mile (1.6 kilometers) long on each side.

B. On the terrace incorporated into the northwest city wall, Sargon's palace, temples, and other residences were built.

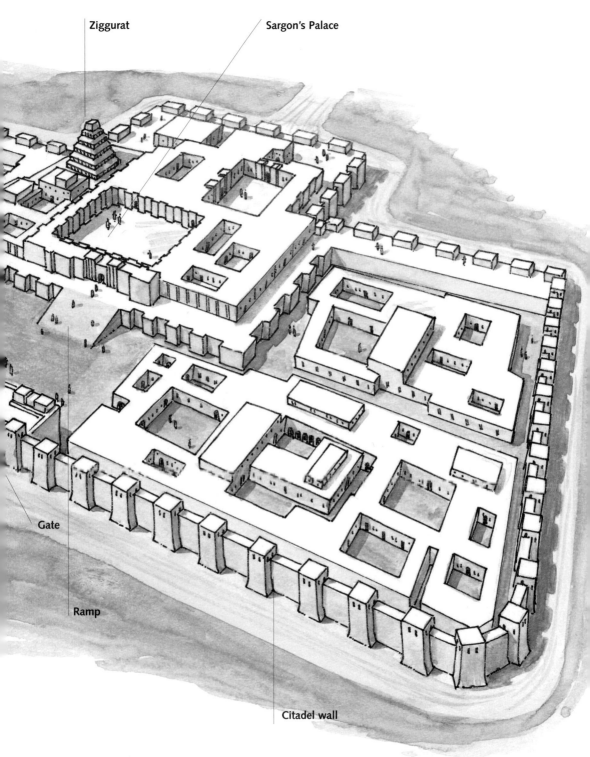

Ziggurat

Sargon's Palace

Gate

Ramp

Citadel wall

larger volume of silver. Perhaps the Assyrian scribal notes were misread, or the silver stripped from the Temple was added to the total.

Lachish fell and Sennacherib moved on to attack another city (2 Kings 19:8). But Sennacherib was most proud of his victory at Lachish, and he later had some seventy linear feet (21.3 meters) of wall reliefs carved to commemorate his success.

Older books sometimes refer to another, later, campaign by Sennacherib into Palestine. Some scholars thought a second campaign was necessary to explain the biblical reference to King Taharqa coming to aid Judah (2 Kings 19:9). They argued that Taharqa was not old enough in 701 B.C. to have been ruling Egypt. According to this "two campaign theory," 2 Kings 18:1-16 related to 701 B.C., but the remainder of that chapter and into chapter 19 told of subsequent events in the reign of Hezekiah. It has since been recognized that when the Bible refers to Taharqa as "king" it is affording him the title that he later held. Sennacherib led only one campaign into Palestine, in 701 B.C.

Hezekiah's dealings with the Assyrian threat are recorded in 2 Kings 18-19, 2 Chronicles 32, Isaiah 36-37; on Sennacherib's prism; and on Assyrian palace reliefs (the excavation of Lachish also adds its own insights concerning the city's siege and fall, see page 122). Putting all these sources together allows us better to recreate this moment in Judean history. We also become aware of some of Hezekiah's political maneuvering that is not recorded in the Bible.

Archaeology also allows us to understand better one episode of political maneuvering that *is* mentioned in the Bible. According to 2 Kings 20:12-13, messengers from Merodach-baladan approached Hezekiah, but the Bible gives no real explanation for this contact. Merodach-baladan was a Chaldean who for a number of years kept declaring himself king of Babylon, and kept trying to end Assyria's control of southern Mesopotamia. The Assyrians would put him

The Taylor Prism in the British Museum in London (15 inches [37.5 centimeters] tall). A nearly identical prism is in the University of Chicago's Oriental Institute Museum. Both prisms are six-sided, made of baked brick, and detail Sennacherib's military campaigns, including his 701 B.C. invasion of Judah.

Sennacherib claims that he attacked dozens of Judean cities, "by means of well-stamped earth-ramps and battering rams brought near to the walls, combined with the attack by foot soldiers. . . ." Sennacherib took special interest in directing the assault on Lachish, and while it was under siege Hezekiah tried to placate Sennacherib with tribute (2 Kings 18:14-16). Sennacherib's prisms expand on the variety of tribute given. It agrees with the Bible concerning the amount of gold handed over, but lists a much

Relief from the ceremonial room at Nineveh devoted to the assault on Lachish in 701 B.C. This central scene from the tableau conflates the attack on the city and its aftermath as Judeans are being led away into exile or are impaled on posts.

Black marble boundary stone, 18 inches (45.5 centimeters) high. Here Merodach-baladan, the man who would be king, is shown on the left conferring a land grant to an official on the right. Emblems of four Babylonian deities are at the top of the stone.

to flight, only to find subsequently that he had returned. When his envoys met with Hezekiah, they were undoubtedly hoping that Judah might ally with them. A second front against Assyria could make it more difficult for Sennacherib to deal with Merodach-baladan. Fortunately, although flattered, Hezekiah stayed clear of this intrigue. Soon Merodach-baladan fled into Elam for one last time.

Earlier kings had palaces at Nineveh but Sennacherib built what he called the "palace without a rival." The palace walls were decorated with carved stone reliefs depicting his military exploits, including his victory over Lachish. Sennacherib commissioned an inner city wall—"wall that terrifies the enemy," he called it—that ran some 7 miles (12 kilometers) in circuit and was fronted by a deep moat. He gave names to the fifteen gates that led into the city. He also had an elaborate system of canals constructed to bring water into Nineveh.

Power struggles for the throne were not exclusive to Israel and Judah. Sennacherib's heir apparent, Esarhaddon, was so slandered by his brothers that he was forced into exile. Only after his father's death did he return, wrest control of the throne, and begin his

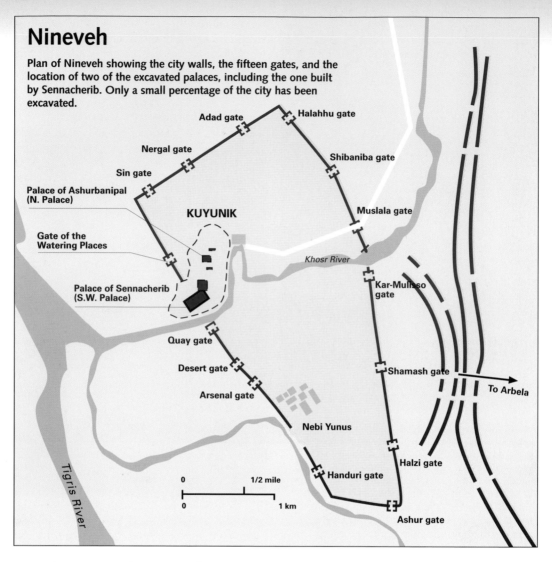

Nineveh

Plan of Nineveh showing the city walls, the fifteen gates, and the location of two of the excavated palaces, including the one built by Sennacherib. Only a small percentage of the city has been excavated.

Adad gate

Halahhu gate

Nergal gate

Shibaniba gate

Sin gate

Palace of Ashurbanipal (N. Palace)

KUYUNIK

Muslala gate

Gate of the Watering Places

Khosr River

Palace of Sennacherib (S.W. Palace)

Kar-Mulisso gate

Quay gate

Desert gate

Shamash gate

To Arbela

Arsenal gate

Nebi Yunus

Halzi gate

Handuri gate

0   1/2 mile

0   1 km

Ashur gate

Tigris River

reign (680–669 B.C.). Manasseh was then king of Judah (697–643 B.C.), and from Esarhaddon's "Prism B" we learn that he was among those conscripted to build a new palace at Nineveh:

> I called up the kings of [Syria] and of the region on the other side of the Euphrates River, to wit: King Balu of Tyre, King Manasseh of Judah. . . . together twenty-two kings. . . . All these I sent out and made them transport under terrible difficulties, to Nineveh . . . as building material for my palace: big logs, long beams, and thin boards from cedar and pine trees. . . .

Esarhaddon blamed Egypt for repeated unrest in Palestine and in 671 B.C. he invaded and appointed local Egyptians to run the new Assyrian province. Empire had extended into Egypt.

Egypt broke free in 652 B.C. when Assurbanipal was king of Assyria (669–627 B.C.). Wanting to reclaim that breakaway province, Assurbanipal would have been concerned that the landbridge to Egypt (Palestine) remained secure. It is therefore most likely that he is the Assyrian king who "captured Manasseh with hooks, [and] bound him with bronze chains" (2 Chronicles

In this tall stele—it is over 9.8 feet (3 meters) high—Esarhaddon is shown facing symbols of the gods, and holding ropes attached to rings through the lips(?) of two small figures (sometimes hooks were used). There is some debate over the identity of the two figures, but the one kneeling might be Taharqa of Egypt. Whatever the correct identifications, the stele is illustrative of action taken against Manasseh, see below.

B.C.) conquered Babylon and with it all of southern Mesopotamia. Assyrian letters and legal documents reveal a throne in trouble: "In the land discord, in the palace strife, depart not from my side. Rebellion and evil plotting are continually contrived against me." A few years later the Chaldeans allied with the Medes (based to the east in modern Iran) and began advancing on the heartland of Assyria. Nineveh came under siege in 612 B.C. and collapsed within three months. The Assyrian empire had fallen.

THE RISE AND FALL OF THE CHALDEAN EMPIRE

The Chaldeans (also called Babylonians or Neo-Babylonians) moved to take over the former Assyrian empire. At the outset of his reign, Nebuchadnezzar (or Nebuchadrezzar, 605–562 B.C.) advanced west and encountered the Egyptian army at Carchemish. The Egyptians were also trying to step into the vacuum left by a collapsed Assyria, but their dream of reestablished empire ended when the Egyptian army was crushed at Carchemish (see Jeremiah 46). As Nebuchadnezzar advanced toward Egypt proper, he paused in Jerusalem, took hostages and made its king, Jehoiakim (609–598 B.C.), declare his loyalty to a new master. The Chaldeans continued the Assyrian practice of deportation, and a teenager named Daniel was among those taken into exile. Judah had experienced freedom following the Scythian raids of 626 B.C., but that independence was now over.

This newly formed empire had to deal with repeated uprisings. In early 598 B.C., for example, Jehoiakim stopped paying tribute, provoking the Chaldean army to march on Jerusalem. A cuneiform tablet provides only the barest details of what happened. Concerning Nebuchadnezzar, "He seized the town on the second day of the month Adar. He captured the king. He appointed there a

33:11). Either Manasseh had gotten caught up in the general unrest and was being punished, or he was being cautioned not to get out of line. The stele of Esarhaddon shown above provides a graphic description of the humiliation Manasseh suffered.

In spite of the apparent power of Assyria, the precipitous fall of both empire and nation was about to begin. In 626 B.C. people known as the Scythians stormed down from the north and rapidly tore the western regions free of Assyria. That same year a Chaldean named Nabopolassar (626–605

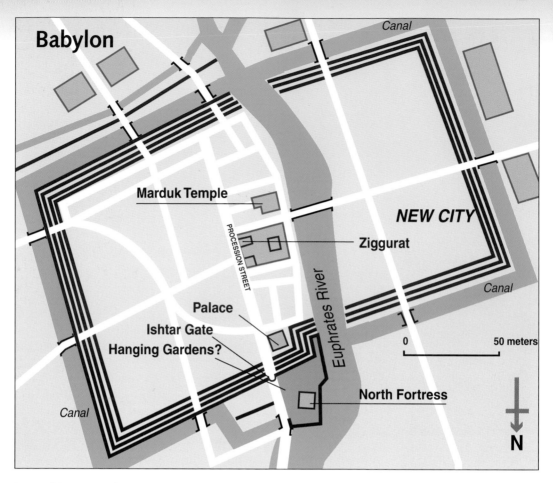

Babylon

Canal

Marduk Temple

PROCESSION STREET

NEW CITY

Ziggurat

Euphrates River

Palace

Ishtar Gate

Hanging Gardens?

Canal

0   50 meters

North Fortress

Canal

N

king of his own choice. He took much booty from it." The biblical account (2 Kings 24:10-17) describes some of the treasures taken, tells us that thousands more were herded into exile, and identifies Zedekiah (597–586 B.C.) as the new vassal king. Elsewhere we learn that Ezekiel was among those who were taken into the Babylonian captivity.

A few years later Zedekiah stopped paying tribute and, not surprisingly, the Chaldean army again set out for Jerusalem. In 586 B.C., after a siege of eighteen months, Jerusalem fell. The city was looted and the Temple torn down. Still more Judeans were deported, and this time one of the Judeans left behind was appointed as governor, not king. Judah was no more.

Babylon has a long history: Hammurapi ruled from there early in the second millen-

nium B.C. But it is the Babylon of Nebuchadnezzar that we can see today. Nebuchadnezzar was proud of how he enhanced the strength and beauty of the city:

A great wall which like a mountain cannot be moved I made of mortar and brick. . . . its top I raised mountain high. I triplicated the city wall in order to strengthen it. I caused a great protecting wall to run at the foot of the wall of burnt brick. . . . A third great moat wall . . . I built with mortar and brick. . . . The palace . . . I rebuilt in Babylon with great cedars. . . .

Excavators found that the inner city occupied approximately 500 acres (205 hectares) and was defended by triple walls and a moat. The whole city covered some 3,000 acres (1,230 hectares) and the wall surrounding this larger area was about 10 miles long in

City of Babylon

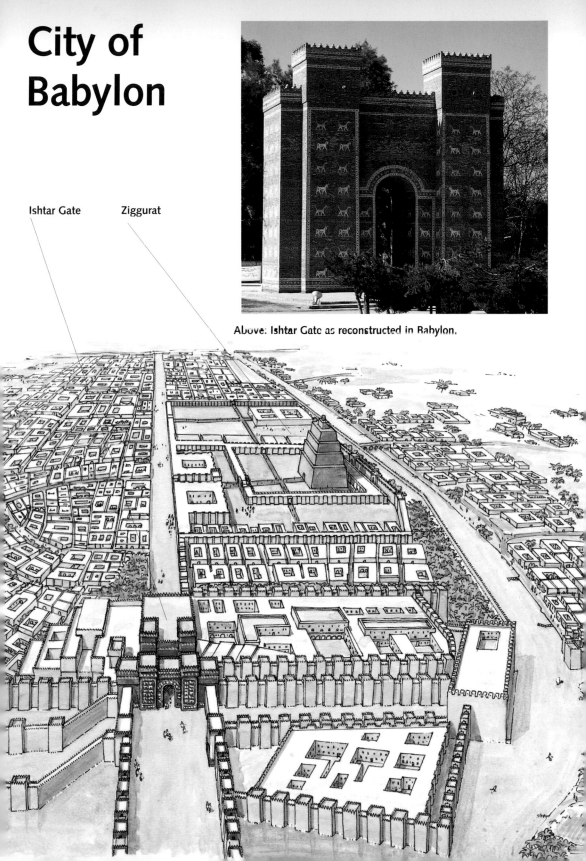

Above: Ishtar Gate as reconstructed in Babylon.

Ishtar Gate   Ziggurat

Administrative tablets found in Babylon list deliveries of oil by the royal household. This very fragmented cuneiform tablet lists delivery to "Jehoiachin, king of Judah," and to the "sons of the king of Judah."

circuit. This outer wall is said to have been wide enough at the top for chariots to pass each other as they moved along the ramparts. Of the gates that gave access to the inner city, the Ishtar Gate is the best preserved. The walls of this gate, and of the Processional Street that led to it, were decorated with glazed relief panels of bulls, lions, and "dragons." In sharp contrast with earlier Assyrian decorations, there were no reliefs of bloody victory over enemies; rather, the decorations were more to please the eye. Nebuchadnezzar's palace was adjacent to the Ishtar Gate. The palace was built around five courtyards and Nebuchadnezzar called it his "shining residence, the dwelling of majesty." Today the ziggurat at Babylon is a disappointment; little remains of it. Contrary to what had been thought, the location of the famous "hanging gardens" (one of the seven ancient wonders of the world) is not certain.

Little is known about the last years of Nebuchadnezzar, but his affliction with boanthropy (a form of illness in which a man believes himself to be an ox; Daniel chapter 4) can be placed within that obscure period. There was some jockeying for the throne following his death, and Evil-Merodach was one of those to come briefly into power (561–560 B.C.). Jehoiakim had died just before Jerusalem fell in 598 B.C., and it was his son Jehoiachin whom Nebuchadnezzar had captured and sent into exile (2 Kings 24:15). Evil-Merodach later released Jehoiachin from house arrest in Babylon (2 Kings 25:27-30). Despite the astronomical odds against such a recovery, archaeologists found ration lists in Babylon that recorded provisions given to Jehoiachin and his family.

In 556 B.C. Nabonidus ascended the Chaldean throne. Scholars are divided in their evaluation of the man. Utilizing the same data they have variously concluded that he was everything from stupid to the most wise of rulers. But if wise, why did Nabonidus do nothing to halt the flow of history that was being set in motion? At the very time Cyrus the Persian was moving west from Iran, and slowly laying claim to more and more territory, Nabonidus removed himself to Tema, deep in the Arabian desert. One scholar finds this move "totally inexplicable."

The Babylonian Chronicles report that Nabonidus left his son Belshazzar as coregent in Babylon. The Bible refers to Belshazzar as king, and for all practical purposes he was. But Belshazzar was not able to stem the growing power of Cyrus. When Belshazzar ordered a banquet (Daniel 5:1), the Persians were just then pressing on Babylon itself. Knowing the defenses of the city, we can perhaps understand how Belshazzar could think himself safe. But only hours after Daniel saw the handwriting on the wall (probably in the central court of the palace) the city of Babylon fell. Belshazzar was killed in battle; the fate of Nabonidus is unclear. The year 539 B.C. marks the end of the Chaldean empire.

The Persians maintained control of Mesopotamia until 331 B.C., when they were defeated by Alexander. A few years later, when Alexander died in Babylon, political control passed to the Seleucids (311–126 B.C.). Under the Seleucids there was an influx of Greeks into Mesopotamia. Cities were laid out according to the *polis* plan, and older cities such as Babylon were partially depopulated to fill new centers of trade and culture. Seleucid interests shifted toward the Mediterranean and they began their role in Intertestamental history. By 126 B.C. the Parthians were in control of Mesopotamia and, in time, they became involved in the pre-king years of Herod the Great. More foreigners entered Mesopotamia, and more cities were built with a citadel and agora. Citadels were even perched atop old ziggurats! Cuneiform writing flickered out about A.D. 75 and Babylon was deserted before A.D. 200.

3

EGYPT
AND THE BIBLE

EGYPT AND THE BIBLE

Egypt is much better known to the general public than is Mesopotamia. Pyramids, pharaohs, and mummies have long been staples of the popular press, and readers of the Bible are aware of the Israelites being in bondage in, and then escaping from, Egypt. There is much more to the story. In fact there is a sense in which several different "Egypts" are portrayed in the Bible. As in chapter two, this chapter begins by summarizing what God allowed to form before his people began interacting with the land of the Nile.

One of the pre-dynastic ceremonial slate palettes which recorded "history." In this example a victory by Upper Egypt over the north seems to be commemorated; the men on the upper left are held by standards which, in later reliefs, clearly identify southern *nomes* (districts) in Egypt. In dynastic times pharaoh could be represented as a lion or a bull, an imagery that was already in place. It has been suggested that the incomplete figure on the far right is dressed in a Mesopotamian garment.

One side of another ceremonial palette. Narmer's name is at the top center of each side. The customary interpretation of the palette is that it commemorates Narmer's military victory over Lower Egypt. On this side he is shown wearing the tall White Crown of Upper Egypt, and on the other side he wears the Red Crown of Lower Egypt. From this point on the two crowns were often joined into a single headdress, signifying the union of the Two Lands. This motif, the mace-wielding pharaoh and the exaggerated size of the main figure in a scene, continued even past dynastic times. Notice also that the characteristic Egyptian rendering of a person, with the torso in frontal view and the rest of the body in profile, had already begun.

EGYPT PRIOR TO ABRAHAM

Predynastic Egypt

Because much of early Egypt is deeply buried under Nile mud, it has not been possible to push as far back in time as can be done for Mesopotamia. Most of what is known about Egypt prior to 3100 B.C. is derived from cemeteries located back from the reaches of the Nile's yearly inundation. What we find is that the graves gradually became more elaborate and more filled with objects. Food offerings, and such essentials of daily life as tools, combs, and cosmetic kits, imply some belief in an afterlife. It is also clear that the south (Upper Egypt, the Nile Valley) was materially richer and culturally distinct from the north (Lower Egypt, the Delta area). The dividing line between the "Two Lands," an ancient Egyptian designation, was just south of modern Cairo.

Development began accelerating toward the end of the predynastic period. Cylinder seals, specific artistic designs, and monumental architecture give rise to the conclusion that Mesopotamia (which was then in the later stages of its Protoliterate period, see page 32) played some role in this advance. Some scholars would also credit Mesopotamia with introducing the concept of writing into the Nile Valley.

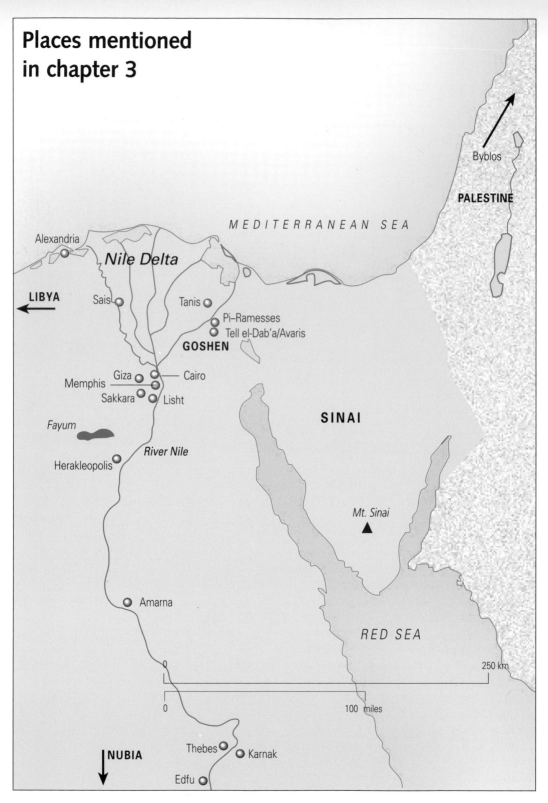

Places mentioned in chapter 3

Byblos

PALESTINE

MEDITERRANEAN SEA

Alexandria

Nile Delta

LIBYA

Sais

Tanis

Pi–Ramesses
Tell el-Dab'a/Avaris

GOSHEN

Giza — Cairo

Memphis

Sakkara — Lisht

SINAI

Fayum

River Nile

Herakleopolis

Mt. Sinai

Amarna

RED SEA

0

250 km

0

100 miles

Thebes

Karnak

NUBIA

Edfu

The sphinx. The human face is assumed to be that of Khafre.

Early Dynastic
(c. 3100–2700 B.C.)

Dynasties 1–2

The division of Egyptian history into dynasties is attributed to a late third century B.C. Egyptian priest named Manetho. Although some of his divisions seem arbitrary, they are now so ingrained that they continue to be used. Narmer (probably the legendary Menes), who was based in Upper Egypt, is generally credited with forcibly uniting the country and founding Dynasty 1. Little can be said about the first two dynasties, but it would appear that battles and rebellion were characteristic of the time. This also seems to have been the time when the concepts of divine kingship and *ma'at* (truth, justice, order), which theoretically would remain unchanged for centuries, were fully formulated.

The Old Kingdom
(c. 2700–2200 B.C.)

Dynasties 3–4

There was apparently a smooth transition to Dynasty 3. Djoser, a third-dynasty king, repeatedly revised the plan of his tomb. The final result was the 204-foot (62-meter) tall "step pyramid." The pyramid was only one part of a funerary complex; it, and several auxiliary buildings, were set within a perimeter wall over a mile in length. During the Old Kingdom the Egyptians believed their pharaoh was a god; they used the same term to designate a god and a king. This belief helps explain how such huge structures could have the support of the people.

71

Giza

Pyramid of Khafre (center) and Khufu (right) at Giza.

Giza, just west of modern Cairo, is famous for its pyramids, which are the sole example of the Seven Wonders of the Ancient World to remain largely intact. These pyramids were built for three pharaohs of the fourth dynasty: Khufu (Hellenized as Cheops), Khafre (Chephren), and Menkaure (Mycerinus). Khufu's pyramid (sometimes called the Great Pyramid) is slightly larger than Khafre's, and stood 481 feet (146.6 meters) tall when its capstone was in place. Of the pyramids, only that of Khafre still retains some of the smooth white limestone casing stones. The now exposed inner blocks average 2.5 tons (2.5 tonnes) each. The pyramids are basically solid except for passageways to their burial chambers.

There is nothing mysterious about how the pyramids were constructed. Ramps and sledges were used to move the blocks into place, and simple water levels ensured a flat construction site. The 13-acre (5.3 hectare) site on which Khufu's pyramid rests is only one inch (2.5 centimeters) out of level for its far corners.

The pyramids are only one part of a complex. Funerary temples on the east side of each pyramid were linked by covered causeways down to valley temples. And, as with Djoser's pyramid complex, there were perimeter walls. The pyramid field also boasts the Sphinx, carved from a rock outcropping, which sits near Khafre's Valley Temple. The human face on this recumbent lion is assumed to be that of Khafre. Additionally, queens were interred in small satellite pyramids adjacent to the main pyramids, and several funerary boats were buried at the base of Khufu's and Khafre's pyramids. Dozens of *mastabas* (tombs) of courtiers and officials also fill the area.

Contrary to what has sometimes been written, the pyramids were not built by slaves, and space considerations require that only a few thousand Egyptians could have labored at any one time. Recent excavation south of the stone causeway uncovered a town for permanent workers and a barracks area thought to have been for a rotating labor force.

The pyramids have attracted a number of eccentric theories: that they were astronomical towers; that they were built by ancient astronauts; or that pyramid-shaped structures possess healing powers. There are even groups who claim God has written a prophetic timeline in the Grand Gallery within Khufu's pyramid, and that the timeline is based on the "pyramid inch." Such aberrations are best avoided.

The Step Pyramid and part of its surrounding wall at Sakkara.

Plan of Giza

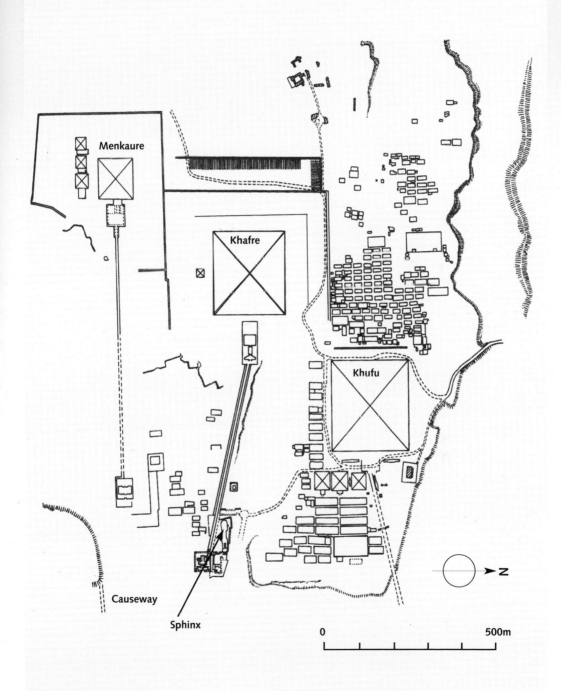

Menkaure

Khafre

Khufu

Causeway

Sphinx

0   500m

N

Dynasties 5–6

The Egyptian "Instructions" were begun in the Old Kingdom and continued to be written well into the first millennium B.C. These Instructions contain advice from a father to his son concerning how to behave in the world. Some of the advice, as in the Instruction of the Vizier Ptah-hotep, is timeless:

> *Ma'at* [Justice] is great, and its appropriateness is lasting; it has not been disturbed since the time of him who made it, whereas there is punishment for him who passes over its laws. . . . If thou art one to whom petition is made, be calm as thou listenest to the petitioner's speech. Do not rebuff him before he has swept out his body or before he has said that for which he came. A petitioner likes attention to his words better than the fulfilling of that for which he came.

During the Old Kingdom Egypt had to repel incursions from Sinai, and may have resorted to military force to maintain its commercial interests in Palestine and Nubia. The Egyptians established a colony at Byblos (near modern-day Beirut in Lebanon) to facilitate trade in cedar, which the Egyptians prized for their boats and coffins. Theoretically, pharaoh was an absolute ruler but beginning in the fifth dynasty that theory began to break down. Various reasons are given for a growing decentralization: for example that the long length of the Nile fostered a growing independence as nobles and officials hundreds of miles from pharaoh could not always wait for his directives to reach them from the capital at Memphis. Their increasing independence can be seen in the way it became less essential that their tombs cluster near the king's pyramid. Toward the end of the Old Kingdom, trade disruptions, together with the increasing burden of building pyramids and exempting temple estates from taxation, began to destabilize the economy. Additional factors are also cited as causes and, whatever weight one chooses to give to each, the Old Kingdom fell.

First Intermediate Period (c. 2200–2100 B.C.)

Dynasties 7–11

For a time Memphis clung to the fiction that it still ruled all of Egypt, but the country split and ruling houses were established at Herakleopolis in the north, and Thebes in the south. People from Syria-Palestine began filtering into the eastern Delta with their flocks. The rapid turnover in pharaohs, and the small, poorly built pyramids point to the troubled times and further decline in the power and prestige of the throne. Thebes finally pushed north and reunited the country. (Scholars generally divide Dynasty 11 between the First Intermediate Period and the following Middle Kingdom.)

EGYPT IN THE TIME OF ABRAHAM

The Middle Kingdom (c. 2100–1800 B.C.)

Dynasties 11–12

The Theban reunification of the country seems to have been both bloody and swift. It was followed, however, by one of the more peaceful and prosperous periods in Egyptian history. The nobles and officials were reined in, and the long years of rule by Dynasty 12 pharaohs imply that stability had been regained. Coregency became a regular practice as the kings tried to ensure dynastic succession. (Centuries later the kings of Israel and Judah would likewise employ coregency to ensure a smooth transition of power.)

Thousands of acres of new land were put into agricultural use and foreign trade expanded. Caravans and ships reached out into neighboring areas and added to the prosperity of the times. Egypt also expanded militarily: a string of forts was established in Nubia along a hundred-mile stretch of the Nile to claim the second cataract as Egypt's new southern border. A line of forts, the "Walls of the Ruler," was

Reliefs from dynasty tomb of Nefer at Sakkara. Since much of what we know derives from tombs, the Egyptians are sometimes perceived as living in constant anticipation of death. On the contrary they loved life and believed they could project their present into the future. These scenes from the fifth dynasty tomb of Nefer depict (top) men constructing a papyrus boat, animal husbandry, and (bottom) women dancing, and men jousting from boats. Other reliefs on the tomb walls picture further aspects of daily life that Nefer expected to have available to him after his death.

Models of houses, fully-rigged ships, and workers engaged in various industries have been found in Middle Kingdom tombs. Like the tomb wall reliefs and paintings, the models provide rich insight into the activities and scenes of daily life. This model is of a Nile funerary boat.

also built to monitor the frontier facing Palestine, but those who had already entered the eastern Delta were apparently assimilated into the population.

The Middle Kingdom pyramids retained the main features of those in the Old Kingdom, but elaborate safeguards signal an increasing concern over protecting the burials from robbery. The largest of the Middle Kingdom pyramids stands about 200 feet (61 meters) tall. As a consequence of their finished stone veneer being placed over a rubble core, all are poorly preserved today.

Abraham entered Egypt to escape a famine. A border dispatch from somewhat later on records the admission of Bedouin tribes from Palestine "to keep them alive and to keep their cattle alive." Perhaps some such accounting was made when Abraham and his entourage were allowed past the Walls of the Ruler. Abraham would have stopped in the eastern Delta where other people from Palestine had relocated from time to time. As noted above, he entered a land that had regained its stability, and was making a concerted effort to continue in the spirit of the Old Kingdom. The capital had been moved upriver to Thebes, but it was returned back north to a spot near Memphis (Lisht). Pharaohs began to have seasonal residences in the eastern Delta.

There has long been speculation concerning pharaoh's interest in Sarah. One commentary found with the Dead Sea Scrolls says he was attracted to her fingernails! It is more likely that the Egyptians saw Abraham as potentially useful to their commercial dealings with Palestine. An exchange of women was one way to seal agreements between two parties, and this could explain

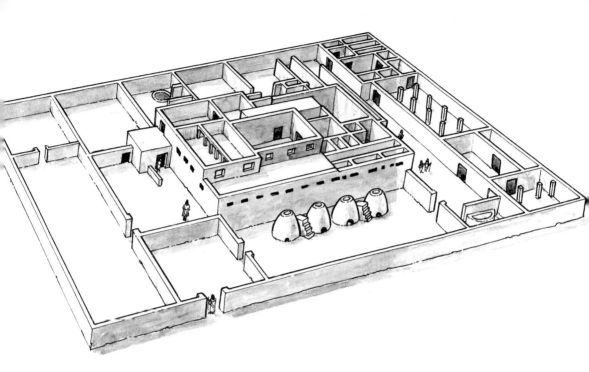

Cutaway of an Egyptian estate.
This illustration is based on an estate excavated at Amarna. Although the site of Amarna dates later than the time of Joseph (see below), it provides a visual setting for his employment with Potiphar. The main building has vents near the first floor ceiling so that hot air can escape the rooms, but large windows are provided upstairs. (The roof has been omitted to show the interior construction.) The circular structures in the foreground are silos. Their staircases allowed the newest grain to be poured into the top while the oldest grain could be extracted through the lower doors. Storerooms, workrooms, and servant quarters are adjacent to the main building.

Hagar's entry into the family. In any event, it was probably not very long before Abraham's deception was discovered and he was escorted out of the country.

As with the Old Kingdom, various reasons have been suggested to explain the fall of the Middle Kingdom: the royal bloodline thinned out, there was royal infighting, trade with the north was disrupted.

EGYPT IN THE TIME OF JOSEPH

Second Intermediate Period (c. 1800–1570 B.C.)

Dynasties 13–17
Egypt again split into competing claimants, and then a wave of Canaanites, called Hyksos by the Egyptians, took control of at least all of Lower Egypt. They ruled from Avaris in the eastern Delta, but how far their control reached into Upper Egypt is not certain. Although the Hyksos assimilated various facets of Egyptian culture (for example,

An Egyptian Silo.
In this Middle Kingdom granary model a worker carries grain in a pot. Egypt's dependence on the Nile's annual inundation, and memory of earlier years of famine, made them very sensitive to the possibility of the recurrence of a time in which, as one of their texts states, "everything that they eat was short."

they used Egyptian hieroglyphics, Egyptian titles, and worshiped the Egyptian god Seth), when they were finally expelled there was a concerted effort to erase this period from history. One ancient Egyptian king-list, for example, jumps from the end of the Middle Kingdom to the first ruler of Dynasty 18.

The caravan that brought Joseph into Hyksos controlled Lower Egypt (Genesis 37:28) brought him to an Egypt politically quite different from the one Abraham knew. Joseph attained a comfortable status for a slave and functioned well until he was falsely accused by Potiphar's wife and thrown in jail.

Joseph was put in the same jail as two of pharaoh's officials: his "chief cup-bearer" and his "chief baker." These are well-known Egyptian titles. The Egyptians believed that dreams were one way the gods communicated with people, and it was Joseph's demonstrated ability in interpreting dreams (first for the two officials and then for pharaoh) that catapulted him from prison into high office. Egyptian texts record other instances of upward mobility by foreigners in society, but it certainly did Joseph no harm that he had come from the same geographical area as the Hyksos. Genesis 41:42-43 records Joseph's investiture: examples of signet rings and chariots have been found; tomb paintings show the fine linen garments, the gold chain (the Egyptian "Gold of Honor") bestowed on favored people, and the bowing of the knee to those in authority.

For seven years Joseph was in charge of storing supplies of grain in anticipation of the coming lean years. So much grain was gathered that the scribes ceased trying to keep an accounting (Genesis 41:49).

Since the Hyksos originated in Syria-Palestine, it is not surprising that they were willing to share their food supplies with people from that region (Genesis 42). Joseph's family was settled in the same eastern Delta (Goshen) where Abraham had resided decades earlier. The chapters relating the life of Joseph in Egypt, from his servitude in Potiphar's house, through his rise as a non-Egyptian to high office, to the embalming and mourning for Jacob and then for Joseph himself, faithfully mirror what is known of the culture of that country. For example, according to Genesis 50:26, Joseph was 110 years old when he died this specific number was an Egyptian expression for a long or ideal life span, not necessarily a statement of actual age.

EGYPT IN THE TIME OF MOSES

The New Kingdom (c. 1570–1069 B.C.)

Dynasty 18 (c. 1570–1318 B.C.)
The Hyksos were in Egypt for approximately one hundred years, and some Egyptians adjusted to their presence. In Upper Egypt, however, frustration over their rule of part of the country grew into hatred and then finally to what has been characterized as "wars of liberation." Ahmose, often identified as "the pharaoh who did not know Joseph" (Exodus 1:8), is credited with the expulsion of the Hyksos from Egypt, and the founding of Dynasty 18.

In some ways Dynasty 18 took up where the Middle Kingdom had left off: art and architecture, for example, repeated earlier themes. However, no more pyramids were built. Instead, the pharaohs were buried in the guarded Valley of the Kings at Thebes; their tomb entrances were hidden, and their mortuary temples placed outside that valley. Also changed was Egypt's attitude toward

foreigners; they could no longer be patronized. Egyptian troops became more aggressive both to the south and to the north. Within Egypt, foreigners still living in the land were put to work on government projects, and not too many years later a move was made toward population control. Within that atmosphere of increasing oppression Moses was born.

The princess who found Moses is not named, and it is fruitless to speculate as to her identity since there would have been several princesses at any given time. Moses was brought into the royal court and despite being "educated in all the learning of the Egyptians" (Acts 7:22), he did not lose his Hebrew heritage.

Thutmose III was the fifth pharaoh of Dynasty 18, but initially he was shunted aside by his stepmother, Hatshepsut. Theoretically the two co-ruled the country but in actual fact she was the one in control. During her reign the emphasis was on building projects and commerce with the outside world. Interestingly, Hatshepsut ruled Egypt as king, not queen; masculine pronouns were used in reference to her, and artists rendered her as decidedly masculine.

When Hatshepsut died and Thutmose III gained full control of the country, there was an immediate and dramatic shift in state policy. Empire became the operative word. In less than three months Thutmose III led an army into northern Palestine where he routed a coalition that had gathered at Megiddo. In fourteen of his next sixteen years the Egyptian army marched north over Palestine's coastal highway, once even going as far north as the Euphrates River to engage the Mitannians, an emerging power in western Mesopotamia. Garrisons were strategically placed in Palestine and native princes were brought back to Egypt to ensure the loyalty of their fathers. By relocating them, it was also hoped that a pro-Egyptian mindset could be inculcated for future use. The training that Moses received can be seen as a forerunner of this policy.

Top: Thutmose III.
Thutmose III is shown in this relief from the Karnak temple bashing Syro-Palestinian prisoners. He assumes a similar pose to that taken by Narmer centuries earlier (see page 69).

Bottom: Amenhotep II.
Amenhotep II's skill with the bow was memorialized in both word and relief. One text tells of his drawing 300 bows to test their quality, and then climbing into his chariot and shooting arrows through copper targets nearly 3 inches (7.6 centimeters) thick, "a deed which had never been done nor heard of." This relief, also from the Karnak Temple, depicts how he unerringly hit poles and other targets. In the lower right his arrows are shown protruding several inches through a thick copper target.
By kind permission of James Hoffmeier.

Tomb painting dating to the reign of Thutmose III. The scene depicts the various stages of brick-making, from mixing water and mud, to forming the mixture in molds, and then setting the bricks out to sun dry. Finally, the bricks were gathered for use. Sometimes mud is of such a consistency that straw does not need to be added, but usually it is required as a binder to keep the bricks from breaking as they dry. Exodus 5 records that the Egyptian taskmasters stopped supplying straw to the Hebrews, but they did not lower the demanded number of finished bricks. An Egyptian text dating later in the New Kingdom informs us that fifty bricks per worker was then considered the daily quota.

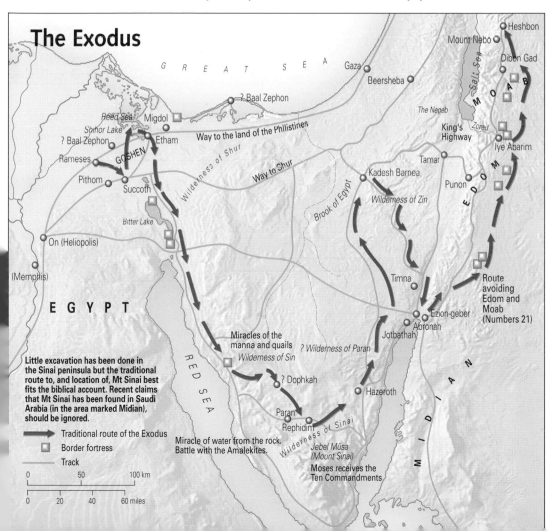

The Exodus

Heshbon
Mount Nebo
Dibon Gad
GREAT SEA
Gaza
Beersheba
MOAB
? Baal Zephon
The Negeb
Reed Sea Migdol
King's Highway
Zered
Shihor Lake
? Baal Zephon Etham
Way to the land of the Philistines
Iye Abarim
Rameses GOSHEN
Wilderness of Shur
Tamar
Pithom
Way to Shur
Kadesh Barnea
Succoth
Brook of Egypt
Wilderness of Zin
Punon
EDOM
Bitter Lake
On (Heliopolis)
(Memphis)
Timna
Route avoiding Edom and Moab (Numbers 21)

E G Y P T
Ezion-geber
Abronah
Jotbathah
RED SEA
Miracles of the manna and quails
Wilderness of Sin
? Wilderness of Paran
M I D I A N
? Dophkah
Hazeroth

Little excavation has been done in the Sinai peninsula but the traditional route to, and location of, Mt Sinai best fits the biblical account. Recent claims that Mt Sinai has been found in Saudi Arabia (in the area marked Midian), should be ignored.

Paran
Rephidim
Wilderness of Sinai

Traditional route of the Exodus
Border fortress
Track

Miracle of water from the rock.
Battle with the Amalekites.

Jebel Mûsa (Mount Sinai)
Moses receives the Ten Commandments

0   50   100 km
0   20   40   60 miles

Following the "early date" of the Exodus (1447 B.C.) Thutmose III has been identified as the "pharaoh of the oppression" and, therefore, the pharaoh from whom Moses fled (Exodus 2:15). His hostile attitude toward non-Egyptians certainly fits the biblical picture. One Egyptologist rates Thutmose III as "incontestably" the greatest of all Egyptian pharaohs, and "Napoleonic" in both his accomplishments and stature. Egyptian texts cast Thutmose III as a militarist, and also as a sportsman; one account relates that he hunted 120 elephants in northern Syria (after that, the last reference to elephants in that area dates to the eighth century B.C.).

Thutmose III was followed by his son Amenhotep II. Following the "early date" of the Exodus, Amenhotep II would be "the pharaoh of the Exodus." Like his father he was a militarist; he took his army north across the Orontes River in Syria, and south almost to the fourth cataract in Cush. His "press clippings" picture him as even more a sportsman than his father. It would seem he spent his life excelling in every form of competition. His strength as an oarsman was amazing; he could not be beaten in a footrace, and his feats of archery were simply superhuman. These reports of his deeds are certainly exaggerated, but one wonders how much he felt it was necessary to give substance to them. Moses' reluctance to confront pharaoh is understandable, and pharaoh's response to Moses' request is in keeping with his official image (Exodus 5:2).

The Hebrews had been assigned to forced labor, specifically to build store cities. Excavations at Tell el-Dab'a (Avaris) have found fortifications and storage facilities that were begun first for Ahmoses, and then continued in use through following reigns as Egypt campaigned into Syria and Palestine. Those structures may have been some of the ones built by the Hebrews.

The plagues that followed pharaoh's intransigence have something of a natural order, and the Bible does not state how extensively the country was affected. Several of the plagues could have been interpreted by the Egyptians as evidence that the gods of Egypt were no match for the God of Moses. Following the tenth plague pharaoh temporarily relented and gave permission for Moses to take his people out of Egypt. But before they left he changed his mind and God intervened to give the Hebrews safe passage.

EGYPT AFTER MOSES

Dynasty 18 after Moses

Amenhotep II was followed by his son Thutmose IV, who was not the eldest son (Exodus 11:5). The next king, Amenhotep III, used marriage to forge diplomatic ties; princesses from both Mitanni and Babylonia were added to his harem, but he became preoccupied with enjoying the wealth that had poured into Egypt from the recently created empire. Consequently, Egypt's hold on Palestine began to loosen.

In his last years, Amenhotep III was assisted by his son. However, this son, Amenhotep IV, continued the neglect and neither father nor son gave much attention to the political turmoil that was then shaking Palestine (see page 107). Amenhotep IV precipitated the short-lived "Amarna revolution." He raised the sun god Aten to preeminence, changed his own name to Akhenaten (glory of Aten), closed temples to other gods, and moved the capital to a new site north of Thebes (Amarna). Scholars are divided over whether these changes should be seen as a move to monotheism. They are also divided over whether Akhenaten was motivated by religious zeal, or whether he was attempting to break the power of the Theban priesthood. Some who have argued for a "late Exodus" have tried to find the origin of Moses' monotheism in "Atenism," but the prominent Egyptologist Donald Redford finds the essential features of the two religions too dissimilar for any influence to have been possible.

Smenkhkare took the throne only to be soon replaced by Tutankhamun. Amarna was abandoned and the capital moved back to Thebes. The worship of Amon was resumed and Atenism was declared a heresy. While Tutankhamun and two additional rulers played out the end of Dynasty 18, political changes were taking place north of the country. Mitanni fell and the Hittites (see chapter 7) began exerting pressure in areas the Egyptians had claimed earlier in the dynasty.

Dynasties 19–20 (c. 1318–1069 B.C.)
The last king of Dynasty 18 chose Ramses I as his successor, but Ramses I ruled less than two years before his son, Seti I, became pharaoh. Thebes remained the religious capital, but the seat of government moved north to Memphis. Farther north, in the Delta, Seti I built a summer palace at Avaris, the previous Hyksos capital. He also renewed Egypt's interest in empire as armies again moved north along Palestine's coastal highway. They paid little attention to the hill country where the Hebrews had by this time settled. Rather, their focus was on Syria, into which the Hittites had extended their control.

Seti I ruled fourteen years, and was followed by Ramses II, who reigned sixty-seven years. Ramses II was a prolific builder, and he incorporated his father's summer palace at Avaris into a new capital, Pi-Ramesses, which became one of the largest cities in the ancient Near East. Egyptian armies continued their marches northwards and repeated battles were fought with the Hittites for control of Syria. In one of those battles Ramses II rode into an ambush and nearly lost his life. After he returned home, however, both texts and wall reliefs transformed the near debacle into glorious victory. Concern over the rising power of Assyria eventually led the two sides to sign a peace treaty. Ramses II married a Hittite princess but, in keeping with Egyptian policy, he did not send an Egyptian princess

to the Hittites. (Following the "late date," 1290 B.C., Ramses II is identified as the Pharoh of the Exodus. The archaeological supports for this date are no longer accepted. Further, the "late date" requires a compaction of the period of the Judges far beyond what is reasonable.)

Merenptah followed his father, Ramses II, to the throne. Early in his reign Merenptah beat back an attempted immigration from Libya to the west. The "Merenptah Stele" records both this victory, and his encounter with the Israelites in Palestine.

The founder of Dynasty 20, Setnakht, ruled only two years and then he was followed in unbroken line by Ramses III through XI. Ramses III had repeatedly to defend his country. Twice early in his reign Libyans tried to settle in the Delta. Also early in his reign (about 1200 B.C.) people the Egyptians called "Sea Peoples" came out of the Aegean and attempted to enter Egypt. Ramses III was able to hold them off, and with great bravado proclaimed his victory in both text and sprawling wall reliefs. Some of the Sea Peoples who survived became mercenaries in the Egyptian army, while others settled along the coast of Palestine. Of the several groups that constituted the Sea Peoples, the Philistines are best known because of their appearance in the Bible (see pages 110, 112).

Ramses III was the last effectual Ramesside pharaoh. In the reigns that followed him there are reports of worker strikes, harem conspiracies, and tomb robberies. During the reign of Ramses XI the Theban priesthood and the south effectively became independent. Egypt was again divided.

Third Intermediate Period (c. 1069–656 B.C.)

Dynasty 21
Beginning with Dynasty 21, the pharaohs were buried at Tanis, the Delta capital, rather than in the Valley of the Kings. In the

Three Egyptian rulers

Following the "early date" of the Exodus, these three personages lived during the early years of the Judges.

Below: Akhenaten, wearing the white crown of Upper Egypt, holds two libation vessels as he worships the sun disk, the Aten, which hovers over him. Hands of the sun rays extend toward his offerings, and nefer, the sign for life, is held to his nose. Behind Akhenaten is his wife Nefertiti and one of their daughters. Although short-lived, three stages have been discerned in Amarna period art. Shown here is the second stage in which the king is almost grotesquely rendered. Several theories have been proffered in explanation, but almost all agree Akhenaten had some physical problem.

Right: Gold face mask of Tutankhamun. He wears the royal nemes headdress, a striped linen wig cover, as well as the ceremonial false beard. Tutankhamun died while still a teenager and his reign would have largely been ignored if his tomb had not been found still crammed with most of its grave offerings. The riches found in his tomb give some hint of the treasures that must once have graced the burials of more prominent pharaohs.

Lower right: The famous bust of Nefertiti. She wears her customary tall blue crown, and is much more realistically rendered than in the relief. The Amarna-period emphasis on the royal family is unprecedented in earlier Egyptian art.

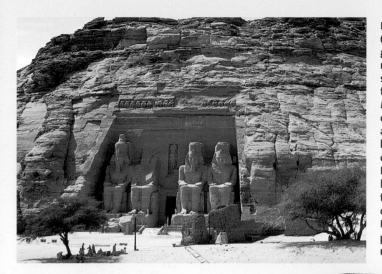

Below: The Merenptah Stele (Israel Stele). Made of black granite, this is 7.5 feet (2.2 meters) tall. The god Amon is shown twice at the top center of the stele. On the left he faces Merenptah and the goddess Mut, on the right he faces Merenptah and the god Horus. Toward the bottom the stele reports a campaign along the coast of Palestine. The next to the last line of the inscription contains the claim "Israel is laid waste;" definitely placing Israel in Palestine about 1220 B.C., but providing no indication of how much earlier Israel had arrived.

Abu Simbel

Top: The Egyptian landscape is dotted with structures dedicated to Ramses II, but Egyptologists note that some were hastily built, some were built with blocks taken from earlier buildings, and on some his name was simply put over that of a previous king. Abu Simbel, pictured here, was cut into a cliff just north of the Nile's second cataract. This temple was the focus of international attention in the 1960s since it was in danger of being covered by Lake Nassar when the Aswan High Dam was completed. Abu Simbel was rescued by cutting it apart into blocks and then reassembling the blocks atop the cliff, above the projected new water line. This illustration shows the temple in its original setting. Each of the four statues of Ramses II is over 65 feet (19.8 meters) tall.

85

Thebes and Its Temples

The city of Thebes began on the east bank of the Nile, probably where the Karnak temple now sits. The west bank became the main cemetery for the city and, in time, the whole area grew to hold the largest concentration of temples in Egypt. Beginning in Dynasty 18 and continuing through Dynasty 20, pharaohs were buried in the Valley of the Kings. The royal tombs were separated from their mortuary temples, which were set outside the valley and back from the edge of cultivation (some of the better preserved mortuary temples are indicated). The mortuary temple of Amenhotep III must have been one of the finest, but today only the "Colossi of Memnon" from its entrance avenue remains.

Top right: Der el-Bahri temple. The mortuary temple of Hatshepsut consists of terraces that are connected to one another by ramps. The covered porticos on each level are richly reliefed with scenes depicting highlights of her reign. This architectural plan was never used again. The Valley of the Kings was on the other side of the cliffs against which her temple was built.

Bottom right: The Luxor temple. Sited south of the Karnak temple, this was begun by Amenhotep III but Ramses II subsequently added a forecourt and this pylon to the entranceway. Grooves in the pylon once held flagstaffs from which banners waved. Each of the seated statues of Ramses II is 76 feet (23 meters) tall. Originally there were two obelisks, but one was transported to Paris early in the nineteenth century.

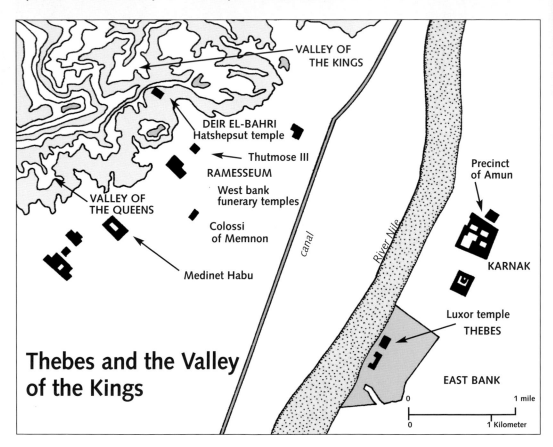

VALLEY OF THE KINGS

DEIR EL-BAHRI
Hatshepsut temple

Thutmose III

RAMESSEUM

West bank funerary temples

VALLEY OF THE QUEENS

Colossi of Memnon

Medinet Habu

Precinct of Amun

Canal

River Nile

KARNAK

Luxor temple
THEBES

EAST BANK

Thebes and the Valley of the Kings

0 ———————— 1 mile

0 ———————— 1 Kilometer

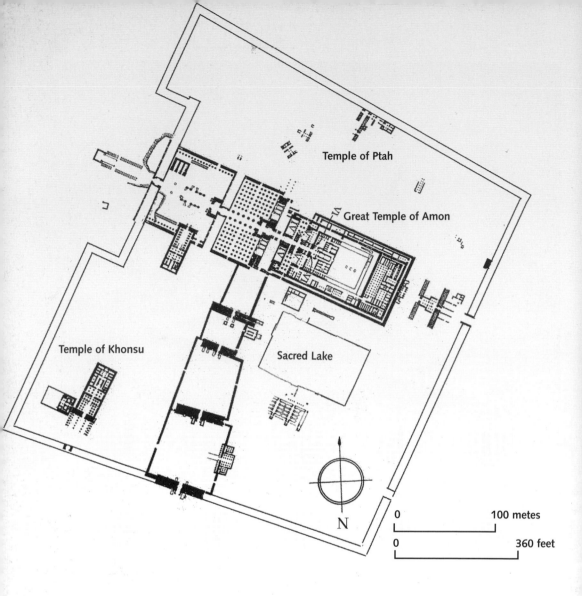

Temple of Ptah

Great Temple of Amon

Temple of Khonsu

Sacred Lake

N

| 0 | 100 metes |
| 0 | 360 feet |

Great Temple of Amon

Above: Plan of the Great Temple of Amon at Karnak. Construction at Karnak began in the Middle Kingdom and continued into the last centuries B.C. as pharaoh after pharaoh added to the complex.

Opposite: Wall relief from the Karnak temple. Shortly after the death of Solomon, Shishak invaded Palestine. This wall relief commemorates his campaign and depicts Shishak brandishing a sword and holding ropes connected to nearly 200 cartouches (ovals), each containing the name of a place in Palestine he claimed to have defeated. Bound bodies are attached to each cartouche. The relief amplifies the biblical account of this raid (see page 119).

south a line of high priests ruled from Thebes in the name of Amon. Contact between north and south was usually peaceful and even resulted in intermarriage. Early in the dynasty Wen-Amun, a Theban official, was sent to Byblos where for centuries the Egyptians had maintained commercial ties. As he sailed along the coast of Palestine he was robbed, and then scorned at Byblos as that city's prince repeatedly demanded his departure. The prince of Byblos made it clear that the respect once shown the Egyptians (see Sinuhe, pages 105–106) was no more: "I am not your servant! I am not the servant of him who sent you either!" Egypt had become a "crushed reed" long before that imagery was used in the Bible to describe the country (2 Kings 18:21; Isaiah 36:6).

In Dynasty 21 Egypt provided asylum for Hadad of Edom when he fled from David. Hadad married into the royal family and his son was raised in the Egyptian court. At the death of David, Hadad returned to Edom where he was an "adversary to Israel all the days of Solomon" (1 Kings 11:14–22, 25). Siamun, the next to last king of Dynasty 21, has been identified as the pharaoh who, in giving a daughter in marriage to Solomon (see page 116), broke a centuries old point of foreign policy. He also gave Gezer to Israel as a dowry, thus relinquishing Egypt's last vestige of empire.

Black granite head of Taharqa. This is the king who came to Hezekiah's aid when the Judean king was attacked by Sennacherib of Assyria. Taharqa wears the cap-like crown favoured by the Cushite kings. He was twice forced to flee upriver to escape the Assyrians. Thebes was sacked four years after his second escape, ending Dynasty 25. The head is 13.75 inches (35 centimeters) high.

Dynasties 22–23

More and more Libyans had been finding their way into the Delta and the Fayum. They became so thoroughly assimilated into the Egyptian population that only their names give evidence of their foreign origin. The family of Shishak (Shoshenq) had been in Egypt for five generations, and when he founded Dynasty 22, the transition to power was smooth. In his day Merenptah claimed to have totally destroyed the Libyans. In Shishak's time, however, much of Egypt was ruled by Libyans even more acculturated than the Hyksos had been. The fears of the "pharaoh who knew not Joseph" came true in a way Merenptah would never have anticipated.

Surprisingly little is known about the two Libyan dynasties. Shishak provided their main intrusion into biblical history. He gave refuge to Jeroboam when he fled from Solomon (1 Kings 11:40) and then, five years after the death of Solomon, he sent an army into Palestine (see page 119). During the reign of Osorkon I Egypt launched a failed attack on Judah (2 Chronicles 14:9-15). Osorkon IV is probably the "So king of Egypt" (2 Kings 17:4) from whom Hoshea sought help in the dying days of Israel.

Dynasties 24–25

A line of Cushite kings developed in Nubia where a gradual Egyptianization had taken place. Piankhy, ruling from Napata, below the fourth cataract, advanced north and conquered Egypt in the name of Amon. These Napatan kings considered themselves legitimate pharaohs of Egypt; they wrote their language in Egyptian hieroglyphics, and they were buried in small steep-sided pyramids.

As Assyria began bearing down on Syria-Palestine, the Dynasty 25 kings initially stayed neutral, but during the reign of Hezekiah they tried to come to Judah's aid (2 Kings 19:9; Isaiah 37:9). Further encounters between Egypt and Assyria followed, and at one point Thebes was even sacked. Assyria's attempt to turn Egypt into a vassal nation proved to be both troubled and short-lived.

Late Dynastic
(c. 656–525 B.C.)

Dynasty 26 [Saite]

Dynasty 26 (or Saite, after its capital city, Sais, in the western Delta). When the Assyrians were not able to maintain control of Egypt, the country was united again, this time under Psamtik I. Stability and prosperity characterize the dynasty, conditions that were due, at least in part, to an increasing foreign population. The pharaohs of this dynasty, whose names reveal a Libyan or Napatan heritage, were protected by Ionian Greek bodyguards. The country's security relied more and more on mercenary armies and fleets. A Jewish garrison at Elephantine guarded the first cataract, once again the southern border of Egypt. Greek and Ionian merchant colonies sprang up in the Delta, and Upper Egypt became an "agricultural granary."

An archaizing tendency in art, architecture, and religious texts had been in evidence for some time, but the trend became even more pronounced as Egypt became increasingly cosmopolitan. This neoclassicism was so well executed that some recovered Dynasty 26 works of art were initially thought to date to the Old or Middle Kingdoms.

When Assyria began its precipitous collapse, Pharaoh Necho's attempt to step into the vacuum and take possession of Syria and Palestine resulted in a confrontation with Josiah and the death of the Judean king. A puppet king was put on the throne in Jerusalem, but Egypt's dream of a revived empire was soon crushed by Nebuchadnezzar and his Babylonian army at Carchemish, and Egypt narrowly escaped invasion. Egypt did not come to Jehoiakim's support when the Babylonians attacked Jerusalem, but Apries did send an army to aid Zedekiah when the city came under siege. It was to a Saite Egypt that Jeremiah was taken after the fall of Jerusalem in 586 B.C.

The Last Dynasties
(c. 525–332 B.C.)

Dynasties 27–31

The fall of Babylonia was unexpectedly swift, and only a few years later, in 525 B.C., Egypt found itself added to the new Persian empire. Dynasty 27 began when Cambyses II, the son of Cyrus the Great, conquered the whole country, a feat the Assyrians and Babylonians had not managed. Greek historians had nothing good to say about Cambyses, but modern scholars paint a more positive picture of his rule. Whatever the truth, Cambyses' reign over Egypt was brief (the Bible ignores him completely, see Ezra 4:5), and Darius the Great was next on the throne of Persia. Darius tried to pose as legitimate pharaoh of Egypt, going as far as to build a temple and commission reliefs depicting him making offerings to the gods of Egypt.

Dynasty 27 was not without interruptions. Egypt revolted following Darius' defeat at Marathon, and it was left for his son Xerxes to restore the *satrapy* (a province into which the empire was divided). Egypt revolted again when Xerxes died, and it was a few

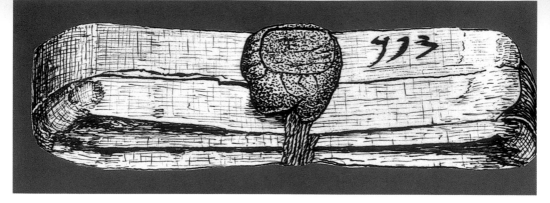

One of the Elephantine papyri.
Written on papyrus and in Aramaic, the papyri were folded, tied, and sealed to guard their contents. In addition to contracts and deeds, the papyri also contain private and official letters. Taken together, they provide great insights into the daily and religious life of the Jewish community living at Elephantine. Written in the fifth century B.C., the papyri also constitute one of the evidences that many Jews, probably the majority, did not rush back to Palestine when return became possible.

years before Artaxerxes reclaimed the territory. Near the end of the dynasty Jews at Elephantine began writing the "Elephantine Papyri." Among these documents were letters to Jews in Jerusalem who had returned from exile. The letters tell of problems and needs in Upper Egypt, but they give no hint of any desire to return to Palestine.

Only one king is listed by Manetho for Dynasty 28, but little can be said about him. What is clear is that Egypt declared itself again free and, through Dynasty 30, struck alliances with Sparta, Athens, and other parties in an effort to maintain that independence. Through it all the Persians considered Egypt a rebellious satrapy and on his second try, in 343 B.C., Artaxerxes III succeeded in reclaiming the country.

Manetho's dynastic list ends with Dynasty 30, but the brief renewal of Persian control, which lasted only nine years, is sometimes called Dynasty 31. This final dynasty was extinguished by Alexander the Great in 332 B.C. Alexander was welcomed as a deliverer by the Egyptians, but he stayed only briefly before continuing on to conquer what remained of the Persian empire. One of his generals, Ptolemy, was left in charge. Still another "different" Egypt was about to begin.

THE INTER–TESTAMENTAL PERIOD

Ptolemaic Egypt (c. 304-30 B.C.)

When Alexander died a few years after conquering Egypt, his dream of a united world did not long outlive him, and Ptolemy became king of Egypt. At first Egypt prospered. Alexander had taken time to found Alexandria and this seaport grew to become one of the largest cities in the world. It not only became Egypt's capital, but also a cultural center to rival Athens. Ptolemaic control initially extended into Palestine and a large number of Jews were deported from Jerusalem and Judea and resettled in Alexandria. Many more joined them voluntarily, and their community became one of the most important within the Diaspora. In time they began speaking Greek and it was for them that the Old Testament began to be translated into Greek (the Septuagint).

Under the Ptolemies, the Greeks spread south from the Delta and took their language and culture with them. At the same time, though, the Ptolemies were attracted to Egypt's past and they tried to be accepted

The temple to Horus at Edfu.
In the Ptolemaic period the Hellenistic world increasingly intruded into the land of the Nile. In art there were awkward attempts to merge Egyptian and Hellenistic styles. At the same time, this temple, begun early in the Ptolemaic period, exhibits much that is familiar, including the 118-foot (36-meter) high pylon with reliefs of the pharaoh in a striding and enemy-bashing pose. Fourteen volumes were required for the Egyptologists to publish the reliefs and hieroglyphic inscriptions from this one temple.

as legitimate successors to the pharaohs. They enlarged old temples, and built new ones to Egyptian gods. In 198 B.C. Egypt lost control of Palestine to the Seleucids, Greeks ruling another portion of Alexander's short-lived empire, who were by this time operating from Antioch on the Orontes. During much of the second century B.C., and continuing into the first century B.C., Ptolemaic infighting caused Egypt to decline.

The growing power of Rome became increasingly felt in Egypt and it was Rome that more and more began to dictate events. In 168 B.C., for example, when the Seleucids tried to invade Egypt, it was the Romans who ordered them to leave. Cleopatra (actually Cleopatra VII) was the last Ptolemaic sovereign, but she was under the control of the Roman Senate. Cleopatra's desire to recover Palestine for Egypt, and her closeness to Mark Antony, caused great difficulties for Herod who had, by then, been declared king of the Jews by Rome.

ROMAN EGYPT

When Antony and Cleopatra committed suicide in 30 B.C., Egypt became a Roman province, administered in the name of the emperor by a prefect. The Romans made some attempt to pose as heirs of the pharaohs; they added to old temples, put their names on others, and built a few small temples of their own. But the distinctly Egyptian civilization was dying out. The practice of mummification continued, but the mummy portraits that came into vogue were hardly Egyptian. And although temples to the goddess Isis spread into the Roman world, it was a greatly altered form of that deity that was exported. Egypt became a part of Rome's breadbasket, and grain ships began to move along the coastline between Alexandria and Italy. The apostle Paul boarded one such ship when he sailed for Rome.

The Rosetta Stone

The Rosetta Stone carries a decree issued in 196
B.C. by Ptolemy V for priests of Memphis. Its real
importance today is that the trilingual inscription
in Egyptian hieroglyphics, Egyptian demotic (a
cursive form of hieroglyphics), and Greek,
provided the key to deciphering Egyptian
hieroglyphics and recovering much of
ancient Egypt's written history.

4

PALESTINE AND THE BIBLE

Old Testament

PALESTINE AND THE BIBLE

Old Testament

Over the centuries travelers to the Near East have been attracted to the impressive monuments from the past that can still be seen in Egypt and, to a lesser extent, in Mesopotamia. Comparable wonders are not the draw for those who choose to visit Palestine; the greater attraction is to walk in the footsteps of Old and New Testament personages.

PALESTINE BEFORE THE PATRIARCHS

Neolithic Period (c. 8500–4300 B.C.)

Jericho is one of the oldest known cities in the world, but little beyond a stone tower can be seen today. During excavation, however, the archaeologists found simple mud-brick housing. They also uncovered a small shrine containing a *massebah*, a Hebrew term for roughly shaped stones ("sacred pillar" in English) which were used as abstractions of deity. Such stones, then, were part of worship long before Moses warned the Israelites against making such objects when they entered the land (Leviticus 26:1; Deuteronomy 16:22). Figurines excavated at Jericho and other sites suggest that Palestine's Neolithic population was engaged in fertility worship. Plastered skulls, and human statues up to

one-half lifesize, are among the other religious finds from this time period. Taken together they illustrate that almost as far back as we can see into the pre-history of Palestine, iniquity (Genesis 15:16) was already accumulating.

Chalcolithic Period (c. 4300–3300 B.C.)

Dozens of unfortified villages have been found that date to this time range. Publications use terms like "pastoral societies" and "chiefdoms" to characterize the social system. Basically the people were agriculturists and shepherds, but there also seem to have been regional "cottage industries." Among the surprisingly wide variety

Opposite: Stone tower at Jericho. This 30-foot-high (9.1 meter) tower is probably near its original height and is only one part of the earliest known defense system in the world. The tower was built against the inside of a city wall over 6 feet (1.8 meters) wide and still standing to 12 feet (3.6 meters) high at one point. Finally, a 9-foot-deep and 27-foot-wide (2.7 meters by 8.2 meters) trench/moat fronted the wall. Jericho was built beside one of the most powerful springs in all of Palestine. That desirable water source would have attracted many people to the area, people the inhabitants of Jericho felt it necessary to defend themselves against. During excavation, the remains of fifteen bodies were found in the tower's interior staircase (arrows point to its lower entrance and the opening on top).

Copper objects dating to the Chalcolithic period. This sample of copper objects is from a cache of over 400 that were found in a cave on the west side of the Dead Sea, near En-gedi. Understandably, the cave has been dubbed the Cave of the Treasure. Initially, some archaeologists thought that the sophistication of the metallurgy required the objects to have been made in the first millennium B.C. Subsequent study of other objects found in the cave, however, together with C-14 analysis, proved their early date. The objects were probably hidden in the cave by priests who had used them in a temple that has been found at En-gedi. Similar objects have been excavated elsewhere in the country.

of artistic expressions that have been found are ivory carvings, wall frescoes, and elaborate copper objects. The art has been termed "extraordinarily opulent." Some of the figurines imply that religion continued to center around fertility, but the specific object of worship is unclear.

Pottery burial chests. The ossuary was one of several types of interment practiced in the Chalcolithic period. Bodies were first left to desiccate and then the bones of the deceased were gathered and placed in a pottery chest sometimes shaped to imitate a house. This practice of "secondary burial" is not seen again until New Testament times when stone "bone boxes" (see page 194) became popular for a short period of time.

Old Testament Palestine

Dan

ASHER

NAPHTALI

Lake Huleh

Hazor

Sea of Chinnereth

G R E A T   S E A

Kishon R.

ZEBULUN

Mount Tabor

Kedesh

MIDIAN

Beth-shittah

Megiddo

Hill of Moreh

ISSACHAR

Jordan R.

GILEAD

Tob

Taanach

Jezreel

Abel-meholah

Tabbath

Samaria

MANASSEH

Shechem

Succoth

Mount Gorizim

Penuel

Jabbok R.

Zererah

EPHRAIM

Shiloh

Jogbehah

Bethel

Ai

AMMON

Gezer

Ajalon

Benjamin

Ramah

Timnah

Zorah

Gibeah

Jebus

Jericho

Heshbon

(Jerusalem)

Kiriath-Jearim

Bethlehem

Ashkelon

PHILISTIA

Lachish

JUDAH

Salt Sea

Gaza

Hebron

MOAB

Gerar

Engedi

Arnon R.

Aroer

Sodom?

Beersheba

0		25		50 km

0	10	20	30 miles

Canaanite "high place." This circular raised platform at Megiddo is about 26 feet (7.9 meters) in diameter, and is the earliest "high place" (*bamah* in Hebrew) known. When excavated, the area around the base was strewn with animal bones, the remains of Canaanite worship.

Early Bronze Period (c. 3300–2300 B.C.)

During this period there was intensive settlement and rise in population, and formidable defense systems became more of a necessity. Unfortified agricultural villages became overshadowed and controlled by "city-states." Scholars are divided concerning how to explain this shift to urbanization; everything from indigenous adaptation to outside forces has been posited. This land between Mesopotamia and Egypt was experiencing some commercial contact from both sides, but whether it was more than that is unclear. Multiple burials became common and some tombs show evidence that they were used for several generations. The large number of pottery vessels found in the tombs would originally have been filled with food and drink offerings, clear evidence of belief in an afterlife. Such "family tombs" were also popular when the patriarchs began to bury their loved ones at Hebron several centuries later.

Middle Bronze I (also called Early Bronze IV) Period (c. 2300–2000 B.C.)

Suddenly the city-states collapsed and almost all the cities west of the Jordan River were abandoned or destroyed. Internal warfare and invasion are among the explanations posited for what has been called "a radical cultural break." Those who favor invasion point to the shift from multiple burials to more individual interments as an indicator of extreme change. Several additional changes are cited by those who argue that an "ethnic invasion," namely, the arrival of Amorites, had taken place. But other scholars do not believe that they became part of Palestine's population (see Numbers 13:29) this early. Clearly, however, during these centuries Palestine underwent a period of deurbanization and "chiefdoms" again characterized the social order.

THE PATRIARCHAL AGE

The patriarchal narratives fit within the Middle Bronze II period (c. 2000–1550 B.C.). In several ways, what is known about this archaeological period parallels and amplifies our understanding of patriarchal life. For example, during Middle Bronze II (hereafter MB II) Palestine experienced a gradual reurbanization and finally a return to the city-state model.

Of the several hundred MB II sites that have been identified, about twenty are large urban centers estimated to have held over half the total population of Palestine. As city-states, these centers dominated surrounding towns and villages. It would be incorrect, therefore, to visualize Palestine as a land filled with tent dwelling nomads. There have been nomads in all periods of ancient Palestine, just as there are today, but they did not constitute a large percentage of patriarchal Palestine's population. Also, living in a tent does not necessarily signal a nomadic lifestyle; some people just prefer that form of housing. The places where Abraham resided after his return from Egypt were relatively close to one another, making it clear how little he moved about in southern Palestine. Further, although the patriarchs sometimes lived in tents, at other times they chose more permanent structures (as in Genesis 33:17).

Archaeologists have found that all but the smallest MB II settlements were fortified, and in some cases it is estimated that the city walls required hundreds of thousands of hours to erect. The gateway was a necessary break in the outer defense wall, and it figures in three patriarchal episodes (Genesis 19:1; Genesis 23; and Genesis 34:20–24).

Through the centuries the gateway underwent design change. Early in MB II the approach was angled to prevent an enemy from making a straight run at its gate door with a battering ram. Later in MB II the three-piered gateway was introduced. Although this meant a straight line of approach, an attacker would have to break down three doors to gain entrance to the city.

The prevalence of fortifications throughout the land is characteristic of a feudal society in which city-states clashed with one another as they tried to enlarge their holdings. Archaeologists have found MB II to have been one of the more prosperous times in Palestine, but the emphasis on defense clearly implies that it was also a precarious time in which to live. This insecurity is reflected in the statement that Abraham had over 300 "trained men" available to rescue Lot (Genesis 14:14). Also, Esau approached Jacob with 400 men, some of whom he offered to leave with Jacob (Genesis 33), and later Jacob complained that his men were "few in number" and would not be able to ensure his household's safety in an attack (Genesis 34:30).

In the story of Sinuhe (see below) there is mention of crime, attack, murder, plunder, captives, and even picked combat, which brings to mind the contest between David and Goliath centuries later. Both biblically and archaeologically, then, patriarchal Palestine can be seen as a land filled with both wealth and worry.

Abraham interacted with the rulers of Jerusalem (Salem), Sodom (Genesis 14:18–24), and Gerar (Genesis 20). Isaac also had contact with the king of Gerar (Genesis 26). Egyptian texts from this period of time do not happen to mention Sodom or Gerar, but they do identify a ruler of Jerusalem as well as of Shechem. Several other cities are named that appear later in the biblical story.

Archaeologists have uncovered a wide range of housing, both in size and quality. Some of these houses have even been identified as palaces. They have also found that a new houseplan, the "courtyard house," had come into popularity. In at least two instances our knowledge of patriarchal housing helps us understand biblical episodes with more clarity. For example, houses within a city were not free-standing; they were more like row houses. Therefore, that the

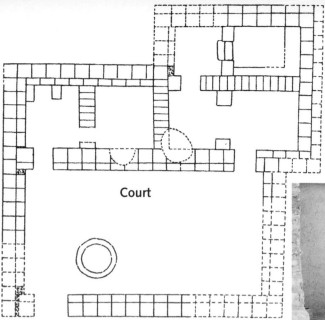

Court

Restoration of a typical interior room. The walls are white-washed and have storage niches. Pottery, and furniture similar to that shown on page 104 furnishes the room.

Ground plan of a typical courtyard house, Tell Beit Mirsim. Available space and wealth naturally dictated the size and quality of housing, but variations on this same house style repeat throughout Palestine. A single doorway gave access into an enclosed courtyard (which in this example is about 40 feet (12 meters) wide where much of the daily activity took place. Rooms behind the courtyard generally served as workrooms and for storage. Upstairs rooms would have been reserved for sleeping areas and leisure activities; playing pieces and remains of a game board were found where they had fallen from the upper floor of this house.

men of Sodom "surrounded" Lot's house (Genesis 19:4), should be understood to mean they were milling around in the street outside his courtyard. When Abimelech looked out a window and saw Isaac in a private moment with Rebekah (Genesis 26:8), the king must have been looking down from an upper floor into an open courtyard (for a later instance where a courtyard failed to provide adequate privacy, see 2 Samuel 11:2).

The Canaanites continued to worship gods of their own imagination, and several temples have been found that functioned in MB II times. Archaeologists have also found that a surprisingly wide variety of offerings were involved. Incense was burned, oil was poured out, and animals were sacrificed. Figurines of doves, cattle, and female deities, as well as several kinds of jewelry, were left at the worship sites. Still, as Genesis 15:16 states, "the iniquity of the Amorite is not yet complete" ("Amorite" was sometimes used as a general term in place of "Canaanite").

By the time of Abraham the land had already seen a good many burials, and some people were not adverse to reusing older tombs. Multiple burials again became popular, but only twenty or so bodies might occupy a single tomb, rather than the hundreds seen in the Early Bronze period. This practice gives literal meaning to the phrase "gathered to their fathers" (for example, Genesis 49:29; Judges 2:10). Abraham chose to purchase a cave in which to bury Sarah (Genesis 23), and in time he and Isaac, Rebekah, Jacob, and Leah would also occupy that family tomb (Genesis 49:31; 50:13).

The Gateway of Dan

In addition to its defensive purpose, the gateway served as the legal and social center of a city. Additionally, an open area was often left just inside the gate to function as a market area. The site of Dan provides a fine example of the gate system that would have been familiar to the patriarchs. Dan's gateway is set within a mudbrick fortification wall still preserved to nearly 23 feet (7 meters) high (center). Traces of the white plaster that originally covered the doorway can still be seen. The gateway is 17 feet (5.18 meters) wide by 12 feet (3.65 meters) high, and the three sets of piers (top) held as many doors. A staircase led up from the surrounding plain to the gateway (bottom), and a shorter interior staircase led down into the city. It is assumed that the top of the wall was crenellated to provide protection for those manning the battlements.

Outside of Gate.

The gateway at Dan from the time of the patriarchs.

Top: Reconstruction of one of the Jericho tombs, from the Rockefeller Musuem.

Bottom: Reconstructions of tomb furniture.
At Jericho a group of family tombs had become so tightly sealed that objects that should have long since perished were still identifiable. Jars contained grain and the residue of liquids. Meat, mostly roasted lamb, still lay on wooden bowls. Woven baskets and scraps of textiles were found. Personal objects like combs, and furniture such as stools, tables (three-legged tables are more stable on uneven surfaces than the four-legged variety), and beds were also recovered. The Canaanites clearly continued to believe that it was necessary to outfit the deceased for their afterlife. There is no reason to think that there would have been any difference between patriarchal possessions and the contents of these tombs.

Adapted from Kenyon

The Story of Sinuhe

Further insights into patriarchal Palestine are available from both Egypt and Mesopotamia. From Egypt comes the Story of Sinuhe, which was composed early in Egypt's Middle Kingdom, but became such a popular piece of literature that copies were made throughout the second millennium B.C. For some unstated reason, Sinuhe, an Egyptian official, fled the country when a certain pharaoh died. Sinuhe spent many years in MB II Palestine and his story is filled with details of life familiar to Abraham and the other patriarchs when they resided in the same land. One useful corrective given by the story has to do with the land itself. Today many people visit Palestine during the summer season and return home with memories of a dry and browned-out landscape. But in the rainy season that same landscape is lush with color and growth. Sinuhe paints a word picture of this rich and variegated land:

> It was a good land. . . . Figs were in it, and grapes. It had more wine than water. Plentiful was its honey, abundant its olives. Every kind of fruit was on its trees. Barley was there, and emmer. There was no limit to any kind of cattle. . . . Bread was made for me as daily fare, wine as daily provision, cooked meat and roast fowl, beside the wild beasts of the desert, for they hunted for me and laid before me, beside the catch of my own hounds. Many . . . were made for me, and milk in every kind of cooking.

Painting from a tomb at Beni Hasan in Egypt. This painting adds to the word pictures. It dates to within about a decade of Abraham's entry into Palestine and depicts an Egyptian escorting a group of Palestinians who had come to Egypt. The painting shows the multicolored clothing and hairstyles then fashionable in Palestine. The men have trimmed beards but no mustache; when Sinuhe returned home to Egypt notice was made that his beard was "plucked." It may be assumed that the patriarchs would have adopted the styles current in their new home; if so, this painting illustrates how they would have appeared. The lyre being carried by one of the men shows that music was part of the lifestyle. When Abraham rescued Lot (Genesis 14), no mention is made of the weaponry his men used. This painting reveals that bows and arrows, spears, swords, and battleaxes were available for warfare. The story of Sinuhe adds shields, javelins, and daggers to the list. Neither source makes note of maces, but excavation has found that the club was a popular weapon and it should be added to the list (see, for example, the maceheads on page 98).

Fish and vegetables failed to receive mention in Sinuhe's story, but they, too, were available for consumption. All in all, Sinuhe's words nicely expand on the Bible's repeated description of the land as a place "flowing with milk and honey" (for example, Exodus 3:8).

Sinuhe was not the only Egyptian living in Palestine and his story gives evidence that several ethnic groups resided in the land centuries before the Bible takes notice of the mixture of peoples (for example, Exodus 23:23). Sinuhe was befriended by an Amorite named Ammi-enshi and married that man's eldest daughter. Similar intermarriage is known from the Bible, for example, Esau married "foreign" women. Despite the dangers inherent in the land, hospitality was still important. Both Abraham and Lot were gracious to travelers, and Sinuhe boasted that he "gave water to the thirsty . . . put him who had strayed back on the road [and] rescued him who had been robbed." Sinuhe's story goes on to recount his years in Palestine, years filled with battles, and increasing family and wealth.

Sinuhe was finally encouraged to return to Egypt because, "It should not be that you should die in a foreign country. . . . You should not be placed in a sheepskin." Before going home Sinuhe transferred his property to his children: ". . . my eldest son being responsible for my clan. My clan and all my property were in his charge. . . ." In the Bible the birthright normally went to the eldest son, who received a double portion of the family wealth at his father's death. He also assumed whatever leadership role his father had exercised.

The Nuzi texts

More than 4,000 cuneiform tablets were found at the site of Nuzi in Mesopotamia. These "Nuzi texts" are dated after the close of the patriarchal period but, because of the static condition of ancient Near-Eastern culture, they reveal societal norms extant for centuries on either side of their actual composition. Most of the texts deal with private contracts and public records—those having to do with adoption and inheritance rights are especially important for the insights they lend to certain patriarchal decisions. For example, a marriage was expected to produce children and if it did not, the man was free to divorce his wife and remarry. But the childless couple also had the option to adopt, and this is the course of action Abraham intended to take with Eliezar (Genesis 15:1-3). In return for being made an heir, the adopted child was expected to care for his new parents in their old age and, when the time came, to give them proper burial. Through adoption the couple also ensured that the family name was not extinguished, a consideration as important as the distribution of the family's wealth. Whether or not the adoption of Eliezer had taken place, God informed Abraham that he would have a son, and that Eliezer would not become his heir (Genesis 15:4). In the Nuzi texts the adoptee lost his primacy if the adopting couple subsequently had a son.

When Sarah gave her handmaid Hagar to Abraham (Genesis 16:2) and Ishmael was born, she was electing another solution acceptable in their milieu. Such surrogate mothers took on the rank of "other wife." It was so important for a wife to produce children that she could be required to provide her husband with another woman: "If Kelim-ninu does not bear [children], Kelim-ninu shall acquire a woman of the land of Lullu as wife for Shennima [the bridegroom], and Kelim-ninu may not send the offspring away." This last stipulation reveals that Sarah was not within her rights when she subsequently pushed Hagar and Ishmael away (Genesis 21:10).

As noted above, the birthright conveyed both wealth and power. Esau gave his birthright to Jacob for little more than a bowl of soup (Genesis 25:29-34). Although there is no direct parallel to this transfer in the Nuzi texts, there are instances where at least part of an inheritance exchanged hands between brothers. In one Nuzi text the exchange seems as unequal as that of Jacob and Esau: Tupkitilla gave Kurpazah an orchard as his inheritance share in exchange for only three sheep.

Jacob lived for twenty years of his life in Haran, and returned to southern Palestine with four wives and twelve children. His twelfth son, Benjamin ("son of the south") was born subsequent to his return. Eventually Jacob moved the Israelites into Egypt where they stayed for several generations and grew in number. By the time they returned to Palestine under the leadership of Moses and then Joshua, the MB II period had ended, and the Late Bronze I period (c. 1550–1400 B.C.) was also just about to end. During LB I Thutmose III imposed control over much of Palestine and began to take Palestinian princes into Egypt for acculturation and future use as puppet kings (see page 79).

THE CONQUEST AND THE PERIOD OF THE JUDGES

The Conquest

Under Moses' leadership the people east of the Jordan River were pacified and the land was granted to two and a half tribes as their inheritance share. By the time Joshua assembled the tribes near the northeast corner of the Dead Sea to cross into the Promised Land, there had been many changes on the other side of the Jordan River. Palestine was economically and politically in turmoil as Egypt's recently established empire slipped into neglect—a neglect that allowed Israel to settle into the land without Egyptian opposition. These chaotic conditions are revealed in the "Amarna Letters," nearly 400 cuneiform tablets from the royal archives of pharaohs Amenhotep III and Akhenaten. Nearly half of the letters were written between the Egyptian court

and various princes in Syria-Palestine. They reveal a Palestine in which caravans were waylaid, armed escorts were necessary, and protection money was demanded. Princes were afraid to leave their cities, others were killed by their own people. Princes who stayed stubbornly loyal to Egypt were not supported, and their pleas for sanctuary were ignored. Abdu-Heba, prince of Jerusalem, wrote:

> To the king, my lord . . . It was not my father and not my mother but the arm of the mighty king that placed me in the house of my father. . . . Let my king take thought for his land! The land of the king is lost. . . . The Apiru capture the cities of the king. . . . Let the king send archers to his land! . . . If there are no archers here this year, let the king send a commissioner, and let him take me to himself together with my brothers, and we shall die near the king, our lord!

There are repeated references in the letters to the land being troubled by Apiru (Habiru in non-Amarna letters). Habiru is etymologically equatable with Hebrew, but what is elsewhere known about Habiru does not correspond with the Hebrews in terms of time, place, or activity. It seems apparent that the Canaanites used Habiru as a "dirty word" directed against anyone they disliked. So although no specific event in the Bible can be tied to any of the Amarna Letters, it is possible that some of their references to Habiru do fill gaps in the book of Joshua's summary account of conquest. At the very least the letters provide a glimpse into the political picture in Palestine at the time of conquest.

Jericho was located at the eastern gateway into Palestine, and it was the first city taken in the seven-year war. Earlier, when Moses' spies had scouted out the land, they reported that the cities were fortified (Numbers 13:28). Archaeologists have found that some cities continued to use defenses from MB times, while other cities merely let the back walls of outer buildings serve for defense. The Bible makes it clear that Jericho was a

An Amarna letter. In this Amarna letter Biridiya, prince of Megiddo, claims he is being attacked by Labayu, prince of Shechem. Biridiya begged desperately for a hundred garrison troops to defend his city. In another letter Labayu wrote of his innocence and swore that he was so loyal to pharaoh that he would even commit suicide if so ordered. The Amarna Letters were written in Akkadian, the diplomatic language in the Near East. It is thought that every main city in Palestine had a scribe who could read and write cuneiform.

walled city, and when Joshua's spies entered Jericho they would have passed through a three-piered gateway similar to that on page 103 (Dan).

In the 1930s an archaeologist claimed that he had found the walls brought down by Joshua, but these were subsequently found to date to a much earlier period. Later it was claimed that, contrary to the biblical account, Jericho was uninhabited at the time of the conquest. In the 1990s, after a re-examination of the excavation records done by Dame Kathleen Kenyon, it was concluded that she misread certain evidences and that Jericho's walls had, in fact, been breached about 1400 B.C.

The conquest of the next city has also been the center of archaeological controversy. In the 1930s the site of et-Tell was suggested as the location of biblical Ai (Joshua 7 to 8). When excavators found that et-Tell was unoccupied between 2200–1200 B.C., liberal scholars began to redact the Bible to fit the archaeological conclusion. Conservative scholars countered that the city could be under the modern city adjacent to the excavated area, or that some other location should be sought. As of this writing, some archaeologists claim to have found biblical Ai at a nearby site. Chapter 1 pointed out that archaeology does not prove the Bible. In fact, here archaeology has presented a problem that we were not aware of—and one that is not yet positively resolved.

The defeat of Ai provided Joshua's forces with a foothold into the central hill country. Several battles were fought in southern Palestine and then Joshua led a surprise attack on a coalition forming in the north under the leadership of Hazor's king. A normal city in Palestine averaged 15 to 20 acres (6 to 8 hectares) in size, but archaeologists found that Hazor occupied about 200 acres (82 hectares). Truly, as the Bible states, Hazor was the "head of all these kingdoms" (Joshua 11:10), and it was imperative that it be neutralized.

The Period of the Judges

Following the death of Joshua, a cycle of subjugation and salvation began. Enemy forces repeatedly took over portions of the land only to be finally repulsed by military leaders called *shophetim* (translated "judges" in English). Early in this period Egypt's interest in empire was rekindled, but there is no mention in the Bible that Egypt was among those troubling Israel. Egypt did set up a network of small forts and administrative strongholds along the coastal highway, but Seti I was focused on territories north of Palestine where Hittite expansion into Syria worried him. Ramses II repeatedly marched along the coastal highway,

Above: Relief of Amenhotep II sitting on the lap of his nurse with his feet on a footstool provided by a defeated enemy. As the southern phase of the conquest was winding down, Joshua followed the Near-Eastern custom of instructing some of his men to put their feet on the necks of the five kings who had been captured (Joshua 10:24; see also Psalm 110:1). In Egypt enemies are often depicted on footstools on which, as here, the pharaoh would place his feet.

Right: Figurine found at Megiddo. Overlaid with gold leaf, it is presumably a representation of El, the chief god of the Canaanites. Texts, temples, and objects like this provide insights into Canaanite religion. Fertility continued to be a main focus in their worship. If Hebrew sacrificial detail seems excessive, Canaanite sacrificial ritual was more so— and sometimes included human sacrifice. God had finally had enough; the "cup of iniquity" was now full, and Joshua's army became the instrument of judgment.

Top: Ramses III commissioned wall reliefs to commemorate his stoppage of the Sea People's attempted invasion. These reliefs allow us to see the dress and weaponry of people who harassed Israel until the days of David. The Philistines wore tall "feathered" helmets, and some are shown wearing body armor. Other reliefs show that women and children were part of the migration.

Below: A collection of Philistine pottery. The pottery shapes and decoration are clearly Aegean in origin. Although it is difficult to distinguish between Canaanite and Israelite settlements, the Philistine material culture distinctively marks their sites.

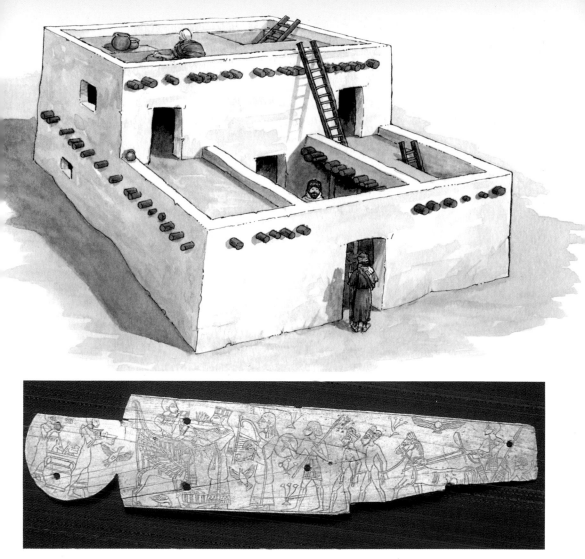

Top: The houses mentioned on the next page are a modification of the courtyard house introduced in the MB II period. For example, pillars were erected so that sheds or more elaborately shaded areas could be added in the courtyard. Archaeological reports speak of "pillared" courtyard houses, and this style became typical throughout the country.

Bottom: Ivory inlay found at Megiddo.
The ivory inlays from Megiddo provide a source for studying the physical appearance, furniture, dress, weaponry, and even the chariots then in style. In this example a Canaanite prince sits on a sphinx-decorated throne, and his feet rest on a footstool. Behind him two servants stand beside a jar and a table on which there are two cups in the shape of

animal heads. The prince is attended by a woman and a musician strumming on a lyre. Captives tied to chariot horses are being led to the prince. In one of the Amarna Letters, the ruler of Jerusalem refers to an enemy who attacked with bows and copper arrows. Copper arrowheads have been found; the metal was no longer too precious to lose. In this inlay the charioteer is armed with a bow, a quiver with arrows, and a spear. "Chariots of iron" mentioned in the Bible (for example, Joshua 17:16, 18) were not made of iron, but the chariot boxes were plated with it to protect the charioteers. The person on the far right in the inlay is carrying a sickle sword, a weapon designed to hack through the body armor that had recently been introduced.

but ignored the hill country where the Israelites had settled. When Egypt and the Hittites signed a peace treaty, they did not specify where their common border ran, but it was probably somewhere in northern Syria. Technically, then, Ramses II claimed Palestine, but he did little to pursue active control. The period of the Judges therefore continued without Egyptian interference.

The sole evidence of contact between Israel and Egypt in this period is found in the Merenptah Stele (see page 85). Perhaps one of the tribes came too close to the Egyptian line of march, but the stele's claim that "Israel is laid waste" is obviously another example of Egyptian hyperbole. Following Merenptah, Egypt's expansionist ambitions again began to fade.

It is shortly after Merenptah that archaeologists assign the beginning of Palestine's Iron I period (c. 1200–1000 B.C.). About 1200 B.C. a mixed group, collectively dubbed Sea Peoples by the Egyptians, emigrated from the Aegean and tried to enter Egypt. When they were repulsed by Ramses III, many settled along Palestine's coastal plain. Some Philistines had been in Palestine since patriarchal times, but more came as part of this migration. The Sea Peoples brought with them the ability to fire furnaces hot enough to smelt iron—an ability that is sometimes said to be their most important contribution to Palestine.

The Iron I period witnessed a building explosion in the central hill country that can be seen at least partly as evidence that Israel was beginning to adopt a more urban lifestyle. Archaeologists are seldom able to tell Canaanite from Israelite settlements and, since the material culture was neutral, there is no reason why Israel's material remains should look different from those of the people around them. What were once thought to be distinctive evidences of Israelite occupation, collared rim jars, pillared courtyard houses, and even the presence or absence of pig bones, are no longer recognized as clear markers.

During the period of the Judges, Palestine became increasingly cosmopolitan. For example, a fragment of the Gilgamesh Epic was discovered at Megiddo, and a piece of a trilingual dictionary was found at Aphek. Archaeologists identify a variety of objects as imports from Egypt, Mesopotamia, and the Mediterranean. Arguably the most important discovery dating to this period, however, was indigenous, not imported. An alphabetic writing system, "one of the great revolutions in the development of human civilization," was invented and had come into use.

THE UNITED KINGDOM

Saul

As instability marked the period of the Judges, the desire for a king grew, even to the point that Abimelech, Gideon's son, led a short-lived attempt at kingship. About 1050 B.C. Samuel anointed Saul as Israel's first king (1 Samuel 10:1). The Bible gives no hint that Saul ever accumulated the regal trappings usually associated with kingship, and archaeology supports the impression that he was a "rustic" king.

Much of Saul's reign found him involved with enemies, both external and internal. The Philistines were Saul's most persistent enemy, and their advantage in military hardware is obvious in the battle of Michmash where only Saul and Jonathan were properly outfitted (1 Samuel 13:22). Until the time of David the Philistines held a monopoly on working with iron, and 1 Samuel 13:19 states, "No blacksmith could be found in all the land of Israel, for the Philistines said, 'Lest the Hebrews make swords or spears.'"

Artist's restoration of Saul's residence at Gibeah. This was found to be small, only 115 by 170 feet (35 by 51 meters), and a fort more than a palace. Nothing found in the excavation would have been out of place in a typical private home of the day. Unfortunately, what remained of the structure was destroyed in the 1960s to make way for a palace King Hussein intended to build on the site. Only a shell of the palace had been erected when the Six Day War of 1967 brought construction to a permanent halt.

David

The best-known encounter between the Philistines and Israel is found in 1 Samuel 17 as the Philistines were trying to gain a foothold into the hill country by controlling the valley of Elah. Conventions of warfare in those days could lead two armies to taunt each other until one side became angry enough to attack. Another alternative was to send out a picked champion from each side to decide the battle's outcome. The losing side would retreat, thus avoiding further bloodshed. In 1 Samuel 17, the Philistines and Israel confronted each other for over a month with Goliath daily taunting the Israelites to send out someone to fight him to the death. The challenge was met when

David finally appeared at the battle site. Goliath wore a helmet and body armor, and carried a "javelin" (there is some dispute over the correct translation of the Hebrew word), spear, and sword. David met him with nothing more than a shepherd's staff, a sling, and a bag of stones.

This confrontation needs to be understood within the context of that day. Despite his bravado, Goliath knew David was approaching him with a deadly weapon. Slingers were common in the ancient Near East and the best ones could "sling a stone at a hair and not miss" (Judges 20:16). The sling had an effective range of over 100 yards (91 meters) and the slingstone could be propelled in excess of 100 miles an hour. Clearly, both men were lethally armed, but David had the

113

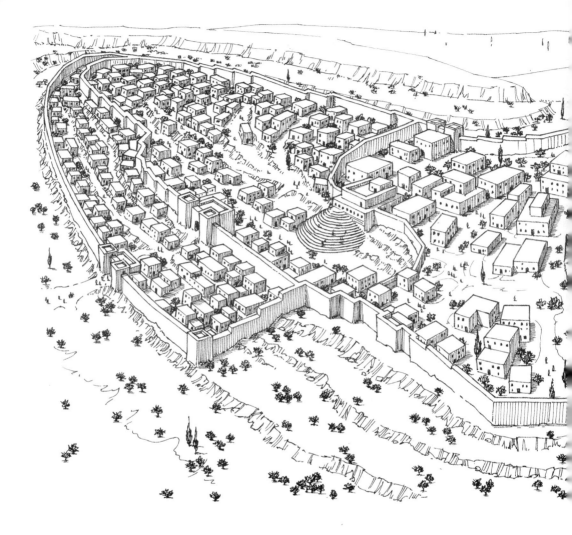

advantage of both mobility and range over any weapon the armor-clad Goliath carried.

After Saul's death David moved to Hebron where he was recognized as king of Judah. For seven years there was civil war until Saul's surviving son, Ishbosheth, was murdered. The Bible records: "Then all the tribes of Israel came to David at Hebron, and said, 'Behold we are your bone and your flesh' . . . and then they anointed David king over Israel" (2 Samuel 5:1, 3b).

One of the first needs for the new king over a unified Israel was a capital city in a more centralized location, one not identified with Judah alone. Jerusalem was chosen. Estimates of the Jebusite city's size range from 9 to 12 acres (3.6 to 5 hectares). Although the city was small, deep valleys on all but the north side provided it with such good protection that the Jebusites boasted the "blind and lame" were sufficient to defend it. The Gihon Spring in the Kidron Valley to the

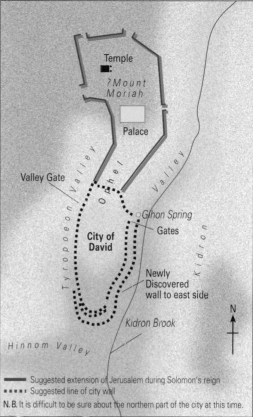

Suggested extension of Jerusalem during Solomon's reign
■■■■ Suggested line of city wall
N. B. It is difficult to be sure about the northern part of the city at this time.

Left: Artist's conception of Jerusalem as seen from the east. A wall surrounds the city. On the east a second wall was built down the slope with towers in the wall and over the Gihon Spring. Much still remains to be clarified. The drawing suggests that the towers were part of the city gateway.

Top: Jerusalem in the time of David and Soloman. The size of David's Jerusalem is indicated by the dotted lines. Solomon extended the city northward (white line).

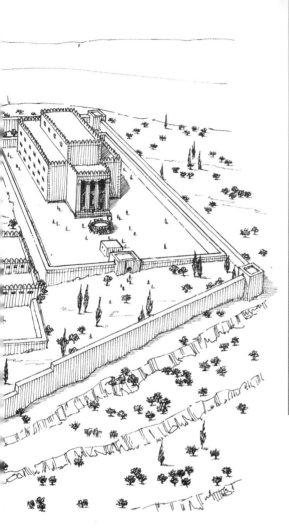

east was Jerusalem's only source of fresh water, and a tunnel had been cut to channel that water from the spring into the city. David chose to launch his attack "through the water tunnel" (2 Samuel 5:8). For years it was thought that the spring lay outside Jerusalem's defenses, but excavation has found an outer eastern wall and at least two towers protecting the spring. The attack on Jerusalem was led by Joab (1 Chronicles 11:6). Perhaps he took a few men past the towers

and into the water system, surprised and over-powered any guards, and then opened the city gates to allow more attackers to swarm in.

David had no intention of being a "rustic" king, and soon he contracted with the Phoenicians for a palace in Jerusalem. Considered the master builders in the Near East, the Phoenicians also controlled the supply of the best wood available, the cedars of Lebanon. David wished also to have a temple built in Jerusalem (excavation seems to indicate that Shiloh was destroyed by the Philistines near the end of the period of the Judges), but by divine revelation he was told to leave the construction of it to his son.

Solomon

David had stockpiled materials for a temple, and commissioned its architectural plans, but Solomon was the builder of the "great and wonderful" Temple to the Lord (2 Chronicles 2:9). It took seven years to build a structure only 90 feet (27.4 meters) long, 30 feet (9 meters) wide, and 45 feet (13.7 meters) tall; in that day size did not determine the greatness of the place of worship. Solomon's Temple is close in plan and size to temples excavated in Syria and, like his father, Solomon made use of Phoenician expertise. Touches of Phoenician decoration could be seen in the Temple but, as was noted earlier with regards to material culture, the architecture itself is neutral. We are told in 1 Kings 8:10-11 that God was well pleased with the results.

It has long been understood that Solomon's (and Herod's) Temples were built where the Golden Dome now stands, but some years ago an argument was made for the Temple having actually been a few hundred feet to the north. The proposed relocation caused considerable religious and political agitation. Later study, however, has confirmed that the placement was as originally thought (see pages 184–185).

Solomon carried out several other building projects in Jerusalem, and 1 Kings 9:15 notes that he also built in Hazor, Megiddo, and Gezer. These three cities have been excavated, and their gateways found to be very similar to one another. At Megiddo the excavators found tripartite buildings (a building divided into three parts), which they identified as "Solomon's Stables." For many years this discovery was linked to 1 Kings 9:19 which refers to "the cities for his [Solomon's] chariots and the cities for his horsemen." Later on, however, the identification became far from certain; for almost as many years scholars have debat-

Illumination of the temple was provided by seven-wicked lamps. The menorah was not in use this early.

ed whether the buildings at Megiddo, and similar structures found elsewhere, could have actually functioned as stables. Some scholars insist tripartite buildings served as storehouses (1 Kings 9:19, also refers to "all the storage cities which Solomon had"); others insist that such a simple architectural plan could have served either purpose. To confuse matters even more, some scholars now believe that the "stables" found at Megiddo actually date to the time of Ahab, and are not linked with Solomon at all.

Gezer is identified as a city Solomon rebuilt after Egypt's pharaoh "had given it as a dowry to his daughter, Solomon's wife" (1 Kings 9:16; see also 3:1). This marriage and dowry carried great significance. Egypt's diplomatic policy allowed a prince to leave the country to strengthen ties with another power; but never a princess. Years before Solomon, for example, as the king of Babylon forged an alliance with Egypt, he sent a princess to the Egyptian court. When he inquired why he had not received a princess in return, he was informed that a daughter of pharaoh was never given in this manner. The Babylonian king went on to make the charge that pharaoh was acting in bad faith. Then he suggested that pharaoh

Solomon's Temple

Earlier reconstructions show the two columns at the front of the Temple as freestanding. Currently the columns are recognized as being within the porch and load-bearing. Storage areas surround the Temple on three sides.

Top right: Groundplans of, from the left, Solomon's Temple, the temple found at Tayinat in Syria, and the Ain Dara temple, also found in Syria. This last temple, like Solomon's, had storage areas on three sides.

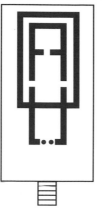

Solomon's Temple

Tayinat temple, Syria

Ain Dara temple, Syria

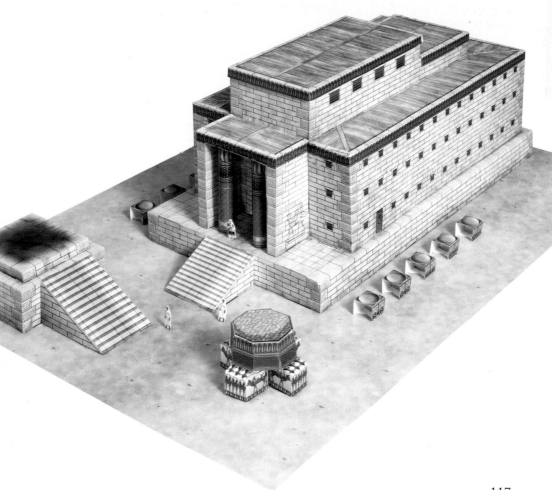

Solomon's Cities

Below: Gateways at Megiddo, Hazor, and Gezer. Unlike in earlier times, four sets of gates now barred an enemy from entry. At Hazor and Gezer casemate walls (double walls joined by cross walls) protected the city. From the outside they appeared as formidable as the solid wall at Megiddo, but they saved in labor and material. In time of peace, the spaces within the two walls could be utilized for storage or housing. In time of war, the casemate wall could be filled in at whatever point the defenses were threatened.

Bottom: One of the "stable" areas as found at Megiddo and (*inset*) a model showing the buildings restored, cutaway to show their interior, and as actually excavated. One objection made to these tripartite buildings being stables is that there would not have been sufficient width in the outer aisles to maneuver stallions past one another. The debate over function shows no sign of resolution.

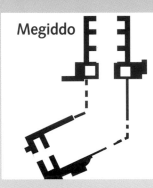

Megiddo

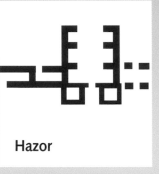

Hazor

Gezer

send a woman who could be passed off as a king's daughter. During Solomon's reign, however, for the first time Egypt faced a power so strong on its northern border that it broke a policy that had stood for centuries. Also, as noted in the previous chapter, Egypt was relinquishing its last vestige of empire.

THE DIVIDED KINGDOM (931–722 B.C.)

Early in Solomon's reign Egypt had thought it wise to defer to Israel and give a princess in marriage to Solomon. However, when Shishak founded Egypt's Dynasty 22 toward the end of Solomon's reign, that marriage would have held no significance for the new pharaoh. After Solomon died in 931 B.C. and the United Kingdom split in two, Shishak must have realized that a potential threat was no longer poised on his northern border.

Jerusalem was now reduced to being the capital only of Judah, and Jeroboam chose Shechem as the capital of the breakaway north, Israel. Five years after the death of Solomon, in 926 B.C., Shishak made his move and "came up against Jerusalem. . . . And he captured the fortified cities of Judah and came as far as Jerusalem," and carried off treasures from the Temple and the palace (2 Chronicles 12:2, 4, 9). The Bible provides no more detail than that, but the figure on page 89 shows a portion of a wall relief, which adds detail to this campaign. In the relief Shishak claims to have attacked close to 200 places. About a third of the preserved place names cluster in the southwest of Judah where archaeologists have found that Solomon established a string of small forts and settlements to support caravans moving between Judah and the Red Sea. One of Shishak's goals was to destroy that network and cut Judah's link to the shipping lanes so that Egypt could regain control over trade with Arabia and Africa.

By plotting out the place names on the relief, Shishak's advance can be followed up into the heart of Judah. Surprisingly, since Shishak had earlier given political asylum to Jeroboam (1 Kings 11:40), the place names indicate that Egypt's march continued deep into Israel before returning home via the coastal highway. Clearly, Shishak's interests were not limited to Judah as one would infer from the Bible; his aim was to impose again Egyptian control over all of Palestine. Although Shishak sometimes exaggerated his military accomplishments by adding names from conquest lists of earlier pharaohs, a stele fragment found at Megiddo proves that his Karnak list can be believed.

Early in the Divided Kingdom Israel closed its common border with Judah and proclaimed Bethel and Dan as new worship centers for the northern nation (1 Kings 12:28–29). Excavation at Dan has uncovered

Fragment of a victory stele found at Megiddo. This fragment contains the birth name of Shishak in the right cartouche, and his throne name in the left one. The throne name distinguishes him from other pharaohs who had the same birth name. Despite his plans, Shishak's campaign proved to be little more than a raid, but his army paused at Megiddo at least long enough to erect a stele.

Carved ivory inlay from Samaria. More than 200 ivories were found during the excavation of Samaria, and they provide an insight into the artistic tastes of the kings and the rich in Israel. Most of the inlays were strong in Phoenician, or, as here, Egyptian motifs. (See also ivory inlay from Megiddo, page 111.)

a stairway and platform that might have been made for the golden calf that was placed in that city.

Jerusalem was the capital of Judah throughout the southern nation's history, whereas in Israel the capital was first at Shechem, then Tirzah, and finally Samaria. Samaria was built by Omri and his son Ahab, but subsequent construction by Herod the Great left little Old Testament period architecture intact. In 1 Kings 22:39 there is mention of "the ivory house" that Ahab built. The reference is not to a house actually made of ivory, but to a house containing ivory panels and inlay. For those who could afford it, furniture, door frames, and the like could be decorated in ivory.

The biblical writers were primarily interested in the religious condition of the various kings, not in their political abilities. It was therefore not until the Moabite Stone was translated that a biblical puzzle was resolved and a little more about Omri as king was revealed. The Bible states that the Moabites fell to David, but that they declared their freedom after the death of Solomon. In the next mention of the Moabites they are paying tribute to Ahab, but nothing is said as to how they came to be subdued again. The Moabite Stone supplied the answer: "As for King Omri of Israel, he humbled Moab many years, for Chemosh [a Moabite god] was angry at his land. And his son [Ahab] followed him and he also said, 'I will humble Moab.'"

During the ninth and eighth centuries B.C. Assyria increasingly intruded into the history of Palestine. Assyria had appeared on the horizon during the reign of Omri, but Ahab was the first to meet that rising power on the battlefield. When he died, Ahab left a strong and prosperous Israel, but only a dozen years afterward Jehu was forced to pay tribute to Shalmaneser. A period of Assyrian weakness allowed a time of relative peace and prosperity during the reigns of Jeroboam II of Israel, and Uzziah of Judah. Then, when Tiglathpileser III ascended the throne of Assyria, the disintegration of Israel began. The final blow was delivered by Sargon II. (For Assyria's repeated involvement in Palestine during the Divided Kingdom, see pages 48–53.)

JUDAH ALONE (722–586 B.C.)

As of 722 B.C. Israel was no longer an entity, and the Assyrians considered all of Palestine vassal territory. When Hezekiah began his reign with a series of religious reforms, he was probably motivated by the knowledge of what had just befallen Israel.

Sargon II continued to send armies into Palestine, but after his death Hezekiah joined in the revolt against Assyrian control. Assyrian reliefs and texts record what happened (see pages 54, 58–59). Excavation in Palestine pro-

The Dan Inscription.
Jehu murdered his way to the throne of Israel and although he enjoyed a respectably long reign for a northern king, he was never politically powerful. He not only paid tribute to the Assyrians, but he also lost portions of his kingdom to the Syrians (2 Kings 10:32-33). These fragments are from a stele set up by Syria at Dan. The stele shows that Dan, a northern city, was within the territory Jehu lost. A second importance of the fragments is that they contain the first recognized extrabiblical reference to David. Ever since the excavation of these fragments in 1993 and 1994, this Syrian reference to the "house of David" has been extremely troublesome to a small group of liberal scholars ("minimalists") who deny the historicity of David.

The Moabite Stone.
Made of black basalt and 3.25 feet (1 meter) high. In the stele, Mesha, the Moabite king, celebrates his successful revolt against Israel. Interestingly, the Bible and the stele present two different viewpoints. Israel acknowledged the revolt after the death of Ahab while, from the Moabite perspective, they were already in revolt during his reign. The stele was originally found whole, but it was shattered before it reached scholarly hands. Fortunately, impressions of the stele had been made before this tragedy, and it was possible to recover most of the inscription.

vides insight into Judah's preparation for Assyria's expected response, as well as graphic evidence of the fury unleashed by Sennacherib, successor to Sargon II.

Hezekiah's preparation of Jerusalem for possible siege included the cutting of "Hezekiah's Tunnel" (also called the Siloam Tunnel) to channel water from the Gihon Spring down into a collection pool at the south end of the city. Today people who walk through the approximately 1,750-foot-long (533.5-meter) tunnel gain a sense of the magnitude of the undertaking. During its Old Testament use, gravity fed water through the tunnel to the pool where people could go to fill their jars. The following inscription (the Siloam inscription) was found on the tunnel wall near the south end:

. . . when the tunnel was driven through. And this was the way in which it was cut through: While . . . were still . . . axes, each man toward his fellow, and while there were still three cubits to be cut through, there was heard the voice of a man calling to his fellow, for there was an overlap in the rock on the right and on the left.

121

A horned altar, a little over 5 feet (1.5 meters) tall, excavated at Beersheba. The top of the altar is charred, indicating that it had been used for burnt offerings. Horned altars are mentioned several times in the Old Testament (for example in Exodus 37:25) but "legal" altars were not to be made of cut stone as seen here (Exodus 20:25). This altar, probably used for pagan worship, was found dismantled, likely as a result of Hezekiah's religious reforms.

Stamped jar handle. Several hundred of these jar handles have been found at various sites in Judah. Before the jars were fired, their handles had been stamped with seals reading *lmlk*, "belonging to the king," together with the name of a specific city. At some sites the handles were found in connection with destruction levels dating to Sennacherib's invasion in 701 B.C. The stamps are understood to be royal seals put on jars designated for the storage of provisions in anticipation of an Assyrian attack on the country.

And when the tunnel was driven through, the quarrymen hewed the rock, each man toward his fellow, ax against ax; and the water flowed from the spring toward the reservoir for twelve hundred cubits, and the height of the rock above the heads of the quarrymen was one hundred cubits.

Dozens of cities in Judah fell to the Assyrians. Excavation at Lachish, one of those cities, adds to the Assyrian account of conquest. Earthen ramps were found where the Assyrians had brought their siege towers up against the city wall, and hundreds of arrow heads were found inside the city where they had been spewed by the Assyrian archers. More graphically, a mass grave containing over 1,500 skeletons is witness to the clean-up necessary after Lachish fell.

Judah continued to exist as a vassal nation and tribute moved from Jerusalem into Assyrian coffers until suddenly the Assyrian empire faltered and fell to a combined attack by the Medes and Chaldeans. Thanks to this collapse, Judah experienced a few years of freedom but that was ended, briefly, by the Egyptians, and then by Nebuchadnezzar, who swept Judah into the new Chaldean empire. Judah festered under Chaldean control and during the reign of Zedekiah withheld tribute one time too many. As Nebuchadnezzar marched west, Judah desperately sought help from Egypt. By this time Lachish had been rebuilt and excavators of the site found twenty-one ostraca (broken pieces of pottery that were used much as notepaper is today) dating to the death throes of Judah.

The Siloam inscription. Late in the nineteenth century, thieves cut the inscription from the tunnel wall. It was soon recovered, but in this damaged condition.

One ostracon from these "Lachish Letters" mentions that a "commander of the host" was en route to Egypt; another refers to the use of fire signals to communicate between cities. Still another ostracon complains that someone in Jerusalem was not supporting the war effort—could this be a reference to Jeremiah? In 586 B.C. Jerusalem went up in flames.

PALESTINE DURING THE EXILE (586–539 B.C.)

Palestine suffered several deportations while under Assyrian and Babylonian control. In the north the Assyrians had brought in people from elsewhere in the empire and they intermarried with Jews who had been

Bulla. Bullae (singular, "bulla") are thumbnail-sized pieces of clay that were impressed with a seal and used, together with string, to secure papyrus documents (see Illustration page 92, and Nehemiah 9:38; 10:1). Hundreds of bullae have been found in Palestine, but in every case the papyrus that they protected had perished. Jeremiah dictated his messages to "Baruch the son of Neriah" (Jeremiah 36:4). This bulla is stamped, "Belonging to Berekhyahu son of Neriyahu the scribe." The "yahu" suffix is an abbreviation for God, so Baruch's full name was "blessed of God." Likewise, Neriah and Neriyahu are one and the same person. An inference drawn from this bulla is that Baruch had been an official royal scribe before he made a career move and began working for Jeremiah.

left behind. These became known as Samaritans. The Babylonians had no policy for repopulating the south, and 2 Kings 25:12 and Jeremiah 39:10 state that only the poorest people were left in Judah. It is true that widespread destruction and abandonment has been found at many of the population centers, but Judah was not as destitute as is sometimes assumed.

THE PERSIAN PERIOD (539–332 B.C.)

Cyrus the Great took control of the Babylonian empire in 539 B.C. For Palestine the transition seems to have been smooth; there are no records of battles fought, and no destruction levels are dated to this time. Palestine became part of the satrapy (province) called "Beyond the River" (beyond the Euphrates River). Phoenicia, Syria, and Cyprus were also included in this satrapy, and Damascus was made its capital. There is irony in that choice; over the centuries Palestine had repeatedly fought off the Syrians and now Palestine found itself governed from the Syrian capital. Palestine was divided into four areas: Galilee, Samaria, Judah, and Idumea. Tyre and Sidon were each given control of several cities along the coast.

The Jews who returned to Palestine in 538 B.C. settled into a narrow strip of the central hill country. They rebuilt the Temple in Jerusalem and, later on, Nehemiah was instrumental in the repair of the city walls. (Archaeologists found that Old Testament Jerusalem reached its largest size during the reign of Hezekiah, but that in the time of Nehemiah it had shrunk back to a size slightly smaller than in Solomon's day.) The Jews were not alone in the land; for example, the Edomites, now called Idumeans, were strongly settled in the region from Hebron southwards.

Regardless of how enlightened the Persians were in ruling their subjects, there

A silver amulet, unrolled. This amulet was found in one of a series of tombs on the south side of Jerusalem's Hinnom Valley. The amulet is presently dated to the seventh century B.C. and bears an abbreviated version of Numbers 6:24-26. It contains, therefore, the earliest biblical text known—it is even earlier than the Dead Sea Scrolls. This amulet, and another like it, testify both to the custom of wearing amuletic texts in Old Testament times, and the personal use of the priestly blessing at least this early.

A silver coin minted in Jerusalem during the Persian period. This coin is only 1/4 inch (0.6 centimeter) in diameter. Not mentioned in the Bible prior to the time of Ezra and Nehemiah (for example, Ezra 2:69; Nehemiah 7:70), coinage is thought to have been invented in Asia Minor in the sixth century. It spread as a medium of exchange under the Persians. In this example a lily is on the obverse; on the reverse is a falcon and, in Aramaic, *Yehud* (Judah).

were periods of unrest. A number of destructions in central Palestine, for example, date to 485 B.C. when the Persian army put down a rebellion that followed the death of Darius the Great. In 359 B.C. the persistent Egyptian dream of controlling Palestine caused a Dynasty 30 pharaoh to lead 10,000 Greek mercenaries as far north as Sidon before he was finally stopped.

THE LAST CENTURIES BEFORE THE NEW TESTAMENT

Alexander the Great swept through the Near East, and 332 B.C. marks the year that Palestine and its Jewish population were transferred from Persian to Greek control. When Alexander died a few years later, Palestine came under the rule of Ptolemy I, one of Alexander's generals, who took control of the Egyptian portion of the empire. Ptolemy I was one of the more enlightened of Alexander's successors, and he continued the liberal policy the Jews had known under the Persians. This same policy was also maintained by the succeeding Ptolemaic rulers.

Greeks had been trading along the eastern Mediterranean for centuries and some trading colonies had even been established along the coast, but Hellenism (it was then the "golden age of Greece") and Judaism now came into more immediate contact. Some Jews accepted Hellenistic culture, while others argued that it was not compatible with Judaism.

Another of Alexander's generals, Seleucus I, established himself to the north and was the founder of Antioch (see Antioch of Syria, pages 237–238). Both the Seleucids and the Ptolemics needed mercenaries as garrison troops and as reinforcements for their military campaigns, and they encouraged entire Greek and Macedonian towns to immigrate into their lands. Estimates of the number of men, women, and children who relocated run as high as a quarter of a million people. As expected, they brought their own lifestyle with them, and this large influx of Hellenism added to the cultural tensions in Palestine.

The Seleucids repeatedly tried to take possession of Palestine and to that end

125

Opposite: Tomb at Marisa. Judaism stayed strongly linked to the Old Testament, but much of the cultural background of the New Testament had its origin and development during the last centuries B.C. Marisa, about 21 miles southwest of Jerusalem, provides an example of Greek culture that was grafted into Palestinian soil. A Greek inscription found within the city identifies a man as Marisa's "agora official." The tomb plan (*bottom inset*) is very different from anything that had ever been seen in Palestine. Low benches ring the walls of the three main chambers and forty-one burial slots extend out from the chambers. The interior walls of the tomb were decorated, and short inscriptions were found by the burial slots: "Let no one disturb [my daughter];" "This too is occupied." This tomb plan would become popular by New Testament times (see page 194). The photograph is taken from the entryway (A) and looks into the main chamber (D).

fought five major battles with the Ptolemies. The Jews were caught in this political struggle, and some even wished for Seleucid victory in the hope that it would end the heavy taxation that the Ptolemies were exacting to support the war effort. In 198 B.C. the Seleucids finally took control of Palestine. There was no change with regard to religious freedom, but culturally the Jews continued to argue among themselves about whether or not Hellenism was acceptable. The Sadducees said yes; the Pharisees said no.

The centuries of religious freedom ended when the Seleucid king Antiochus IV began to plan for a pan-Hellenic league able to withstand the encroaching Roman legions. He felt that by compelling his subjects to adopt Greek ideals and customs, he would bring about greater unity in his realm. Instead, in 167 B.C., his suppression of Judaism precipitated the Maccabean Revolt. Two years later the Jews were again granted their religious freedom, but fighting continued because they now wanted political freedom as well.

By 129 B.C. the Jews had won their political freedom, and John Hyrcanus was proclaimed ruler of a nominally independent Hasmonean kingdom. John Hyrcanus is generally given good marks as a king, but one of his policies was to have serious consequences—he forced the Idumeans either to convert to Judaism, or to leave southern Palestine. The ancestors of Herod converted. At the death of the Hasmonean ruler Queen Salome Alexandra, such intense infighting broke out that various factions made overtures to Rome for help in bringing peace. Pompey responded by taking over Palestine. In 63 B.C. it became part of the Roman province of Syria-Palestine.

Herod's father, Antipater, so ingratiated himself with Rome that he was made governor of Judea, Samaria, and Galilee. After Antipater's untimely death by poisoning in 43 B.C., both Herod, and a Hasmonean named Antigonus, each wanted to be his replacement and made petitions to Rome. Herod's friendship with Marc Antony won the political battle but when Antigonus bribed the Parthians to invade Palestine on his behalf, Herod had to linger in Rome. Finally, in 37 B.C., Rome could spare troops, Antigonus was defeated, and Herod could begin his reign as king.

5

PERSIA
AND THE BIBLE

PERSIA AND THE BIBLE

The Persians were latecomers to the land area now known as Iran. As in other areas in the Near East, archaeology has increased our knowledge far back into the B.C. millennia, but early Iranian history is dependent on neighboring Mesopotamia for substance. It is, for example, from cuneiform texts dating to about 3000 B.C. that we know of various people groups, including the Elamites and Kassites, lining up along the border with Mesopotamia and engaging in peaceful trade. Because, however, of the lack of natural geographic barriers between Babylonia and the plains of southern Iran, the records speak more often of military activity. Sargon, Hammurapi, and others boasted of their armies marching east and invading Elam (southwestern Iran). The records also tell of repeated invaders from the east burning Ur, plundering Babylon, and other cities. During one such attack the Code of Hammurapi (see pages 46–47) was taken as booty from a city north of Babylon. It was recovered during the excavation of Susa.

Over the centuries Iran wrestled for its cultural identity, and cylinder seals are just one of the hallmarks of Mesopotamia's material culture to find their way east. Interestingly, the best-preserved ziggurat is not found in Mesopotamia, but at the site of Choga Zanbil, near Susa.

Persian Empire

Susa and Sardis are connected by the "Royal Road."

THRACE

Byzantium

BLACK SEA

Halys

Hattu:

LYDIA

Pteria

IONIA

Sardis

PHRYGIA

Ephesus

CILICIA

Carchemish

CRETE

CYPRUS

GREAT SEA

ABAR NAHARA

Sidon

Tyre

Jerusalem

Damascu

LIBYA

Alexandria

Memphis

Tema

EGYPT

RED SEA

Thebes

Nile

PERSIAN CENTERS

Ecbatana

Ecbatana is mentioned only once in the Bible (Ezra 6:2). The Medes governed from Ecbatana, and then the city was taken over by Cyrus the Great. The modern city of Hamadan covers the ancient site so no large-scale excavation has been possible. Over the years, however, small finds have surfaced.

Pasargadae

Pasargadae was founded by Cyrus shortly after his conquest of Ionia. The buildings on the site are scattered over an area of approximately 1.25 miles (2 km) but they seem to be the result of a unified plan. A palace set in a large garden, and an *apadana* (audience hall) are among the buildings that have been found. Cyrus' tomb is located a short distance to the southwest. Pasargadae seems to have been little used following his reign.

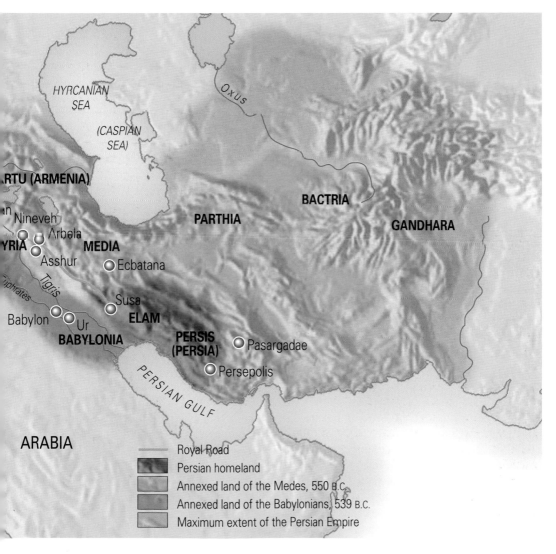

Gold and silver rhyton. Similar drinking cups, some in pure gold, have been found at several Persian centers. Such cups call to mind Esther 1:7, which records that, "Drinks were served in golden vessels of various kinds."

Susa

When Darius became king, he initially resided in Babylon, probably using one of Nebuchadnezzer's palaces, before building a new one for himself. Rather soon, however, Darius moved to the more centrally located Susa. Susa covers more than 173 acres (70 hectares) and consists of four major mounds. Darius built a defensive wall around the city, and perhaps surrounded that with a wet moat. He made some use of the old Elamite palaces and temples, but his palace and *apadana* exhibit an eclectic art-style that would be characteristic of the Persians for the next 200 years. In a text found in the ruins Darius lists how, not surprisingly, he used supplies and employed

craftsmen from all over the empire. Unfortunately, despite extensive excavation, the massive expedition house is the most visible architectural feature at Susa today. In order to "see" the palace, one scholar resorted to the imagery in the book of Esther.

Persepolis

The Susa palace was barely finished when Darius decided to move again. This time he chose a location southwest of Pasargadae. To Darius the city would be Parsa, to the Greeks Perse-polis, the "city of the Persians." Persepolis, like Pasargadae, is not mentioned in the Bible, but it provides the best visual insight into the world that Esther, Ezra, and Nehemiah would have known.

A large terrace, some 1,500 by 900 feet (457 by 274 meters), was partly quarried and partly built of huge stone blocks. The combination of terrace and unbaked brick wall resulted in a defensive system roughly 60 feet (18 meters) high. A monumental double stairway gave access to the terrace. Atop the terrace is a complex of loosely grouped but separate buildings. A palace, *apadana*, and treasury are the major contributions attributed to Darius. The Persepolis *apadana* is similar in plan to the earlier audience halls built at Pasargadae and Susa. Here the columns are 65 feet (20 meters) high and fluted, the mark of Ionian craftsmen. The doorways of Darius' palace south of the *apadana* feature cavetto cornices, an Egyptian architectural feature.

Xerxes finished the *apadana* and built the Gate of all Nations entryway, which greets visitors when they ascend the double stairway. The huge guardian bulls that are part of the gateway are Assyrian in style. Xerxes is also credited with a palace, harem, and the Hall of One Hundred Columns. Artaxerxes I made only modest contributions to the complex.

The staircases of the *apadana* are covered with reliefs of the Immortals, Persian and Median nobles, and delegations from around the empire bearing gifts or tribute. Over 800 figures are involved, and the delegations

Glazed-brick frieze from Susa of life-sized palace guards. This and other glazed wall panels from the palace at Susa give some hint of the grandeur and color summarized in Esther 1:6.

reveal the power and diversity of the empire. There is a monotony in the art, however, as the same scene repeats with only subtle differences. Perhaps, when the reliefs still retained their original paint, that sameness was not as marked. These stairway reliefs, as well as reliefs placed in doorways, are not where people would be inclined to loiter and admire. Persian art was primarily a form of decoration; it did not try to tell a story in the way that reliefs and paintings did in Egypt and Mesopotamia.

THE PERSIANS

There were repeated immigrations into Iran from the north. Two Indo-European tribes, the Medes and the Persians, seem to have arrived late in the second millennium B.C. They settled in northwest Iran where Shalmaneser III (see pages 48–50, 52) mentions encountering them during his eastern campaigns. Later, Sargon II used Median territory as a resettlement area after the fall of Israel (2 Kings 17:6).

Initially the Medes were the stronger of the two groups, and it is they who helped the Chaldeans defeat the Assyrians at Nineveh (see page 61). By the end of the seventh century B.C. the Persians (also called Achaemenids after the founder of their dynasty) had moved south into an area east of Elam. A marriage between the Median and Persian royal houses resulted in the birth of Cyrus II, the man who would allow the Jews to return home from exile.

Cyrus the Great (559–530 B.C.)

Cyrus II began his kingship as a vassal to his Median grandfather, but he soon began making alliances, most notably with Nabonidus, king of Babylon, who wanted Haran, a city held by the Medes since the fall of Assyria. Cyrus, for his part, wanted a weakened Media in order to end his vassalage. Nabonidus took Haran and Cyrus was victorious in two battles against the Medes. Cyrus spared the

Median capital of Ecbatana, but the Persians had become the dominant power.

Cyrus had dreams of empire, and he first set his sights on western Anatolia. He marched west and met the army of Croesus of Lydia near the old Hittite capital of Hattusha. There was a standoff and Croesus retired to Sardis, but Cyrus pursued him and forced a battle just east of the city. Cyrus was victorious and Sardis fell. Then one by one the Greek cities on the west coast of Anatolia (Ionia) also fell, and a Persian empire now stretched west to the Aegean. During this campaign the Persians learned two facts that would prove invaluable in future years: the Greeks had difficulty working together and they could be bought with Persian gold.

Cyrus was not yet satisfied. Persian armies advanced east into what is now India, and west into Mesopotamia. Nabonidus, Cyrus' onetime ally, had departed for Tema and left his son Belshazzar to rule. Cyrus began chipping away at the Chaldean empire until, by 539 B.C., little more than Babylon itself remained free of Persian control. Only a few hours before the city fell, Daniel interpreted the handwriting on the wall (Daniel 5:26-28). Belshazzar died (Daniel 5:30), but the fate of Nabonidus, who had returned home only to be captured, is not clear. Before the end of October 539 B.C. Cyrus made a triumphal entrance into the city of Babylon; palm branches were strewn in his path, and peace was proclaimed for everyone.

Cyrus had carved out an empire larger than anything the Near East had ever seen. Daniel 5:31 reports that "Darius the Mede received the [Chaldean] kingdom" but no such person is known extrabiblically. One suggestion is that the title is simply another designation for Cyrus the Persian. The Persians tried to retain local administrations whenever possible. This explains why, although Daniel's position as "third ruler" (Daniel 5:29) did not outlast the fall of Babylon, the Persians appointed him as one of their officials.

The Cyrus Cylinder. This baked-clay cylinder, 9 inches (23 centimeters) long, records the fall of Babylon: Marduk [the chief god of the Chaldeans] . . . beheld with pleasure Cyrus' good deed . . . and therefore ordered him to march against his city Babylon. He made him set out on the road to Babylon, going at his side like a real friend . . . Without any battle, he made him enter his town Babylon, sparing Babylon any calamity. He delivered into Cyrus' hands Nabonidus, the king who did not worship Marduk. All the inhabitants of Babylon . . . bowed to Cyrus and kissed his feet, jubilant that he had received the kingship . . . I am Cyrus, king of the world, great king, legitimate king, king of Babylon . . . king of the four rims of the earth. . .

Persian policy toward subject peoples differed radically from that of previous empire builders. Whereas previous world rulers had humiliated and oppressed their conquered subjects, Cyrus engaged in what has been called "persuasive propaganda," which helped both to win and maintain empire. Rather than forcing new subjects to take on at least a portion of the conqueror's religion, Cyrus encouraged them to worship their own gods in their own ways. And Cyrus asked that those gods pray that he and his son would have long lives. Similarly, Darius later asked the Jews to pray to God "for the life of the king and his sons" (Ezra 6:10). People were also allowed to return to their homelands. The most familiar biblical example of this policy is the decree Cyrus issued authorizing not only that the Temple should be rebuilt in Jerusalem, but that Jews should be encouraged to go back and begin the task (Ezra 1:2-4; 6:3-5). Incidentally, these verses should not be understood as evidence that Cyrus was converted to worship of the true God. Rather, they are another example, as in the Cyrus Cylinder above, of his "persuasive propaganda."

Cyrus ruled another nine years after the fall of Babylon. Then in 530 B.C. he personally led a march against a semi-nomadic tribe in the northeast. Cyrus was mortally wounded in battle and died three days later.

Cambyses II (529–522 B.C.)

Cambyses II followed his father to the throne, but his short reign is largely a bridge between Cyrus the Great and Darius, the next great Persian king. The biblical account ignores his kingship (Ezra 4:5). Cambyses did realize his father's plan to add Egypt to the Persian empire, and he founded Egypt's twenty-seventh dynasty in 525 B.C. (see page 91). Whether or not Cambyses' rule of Egypt was as disastrous as Greek historians painted it, he was in that country only three years when word reached him of unrest back home. Cambyses started for home, but died en route. The circumstances of his death are not clear.

The tomb of Cyrus at Pasargadae. The windowless tomb rises about 35 feet (10.5 meters) above the garden that once surrounded it. Its entranceway, 4.5 feet (1.3 meters) tall, was originally secured by two swinging stone doors. The inside dimensions are only 8 by 10 by 8 feet (2.4 by 3 by 2.4 meters) high. The tomb is long since empty, but it is reported to have held a tublike golden sarcophagus, and a table for offerings.

Darius the Great (522–486 B.C.)

Cambyses died in 522 B.C. leaving no heir and Darius, from another branch of the Achemaenid line, needed some time to put down the unrest that had caused Cambyses to leave Egypt, and to defeat those who opposed his rule.

Shortly before the Behistun relief and inscription were completed, work resumed on the Jerusalem Temple. When a local Persian governor questioned whether the Jews really had been granted permission for the rebuilding, a letter was sent off to Darius. Ezra 6:1-5 tells of the search that was made and the discovery in the archives at Ecbatana of Cyrus' decree permitting the construction. The Bible does not say how long it took to locate the pertinent document, but the Persian cataloguing system was so efficient that it was later adopted for the library in Alexandria. According to Ezra 6:6-12, Darius not only gave his blessing to the project but also provided aid.

Tolerance for local religions, laws, and traditions greatly helped the Persians maintain peace within the empire. There were some uprisings, however. For example, revolt broke out in Ionia in 499 B.C. and it was not put down until five years later. The Persians preferred to rule with a "velvet glove," but they could be brutal to those who resisted their authority: in Ionia people were resettled, made slaves, eunuchs, or put into harems. Darius blamed the mainland Greeks for the unrest in Ionia and in 492 B.C. his army gained a foothold in Macedonia and Thrace in northern Greece. Then in 490 B.C. his army moved farther south and the famous battle of Marathon was fought. The battle began when the Athenian forces advanced on a run toward the Persian lines.

The Greeks attacked with a weak center and strong wings. The Persians pushed the center back, but then found themselves outflanked by the Athenian wings. The Persians broke and fled. According to the casualty count, 6,400 Persians but only 192 Athenians, died. Such lopsided body-counts are known in antiquity, and the last figure rings true since each of the Greek dead is listed by name. It should be noted that the account of Phidippides' running from Marathon to Athens to proclaim the victory is only legend. Additionally, the distance run in modern marathon races was set early in the twentieth century; it is not based on the distance between the battle site and Athens.

Darius began plans personally to lead another campaign against the Greeks, but he also had a second front to contend with. The news of Marathon had pushed the Egyptians into revolt. Perhaps fortunately for him, Darius died in 486 B.C. before he could deal with either country.

Administration had been one of Darius' strengths. The empire was divided into satrapies (districts), each with a satrap (governor). The satraps were powerful, but they were also closely monitored, each district having a secretary who acted as liaison between king and satrap. With each satrap there was also a commander-in-chief in charge of the local military force. This commander was directly responsible to the king, not to the satrap. There were also "the eyes and ears of the king," inspectors who traveled about the empire, sometimes with their own army. They could drop in unannounced on the various satraps, and they answered only to the king.

Darius was very proud of his "Ordinance of Good Regulations." It was copied on steles, clay tablets, or parchment, and sent to all

The Behistun relief. This relief was placed high on a cliff near Ecbatana, and near where Darius had won a decisive battle. On the left are the bearers of the king's spear and bow. Then Darius, depicted life size, faces his defeated enemies, who are roped together around the neck. A winged figure, presumably the god Ahura Mazda, hovers over the scene. Beside and below the relief is a trilingual inscription, in Akkadian, Elamite, and Old Persian, recording Darius' rise to power. The Behistun inscription helped make the decipherment of cuneiform possible, achieving for cuneiform what the Rosetta Stone had done for Egyptian hieroglyphics.

The Treasury relief from Persepolis. Made from limestone, and just over 20 feet (6 meters) wide, this relief has long been understood to depict Darius receiving a report from a Median official. Immortals, the elite corps within the Persian military, stand at either end of the scene, and Darius' son Xerxes appears behind his father. Behind Xerxes are the royal cupbearer (?) and the holder of the king's battleaxe and bow case.

parts of the empire. What little is preserved of this lawbook suggests that it borrowed from the Code of Hammurapi: Hammurapi's Stele was in Susa when Darius used that city as a capital. The Persians demanded that their judges be totally honest. In a story set in the reign of Cambyses II, a judge was caught taking a bribe. He was killed, skinned, and his skin was cut into strips and tanned. The strips were then used to cover the judgment seat used by the next judge—who was advised to remember upon what he was sitting!

To administer his vast empire, Darius created a network of roads, which were closely patrolled and maintained; portions of certain roads were paved, and in other roads artificial ruts were sometimes cut to guide wheeled vehicles. The "Royal Road" stretched almost 1,700 miles from Susa to Sardis and post stations with fresh horses were placed about every 15 miles along its length. Ancient records reveal that a caravan could travel the length of the Royal Road in ninety days, but a courier made the same distance in a week.

Xerxes (485–465 B.C.)

When Xerxes ascended to the throne, he quickly restored Egypt to the empire. Also early in his reign, he put down two revolts in

After Cyrus, the Persian kings were interred in nearly identical tombs, each cut into cliffs near Persepolis. The door leads into a chamber only large enough to receive the king and his immediate family. The relief above the doorway shows representatives from around the empire holding a platform aloft. On the platform, the king is depicted standing and facing a fire altar.

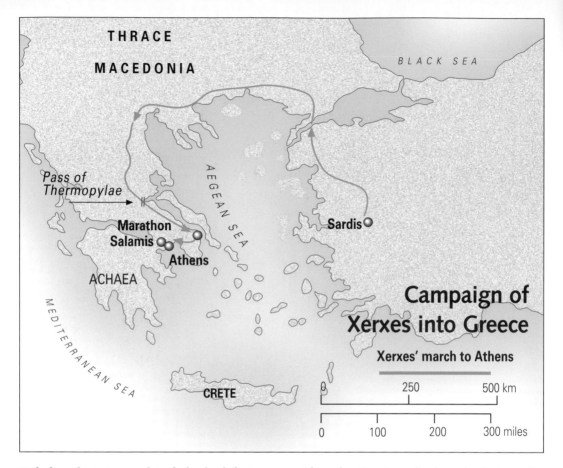

THRACE

MACEDONIA

BLACK SEA

Pass of
Thermopylae

AEGEAN SEA

Marathon

Salamis

Athens

Sardis

ACHAEA

MEDITERRANEAN SEA

CRETE

Campaign of Xerxes into Greece

Xerxes' march to Athens

| 0 | 250 | 500 km |

| 0 | 100 | 200 | 300 miles |

Babylon, but it was his father's defeat at Marathon that most consumed him. In the spring of 480 B.C. the Persians crossed into Greece. According to Herodotus, Xerxes' forces numbered in the millions. Scholars reject such a total, but they cannot agree on what might be a realistic figure. The Persians met little resistance until they encountered the narrow pass at Thermopylae, which was blocked by a few thousand Greeks. The Persians were not able to break through until they learned of a path that came out on the other side of the Greek positions. When it was discovered that the Persian Immortals were advancing along the path, most of the Greeks retired before they could be outflanked. Only Leonidas, a Spartan king, and 300 of his men chose to stand and fight. They were all killed, but their sacrifice is immortalized in Greek history.

After the Persians had pushed through the pass of Thermopylae, they marched on Athens and set fire to the Acropolis. Then the Persian fleet blockaded the Greek fleet within the Bay of Salamis. When the Persians were lured into the narrow straits of the bay, the superior number of their ships proved to be a disadvantage; they had no room to maneuver. As Xerxes sat on a nearby hill to watch the battle, his fleet was defeated. Unnerved, he quickly withdrew with the bulk of his troops to Sardis. Historians fault Xerxes at this point since the Battle of Salamis was only a minor setback and all the Greeks had really won was encouragement. But Xerxes had lost his taste for war. Persian troops left on the mainland continued to fight, but all of Greece and Ionia were eventually lost.

Persepolis

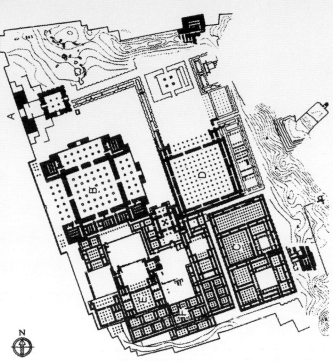

The artificial terrace at Persepolis was accessed by a monumental staircase on the west (A in the plan and photo below). Just to the east of the staircase is the Gate of all Nations (upper right in the photo below, and page 142 top). Also on the terrace is the *apadana* (B), the Treasury of Darius (C), the Hall of One Hundred Columns built by Xerxes (D), the palace of Xerxes (E), and his harem (F).

Above: The Gate of All Nations. Below: Detail of a procession of Mede (distinguished by their round hats) and Persian Immortals from the north stairway to the *apadana*.

Above: Two of the many delegations, here from Gandara and Bactria, bearing gifts of tribute; north stairway of the *apadana*.

Below: Looking west over Persepolis from the cliffs above its east side. The tall columns stand on the *apadana*.

A relief of the king fighting a bull, from a doorway in the Hall of One Hundred Columns.

When Xerxes was back in Persia, he dedicated himself to finishing the works his father had begun at Susa and Persepolis, and also began new buildings in a grandiose style. At Persepolis Xerxes razed a portion of his father's treasury in order to add to the number of suites in what the excavators identified as his harem. Xerxes never again left home, and his personal life became increasingly chaotic. Intrigue within the royal family led to revolt, mutilation, and torture. Toward the end of his life Xerxes

144

One of the many capitals atop the 65-foot- (20-meter-) tall columns in the *apadana*.

was manipulated by the commander of the Immortals and his own cupbearer. In 465 B.C. these two assassinated him.

The book of Esther fits nicely within what is known from Persian and Greek history, and numerous scholars have remarked on the book's great "familiarity with both general and specific features of Persian life." The book is sprinkled with loan words and personal names of Persian origin. The king's name, Khshayarsha in Old Persian, is rendered Ahasuerus in Hebrew and Xerxes in Greek. It is generally accepted that Mordecai can be identified with Marduka, a high official working in Susa. Some would identify Esther with Queen Amestris.

The disastrous Greek campaign fits nicely into the time gap between Xerxes' third year (Esther 1:3) and his marriage to Esther in his seventh year (Esther 2:16). Our knowledge of the turmoil in the king's personal life certainly makes us see that Esther's position was less than attractive. The enlarged quarters at Persepolis bring to mind Esther 4:11 where she tells Mordecai that she has "not been summoned to come to the king for these thirty days." Her novelty had apparently worn off. It is probable that after the death of Xerxes the remainder of Esther's years were spent in some non-functional part of the royal harems.

Artaxerxes I (464-424 B.C.)

After Xerxes was assassinated, his heir apparent was murdered by a younger brother, Artaxerxes. Artaxerxes himself barely escaped assassination before he was finally

145

recognized as king of Persia. In 461 B.C. Artaxerxes moved to Susa where he stayed for most of his reign. Three years later he sent Ezra to Jerusalem with a decree to further the worship of God (Ezra 7:11-26). It was Persian policy to foster local religions, but Artaxerxes had an additional reason for sending Ezra. Egypt, with the help of Athens, had revolted soon after Artaxerxes took the throne, and he wanted Palestine, the land bridge to Egypt, to remain quiet until such time as the Persian army could respond.

Artaxerxes relied on other resources besides Ezra. Repeatedly the Persians found their gold as effective as any man or armed force. Repeatedly, they were able to bribe peoples and cities that should have been allies to fight against one another. For example, since Athens had given aid to Egypt in its revolt, Artaxerxes sent a bribe to Sparta. The Spartans used the money to finance a victory over Athens. In 454 B.C. the Persian army marched through Palestine and the Persian Dynasty 27 was reestablished in Egypt.

In 444 B.C. Artaxerxes allowed Nehemiah to travel to Jerusalem. Nehemiah was a cupbearer for the king (Nehemiah 1:11). As cupbearer, one of his duties would have been to protect the king from being poisoned (Nehemiah 2:1). Holders of such a sensitive position were often eunuchs because, having no prospect of establishing their own dynasty, they were less likely to poison the king. Scholars debate whether Nehemiah was a eunuch, but there is no firm evidence either way. Nehemiah was sent to Jerusalem as governor of Judah, and despite opposition he was able to restore the defenses of the city.

A few years earlier Athens and Persia had agreed to share control of Ionia, but by 441 B.C. they were once again fighting over the territory. When Sparta attacked Athens, all Artaxerxes had to do was watch the two Greek cities try to destroy each other. This time no Persian gold was required.

Gold coin with the image of a Persian king as an archer. Such coins were repeatedly used by the Persians to keep Greek cities at odds with one another. At one point a Spartan complained that he had been driven from Ionia by 10,000 archers—that is, 10,000 gold coins.

Late in Artaxerxes' reign the palace in Susa burned to the ground. He then moved to Persepolis and only left the city so he could die in Susa—of natural causes. Artaxerxes ruled forty years, longer than either Cyrus the Great or Darius the Great. There were no Persian forays into mainland Greece during his reign, but the Persians fostered the love-hate relationship between Athens and Sparta. Artaxerxes I is the final Persian king to play a role in the Old Testament. The Persian empire continued on for almost another century, but the glory days of Cyrus and Darius were but a memory.

6

PALESTINE AND THE BIBLE

New Testament

PALESTINE AND THE BIBLE

New Testament

QUMRAN, THE DEAD SEA SCROLLS, AND JOHN THE BAPTIST

The Dead Sea Scrolls, a cache of ancient documents dating from the first century B.C. to the first century A.D., were found in eleven caves near the Qumran settlement on the northwest shore of the Dead Sea. Cave One was discovered in the spring of 1947 by two bedouin children from the Taamireh tribe near Bethlehem. This cave contained a number of important scrolls of the Bible and other literature of the community that produced them. Most scholars have identified this community of Jewish monastic-type religious devotees with the Essenes, the third largest sect of Jews in ancient Israel, according to Josephus (*War* 2.119-161). This identification, however, is not accepted by everyone.

In an intensive investigation of the area

Qumran and the Dead Sea from Cave One.

The cliffs at Qumran. In the caves were found many of the Dead Sea Scrolls.

Excavations at Qumran.

around the settlement by both bedouin and archaeologists, a few more scrolls and thousands of fragments were subsequently discovered in ten other caves.

Besides the *Manual of Discipline*, some of the more important scrolls include the two scrolls of the *Book of Isaiah*, the *Commentary on Habakkuk*, the scroll of the *War Between the Sons of Light and the Sons of Darkness*, the *Thanksgiving Hymns*, and the *Temple Scroll*.

The Qumran community

The settlement at Qumran was excavated in the mid-1950s by the Jordanian Department of Antiquities, the École Biblique in Jerusalem, and the Palestine Archaeological Museum.

Excavations confirmed that a Jewish community lived here that was engaged in the production of manuscripts of the Bible as well as other religious literature. They were zealous for Jewish tradition but refused to take part in the Temple sacrifices in Jerusalem, feeling that it had been profaned by Roman influence. Several large *mikvaoth* (baptistries) were found in the settlement, connected to each other by aqueducts that fed them from the nearby Judean hills. These were used for ritual purification. The self-described purpose of the settlement, according to chapter eight of the *Manual of Discipline* (or *Community Rule*) found among the scrolls, was to prepare in the wilderness a way for the Lord. They were thus attempting to avoid the defilements associated with Hellenistic society by isolating themselves here in the desert of Judea.

The importance of the scrolls

The Dead Sea Scrolls have been of enormous value in the reassessment of Jewish sectarianism in the Second Temple period (which includes the time of the New

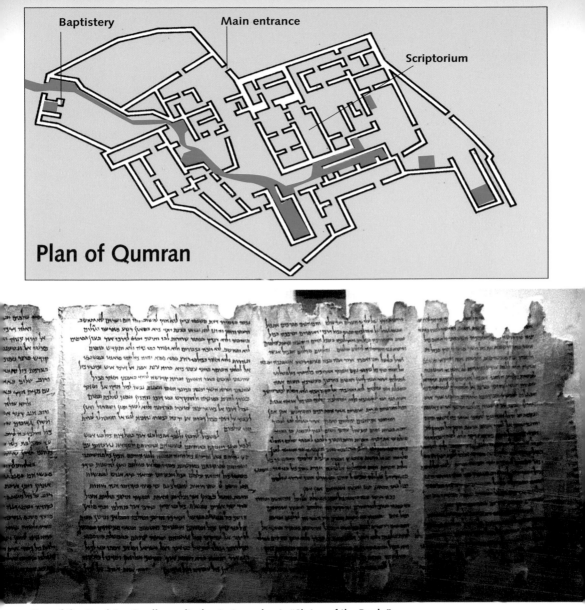

Baptistery   Main entrance

Scriptorium

Plan of Qumran

One of the Dead Sea Scrolls on display in Jerusalem's "Shrine of the Book."

Testament). They have also provided texts of some of the books of the Bible that are a thousand years older than the authoritative Hebrew texts of the ninth century A.D.

In addition the scrolls provide interesting background material for the study of the ministry of John the Baptist, who may at one time have been associated with this group.

Thus far, however, there is no evidence from Qumran that bears directly on either Jesus of Nazareth or the New Testament. The many outlandish claims of Christianity's dependence on Qumran published by early sensationalists have, upon more mature investigation of the scrolls, been shown to be without foundation.

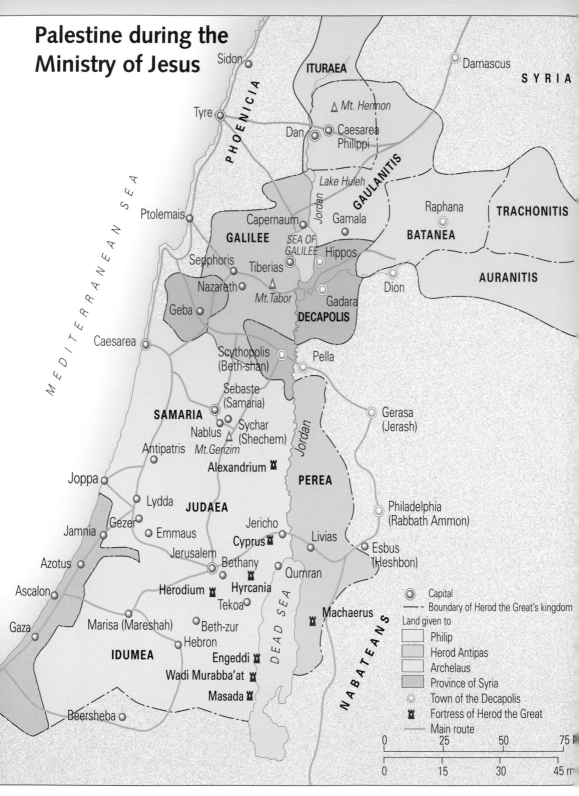

Palestine during the Ministry of Jesus

Sidon

ITURAEA

Damascus

SYRIA

PHOENICIA

Tyre

△ Mt. Hermon

Dan

Caesarea Philippi

GAULANITIS

Lake Huleh

Jordan

Raphana

TRACHONITIS

Ptolemais

Capernaum

Gamala

BATANEA

MEDITERRANEAN SEA

GALILEE

SEA OF GALILEE

Hippos

Sepphoris

Tiberias

Nazareth

△ Mt. Tabor

Dion

AURANITIS

Geba

Gadara

DECAPOLIS

Caesarea

Scythopolis (Beth-shan)

Pella

Sebaste (Samaria)

Gerasa (Jerash)

SAMARIA

Nablus

Sychar (Shechem)

Antipatris

△ Mt. Gerizim

Alexandrium ♜

PEREA

Joppa

Lydda

JUDAEA

Jericho

Philadelphia (Rabbath Ammon)

Jamnia

Gezer

Emmaus

Cyprus ♜

Livias

Esbus (Heshbon)

Azotus

Jerusalem

Bethany

Qumran

Ascalon

Herodium ♜

Hyrcania

Gaza

Marisa (Mareshah)

Tekoa

Beth-zur

Machaerus ♜

NABATEANS

Hebron

IDUMEA

Engeddi

Wadi Murabba'at ♜

DEAD SEA

Jordan

Masada ♜

Beersheba

⊚	Capital
— · —	Boundary of Herod the Great's kingdom

Land given to

☐	Philip
☐	Herod Antipas
☐	Archelaus
☐	Province of Syria
◎	Town of the Decapolis
♜	Fortress of Herod the Great
—	Main route

0   25   50   75 k

0   15   30   45 m

On-going research

A half century has passed since the discovery of the scrolls, during which time they have been controlled by a very few scholars and unavailable to the scholarly world in general. However, pressure by the editor of the Biblical Archaeology Society and others has resulted in their publication and universal accessibility. This has made unlimited study available but is also producing a vast array of opinions and much scholarly debate and criticism. The Dead Sea Scrolls, far from being dead, continue to live and generate front page news. Many established news publications around the world have carried articles about the scrolls. Religious and scientific journals are constantly filled with the latest developments about these esoteric documents.

There appear to be more than 800 manuscripts of these scrolls in Hebrew and Aramaic, compiled between the second century B.C. and A.D. 68, when the Roman army overran Palestine. All of the complete scrolls have been published, but there are thousands of fragments that are now available for study. These fragments are generating excitement and published opinions both from those who are qualified and those who are unqualified.

Release of the documents to the public in 1992, after unbearable pressure was applied to the unproductive publication committee, has predictably unleashed a torrent of speculation, argumentation, exaggeration, and downright fantasy about the nature, date, and value of these scrolls. As might be expected, there is widespread disagreement on almost every question relating to their discovery and interpretation as well as the history and identity of the Qumran community. Those who look back over a half century of familiarity with the scrolls have a sense of *déja vu*. It is as if they have returned to life; again we see them generating the same kinds of unrestrained and often irresponsible speculation that we saw originally.

The Church of the Nativity, Bethlehem.

Star at the birthplace under the apse of the Bethlehem church. Beneath a cross in the apse at the east end of the Nativity Church, this cave has a silver star laid on a marble pavement marking the spot venerated for centuries as the birthplace of Jesus. The cave is large, about 40 feet (12 meters) long east to west, 16 feet (4.8 meters) wide north to south, and 10 feet (3 meters) high. It actually consists of about ten sections, in the westernmost of which Jerome translated portions of the Latin Vulgate. He lived in Bethlehem from A.D. 386 until his death in 420.

BETHLEHEM:
THE BIRTHPLACE OF JESUS

Church of the Nativity

Centuries before the birth of Jesus, the Old Testament prophet Micah wrote by inspiration: "But you, O Bethlehem Ephratha, who are little to be among the clans of Judah, from you shall come forth for me one who is to be ruler in Israel, whose origin is from of old, from ancient days" (Micah 5:2). Jesus, the Jewish Messiah, fulfilled that prophecy, being born in the little village of Bethlehem, about seven miles south of Jerusalem.

The traditional place of the birth of Jesus is marked by the Church of the Nativity, constructed by the emperor Justinian (A.D. 527–565) over the remains of an earlier church built by Helena, the mother of the

emperor Constantine, who reigned from A.D. 306 until his death in 337. During her visit to the eastern provinces of the empire in 326, Helena had her scholars study the traditions and literature available to them while they were in the Holy Land, and they concluded that this cave was the place where Jesus was born. She then had Constantine authorize the construction of a small church there, the remains of which can still be seen inside the present building. She also had another church constructed at the place of Christ's ascension on the Mount of Olives in Jerusalem. Eusebius, the fourth-century church historian, wrote:

> Thus did Helena Augusta, the pious mother of a pious emperor, erect over the two mystic caverns these two noble and beautiful monuments of devotion, worthy of everlasting remembrance, to the honor of God her Savior, and as proofs of her holy zeal, receiving from her son the aid of his imperial power. *The Life of Constantine* 3.43

Shortly after returning from her journey in late 327 or early 328, Helena died in Rome at the age of eighty. The church was finished before 333, when it is mentioned by the Bordeaux Pilgrim who, speaking of Bethlehem, wrote: "There a basilica has been built by order of Constantine."

Due to the scarcity of wood and the expense of constructing stables, it was customary in the Holy Land to build houses above caves, which could be used as stables for housing animals. Both Justin Martyr, in the second century, and Origen, in the third century, wrote about a cave beneath the church as the place where Jesus was born.

In 1875, the population of Bethlehem was about 3,000 and was almost entirely Christian. Bethlehem today is a town of about 30,000 inhabitants, about one-third of whom are Christians. This Christian

Opposite: Aerial View of Bethlehem, showing the Church of The Nativity.

Inset: Interior of the Church of the Nativity.

population is rapidly decreasing as a result of emigration because of the Arab/Israeli conflict. If Bethlehem continues to be divided by the concrete wall built by Israel through the heart of the city, its economic structure, which is almost entirely based on pilgrims and tourists, may not survive.

NAZARETH: THE HOMETOWN OF JESUS

The annunciation

Mary, the mother of Jesus, was living in Nazareth in the southern hills of Galilee when her miraculous conception of Jesus was announced by an angel of God: "In the sixth month the angel Gabriel was sent from God to a city in Galilee, called Nazareth, to a virgin engaged to a man whose name was Joseph, of the descendants of David; and the virgin's name was Mary" (Luke 1:26-27).

Archaeological excavations, which were conducted in Nazareth by Bellarmino Bagatti in 1955 when the new Church of the Annunciation was erected, have revealed evidence of a Byzantine period church beneath this one. The first church built here seems to have been constructed by Joseph of Tiberias, an eminent Jew who converted to Christianity; upon request he was granted the privilege of building churches in Galilee by Constantine.

Excavations beneath the floor of the Byzantine church have shown that it was preceded by a religious site. On the basis of architectural features still in existence, including style and structure, it is suggested that the building dates to the third or fourth century and is a Jewish/Christian synagogue. A Jewish ritual bath (*mikveh*) that may have belonged to a still earlier synagogue was discovered beneath the mosaic floor. It is possible that the synagogue referred to in Luke 4:16, which Jesus attended, may have stood here prior to the fourth-century synagogue. It was customary for Jews to build new synagogues on the site of previous ones.

The Church of the Annunciation, Nazareth.

Excavations conducted in Nazareth have revealed an agricultural settlement of the time of Jesus with numerous winepresses, olive presses, caves for storing grain, and cisterns for water and wine. Some of these stand below the Annunciation Church and the Church of St. Joseph to the north. Christian tradition connects portions of these with the dwelling places of Joseph and Mary. In Nazareth today, there is still in use a well called "The Well of Mary," which has traditionally been held to be one that Mary used. Across the street from this well, beneath the floor of the Cactus Café, a bath complex from the time of Jesus has very recently been discovered, which may affect current assumptions about the rural nature of the first-century village in which Jesus lived and worked for thirty years.

Top: Church of the Annunciation in Nazareth The traditional spot of the annunciation is marked by the erection of the modern Church of the Annunciation, situated in the heart of the modern city, which was only a small village in the time of Jesus. Inside the church, the walls are covered with mosaics and paintings of the virgin Mary sent from countries all over the world.

Right: Excavations beneath the Annunciation Church.

Below right: Well of Mary by the Cactus Café, Nazareth.

159

SEAPORTS ON THE SEA OF GALILEE

Whereas today there are only four small ports on the Sea of Galilee, twenty-five years of research and exploration of the sea have resulted in the discovery of sixteen harbors that lined its shores in antiquity. This exploration has been made possible by years of record-breaking minimal rainfall and subsequent lowering of the depth of the sea, revealing piers, promenades, and breakwaters, along with ships' anchors, weights that were fastened to fishing nets, and mooring stones to which the ships were tied.

Capernaum: the village where Jesus lived with Peter

One of the sixteen harbors discovered is in Capernaum, on the north shore of the Sea of Galilee, where, or near where, the apostle Matthew lived and had his toll station for collecting taxes (Mark 2:1, 13-14; Matthew 9:1, 9; 10:3). The harbor and the nearby roads made Capernaum an important location for collecting taxes.

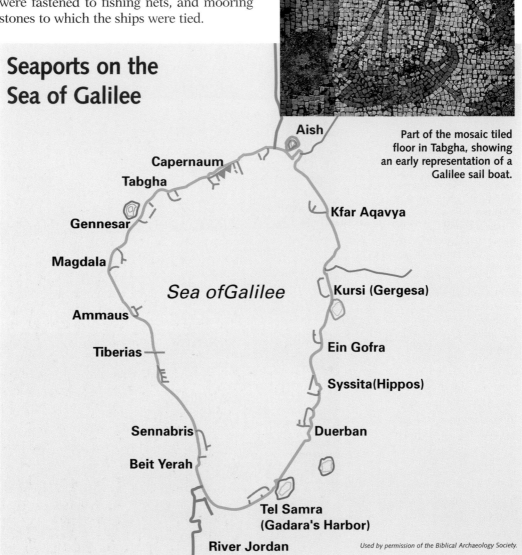

Part of the mosaic tiled floor in Tabgha, showing an early representation of a Galilee sail boat.

Seaports on the Sea of Galilee

Aish
Capernaum
Tabgha
Kfar Aqavya
Gennesar
Magdala
Sea of Galilee
Kursi (Gergesa)
Ammaus
Ein Gofra
Tiberias
Syssita (Hippos)
Sennabris
Duerban
Beit Yerah
Tel Samra
(Gadara's Harbor)
River Jordan

Used by permission of the Biblical Archaeology Society.

The Synagogue in Capernaum.

The Synagogue in Capernaum

Excavations have been ongoing in Capernaum for many years and have recently revealed that the synagogue standing there is from the Byzantine period. Ten thousand coins excavated beneath the limestone floors have shown that the prayer hall dates to the fourth century and the adjoining room on the east to the fifth century. Further recent excavations beneath the structure have revealed walls of basalt stone 4 feet (1.2 meters) thick that belonged to an earlier synagogue. Archaeologists were able to date this earlier synagogue to the first century on the basis of the pottery found beneath the basalt cobblestone floor. Both the first- and fourth-century synagogues were about 60 feet (182 meters) long, 80 feet (24.3 meters) wide and divided into three areas—a large nave and two narrow aisles, one on the east and the other on the west. Since Capernaum was a small village and likely had only one synagogue, this earlier synagogue is probably the one in which Jesus taught (Luke 4:33, 38).

After Jesus was rejected in Nazareth, he went to Capernaum (Luke 4:16, 29-31) the home of Peter and Andrew (Mark 1:29) and probably stayed with Simon Peter (Matthew 8:14-16). Capernaum is called his "home" in Mark 2:1 and 3:20. Almost 100 feet (30.4 meters) south of the synagogue in Capernaum, excavations revealed a smaller

In 1990, the Roman Catholic Church built a huge hexagonal chapel over the earlier fifth century octagonal room, which stood over the room where Jesus is thought to have lived. It is a popular place of pilgrimage for tourists.

The remains of the house of Peter before the Franciscan chapel was constructed above it.

octagonal building constructed over the remains of the stone walls of a first-century house. Excavators working from 1968 to 1998 suggest that this house is probably the house of Simon Peter. This is because, first, the walls are too narrow to support a masonry roof or a second floor, and the roof may thus have been made of wooden branches covered with mud such as the one that was "dug out" to lower the paralytic down to Jesus (Mark 2:4). Secondly, pottery found in the center room of the house shows that by the mid-first century it ceased being used for normal residential living. Thirdly, more than 150 fragments of plastered walls were found containing inscriptions from the mid-third century until the early fifth century. These inscriptions had been scratched on the walls in several languages, predominantly Greek, but also Hebrew, Aramaic, Syriac, and Latin, indicating that the room was a place of public attraction. The presence of Hebrew graffiti may indicate that at this time the build-

ing was being used as a house-church by Jewish-Christians. The inscriptions refer to Jesus as the Lord, Christ, the Most High, and God. One inscription says: "Lord Jesus Christ help thy servant." Another reads: "Christ have mercy." Various symbols, such as crosses in various forms and a boat, were also etched on the walls. In the fifth century, an octagonal structure was built over the room.

The total evidence available at the present time, therefore, seems to suggest that this chapel was built over a first-century house, that was set apart in the middle of that century as a public area. It had then been made into a church and venerated since as the house of Peter.

Excavations adjacent to and east of the synagogue and house have revealed remains of a Roman bath-house, constructed in the first century B.C. A number of buildings oriented in the same direction as the bath-house, and dating to the first century A.D.,

The Galilean Boat

The newly-exposed seashore on Galilee, as a result of lower rainfall, has revealed the remains of a rather well-preserved wooden boat. An interesting example of what this boat might have looked like has been provided by a recent discovery in Galilee. In January 1986 a boat was found buried in mud on the northern shore of the Sea of Galilee, just west of the Kibbutz Ginnosar. Carbon 14 tests dated it between the first century B.C. and the end of the first century A.D., thus in the time of Jesus. It was excavated in February 1986 and found to be 26.5 feet long, 7.5 feet wide, and 4.5 feet high (8 meters by 2.3 meters by 1.3 meters). It is the first work-boat found at an inland lake in the entire Mediterranean area. It was determined that the boat had a mast for sailing and two oars on each side. It would have

The preserved boat at Yigal Allon Museum, Ginossar.

accommodated about fifteen males the size of those who lived in Galilee in the time of Christ—the average male being about 5 feet and 5 inches tall (1.65 meters), and weighing 140

pounds (63 kilograms). Jesus and his disciples could easily have fitted into such a boat, the use of which is mentioned several times in the Gospels. Jesus was probably sleeping in the stern of a boat like this when a storm arose and began filling the boat with water When he was awakened by his disciples, he commanded the storm to subside and "there was a great calm" (Mark 4:37-41). The excavators reinforced the fragile vessel by constructing fiberglass and polyester resin frames wrapped in thin plastic sheeting and sprayed with polyurethane liquid, which hardened into a protective shell. It was then transported 550 yards (500 meters) by sea, from its place of discovery to the Yigal Allon Museum at Ginnosar for proper treatment to insure preservation. A similar boat was found depicted in a first-century mosaic from the city of Migdal (Magdala), only a mile west.

A reconstructed Galilee sailboat on the east shore of the lake.

were discovered nearby on the north side and help to give further definition to the little town of Capernaum where Jesus lived during the last three years of his life.

It is a matter of special interest that this town became the object of Jesus' criticism. He pronounced a curse upon Capernaum as well as Chorazin and Bethesda (Matthew 11:20-24) because they did not repent in spite of the fact that he performed "most of his mighty works" in these villages (Matthew 11:20). These villages still lie in ruins today, while Nazareth, Bethlehem, Jerusalem, Tiberias, Jericho, and others mentioned in the Gospels continue to thrive.

Chorazin: a town cursed by Jesus

Although the site of Chorazin is identified by excavated remains of basalt houses and a third-century synagogue, nothing from the time of Jesus is extant. It is identified with Khirbet Kerazeh, a site in the hills 2.5 miles northwest of Capernaum.

Tiberias on the Sea of Galilee

The city of Tiberias is mentioned only once in the New Testament. The Gospel of John records that after the feeding of the five thousand, which took place on the eastern side of the sea, Jesus perceived that the people were about to take him by force to make him king (John 6:15), so he told his disciples to go by boat across the sea towards the area of Capernaum and Bethsaida while he dismissed the crowds (Mark 6:45). John writes that the next day boats came from Tiberias to the place where Jesus had fed the five thousand, looking for him (John 6:23). So there is no clear evidence that Jesus was ever in the city of Tiberias.

Herod Antipas built Tiberias to replace Sepphoris as his capital. It was probably completed in A.D. 23. Excavations in the southern part of the city have revealed portions of a stone paved road and city gate with two circular stone towers south of the gate, each 23 feet (7 meters) in diameter, all of which were a part of

Synagogue at Chorazin.

Excavations at the stadium in Tiberias built by Herod Antipas.

Antipas' construction. Recent excavations east of the Jordan River Hotel have also uncovered a stadium, built by Herod Antipas.

Tiberias.

Gergesa: where Jesus exorcized demons

Less than ten miles southeast of Capernaum on the eastern shore of the Sea of Galilee, a sixth-century Byzantine church was excavated that was probably built to mark the site of ancient Gergesa, where Jesus cast the demons out of a man and put them into a herd of swine, which immediately ran over "a steep bank" into the sea and drowned (Matthew 8:32; Mark 5:13; Luke 8:33).

The identification of the city has been problematical because three villages with names that are very much alike existed on the east side of the sea, and all three names appear in the accounts of the story in various manuscripts of the Greek New Testament. These names are Gerasa, Gadara, and Gergesa. Since manuscripts in ancient times were copied by hand, either from other manuscripts or from listening to the text, it was easy to misunderstand a pronunciation or misread a written name that looks or sounds like that of another well-known village. This is obviously what happened in the transmis-

The only "steep bank" on the east shore of the Sea of Galilee.

sion of the Gospel texts, and thus we have diverse readings in all the manuscripts.

Since the miracle could only have occurred in one place, the question confronting textual critics of the Greek New Testament is which one of the names represents the actual geographic site of the story. The methodology of textual criticism requires that each of the three Gospel texts containing the term be evaluated in the light of the most probable reasons for scribal errors. The conclusion reached by textual critics is that the best Greek texts have Gadara in Matthew but Gerasa in Mark and Luke. Some of our oldest manuscripts, however, have the word Gergesa in one or more of these verses.

Gergesa

Since it was customary in the Byzantine period to build churches on sites where miracles were performed by Jesus, we are not surprised that in the fifth or sixth century a church was constructed on the site of El Kursi. Eusebius had identified this place in the fourth century with these words: "Gergesa where the Lord healed the demons. A village is even now situated on the mountain beside the sea of Tiberias into which also the swine were cast headlong."

The remains of a Byzantine church were unearthed in 1970, during the construction of a new road about 300 yards (275 meters) from El Kursi. In the small bay nearby, there are remains of a well-constructed harbor. Excavations were begun here the next year, revealing the basilica type church, which had a narthex, an atrium, a nave, an apse, aisles, a baptistery, chapels, domestic rooms and a beautiful mosaic pavement with geometrical patterns, and representations of birds, fish, fruits, flowers, and plants. A mosaic in the baptistery has a dedicatory inscription in Greek that dates the mosaic to 585. Above the village, a number of caves and tombs have been found, matching the Gospel narrative, which says that the man who possessed the demons was living among the tombs (Mark 5:5).

The remains of a Byzantine church at El Kursi (biblical Gergesa).

Excavations at Bethsaida Julius.

Since textual criticism has thus not been able to provide a uniform answer to the question of where exactly this miracle took place, other factors have to be considered as well. On the basis of geography alone, neither Gerasa nor Gadara could be the site, because they do not fit the environmental demands of the texts. Gerasa, modern Jerash in the country of Jordan, is 37 miles southeast of the Sea of Galilee. Gadara, modern Umm Qeis in Jordan, is 5 miles southeast of the sea. Neither site satisfies the text's statement that the pigs ran off a "steep bank" into the sea and drowned. Gergesa, modern El Kursi, is the only site of the three that is located on the Sea of Galilee (on the north end, about 9 miles east of Capernaum) and the only spot on the entire eastern side where the cliff comes out to the sea.

Bethsaida:
the feeding of the five thousand

Excavations in the past decade on the north shore of the Sea of Galilee have uncovered remains of a village that archaeologists have identified as the Bethsaida where Jesus fed the multitudes with five loaves and two fish (Luke 9:10). Fifteen years of excavation have shown that of the various candidates for the site, only et Tel, which was founded in the tenth century B.C., was occupied around the time of Jesus. The village, mentioned as often as Capernaum in the Gospels, is the birthplace of Peter, Andrew, and Philip (John 1:44). The first century A.D. Jewish historian Josephus states that Philip, son of Herod the Great, gave Bethsaida the status of a city in A.D. 30, renaming it Julius in honor of Julia-Livia, the wife of the Roman emperor Augustus. Archaeologists have also discovered a temple, built on a typical Roman temple plan, that may have been erected as a part of the renaming ceremony. Although the site lies 1.5 miles north of the present shore of the Sea of Galilee, the sea extended farther north in the time of Jesus.

167

SEPPHORIS

Excavations conducted in Sepphoris since 1983 have uncovered remains of the city, including a theater that was probably built by Antipas. Though only 4 miles from Nazareth, Sepphoris is not mentioned in the New Testament. However since Joseph, Jesus' earthly father, was a carpenter, it has been suggested that he and Jesus may have been employed in the construction of the city. Some excavators of Sepphoris argue that it may have been the popularity of the theater at Sepphoris that led Jesus to use the word "hypocrite" in his teaching. "Hypocrite," the classical Greek word for "stage actor," meant a person who practices deceit. It occurs seventeen times in the New Testament, all in the sayings of Jesus in the first three Gospels, and is used of people who only pretend to be pious and sincere.

Built on a mound, ancient Sepphoris guarded the western end of the Beit Netofa Valley. This ancient city, which Josephus, in the first century, called "the ornament of all Galilee" became an important capital of one of the five districts into which the country was divided after the Roman general Pompey conquered it in 63 B.C. In the winter of 39/38 B.C., at the beginning of his reign, Herod the Great took the city during a blinding snowstorm. But after Herod's death a rebellion in the city caused the Roman general, Varus, to burn it and sell its inhabitants into slavery. When Herod's kingdom was partitioned at his death, Sepphoris, with all of Galilee, was given to his son Herod Antipas who immediately rebuilt it, intending it to be subordinate to the city of Tiberias, which he eventually built on the Sea of Galilee and named for the emperor Tiberius. The city was almost entirely Jewish at this time, according to Josephus, who wrote that later under Agrippa I, "Sepphoris, by submission to Rome, became the capital of Galilee and the seat of the royal bank and the archives."

Sepphoris, a partially inhabited mound today, has been extensively excavated and turned into a national park with buildings constructed over significant portions of the ancient remains. Among them are impres-

The theater at Sepphoris.

Mosaic "Mona Lisa" of Galilee at Sepphoris.

CANA:
THE MIRACLE
AT THE WEDDING

Only 5 miles northeast of Nazareth, is another village visited by Jesus; in all four of its references in the New Testament it is called, "Cana in Galilee" (John 2:1, 11; 4:46; 21:2). This was the hometown of Nathanael, one of the disciples (John 21:2).

It was in this village that Jesus performed his first miracle, turning water into wine at a marriage (John 2:1-11). A Roman Catholic church and a Greek Orthodox church in the modern village of Kefr Cana (Arabic for village of Cana) have long preserved the memory of that miracle, housing jars reminiscent of the six Jesus filled with wine, and this site has long been regarded as the Cana mentioned in John's Gospel.

There is, however, no archaeological or historical evidence in support of that claim, and in recent years excavators at Khirbet Kana (Ruins of Cana), 9 miles north of Nazareth, are building a case for the identity of that site with the Cana of Jesus' miracle.

sive mosaic floor depictions such as the beautiful female portrait dubbed "the Mona Lisa of Galilee." It is a mosaic panel which was part of the floor of a late third- or early fourth-century public building. The panel comprises about 54 square feet (4.8 square meters)—9 by 6 feet, 2.7 by 1.8 meters—and is 75 percent complete. Mosaics are usually badly damaged due to earthquakes or rebuilding activity after military conquests. This stunning portrait depicts a woman of enchanting beauty, not unlike one found by the present writer in Caesarea Maritima dating to the same period. The opposite end of the panel contained another such portrait, but it was substantially damaged. The panel, containing fifteen separate scenes probably depicting the life of Dionysus, the Graeco-Roman god of wine and debauchery, may have adorned the floor of a banqueting hall.

A jar in the Greek Orthodox church in Cana.

169

Above: New excavations at Khirbet Kana, possible site of the "Cana in Galilee" of the Gospels.

Paneas, near biblical Caesarea Philippi.

CAESAREA PHILIPPI: WHERE JESUS COMMISSIONED PETER

On one occasion, Jesus "came into the district of Caesarea Philippi" (Matthew 16:13) with his apostles and there told Peter "upon this rock I will build my church" (Matthew 16:18). The city lay in the extreme northeast section of modern Israel, in the forested area near the foot of Mount Hermon. According to Josephus, the first-century Jewish historian, Caesarea Philippi was given to Herod the Great by Augustus Caesar (*Antiquities* 15.360). Philip, the son of Herod, received the territory and the city from his father and renovated it (*Antiquities* 18.28).

Above: Distant view of the northern sector of Caesarea Philippi. Remains of a magnificent palace have been excavated here; it has been identified by the white marble still attached to some of the walls as having been built by Herod Agrippa II (the great-grandson of Herod the Great). An inscription discovered in Beirut records Herod Agrippa's practice of building with marble. This is the Agrippa before whom Paul appeared in Acts 26, and who made Caesarea Philippi his capital from A.D. 53–93. Excavated remains include portions of a reception hall, a public bathhouse and large circular towers that fortified the north-south colonnaded street that ran through the center of the city.

Right: The author in the palace of Agrippa II at Caesarea Philippi. Josephus says that Herod built a beautiful temple of white marble "in the region of Paneas" (modern Baniyas). This is probably the temple depicted on a coin found in the excavations there. The view on the coin is of the front of a four-columned temple. Excavations at Omrit in this region, less than 2 miles south of Banyas (Caesarea Philippi) began in 1999 and uncovered a temple like the one mentioned by Josephus. The discovery was first reported in 2003 in the *Biblical Archaeology Review.*

Caesarea Maritima
Center of Roman Rule

The harbor at Caesarea.

One of the most extensively excavated sites in Israel is also named Caesarea, but since it is on the Mediterranean coast it is differentiated from Caesarea Philippi by being given its maritime designation, Caesarea Maritima. This Caesarea, completely built anew from the ground up by Herod the Great, stands on the coast, halfway between Tel Aviv and Haifa and in Herod's time covered about 164 acres (67 hectares).

Some of the street system of Herodian Caesarea has come to light, providing an idea of the layout of the city. The cardo maximus, the major north-south street, was about 13 feet (four meters) wide and was paved with stone in a herringbone pattern. It had mosaic sidewalks 18 feet (5.5 meters) wide, also paved with mosaics. The total width of the street was more than 52 feet (16 meters) and was lined with about 700 columns, many of which now lie in the harbor where they were placed as a breakwater in the Crusader/Arab wars.

Herod's temple, palace, and theater.
Foundations of a temple that Herod built in honor of Roma, the goddess of Rome, and Augustus the emperor were found standing on a terrace above and east of the harbor. Josephus wrote of this

Roman Aqueduct at Caesarea.
A considerable portion of the huge aqueduct Herod built to supply the city with water is still standing on beautifully constructed Roman arches. It brought water from a source

temple: "On an eminence facing the harbor-mouth stood Caesar's temple, remarkable for its beauty and grand proportions; it contained a colossal statue of the emperor . . . and another of Rome." He also wrote that Herod named the city Caesarea in honor of Caesar (Augustus). This is one of the three temples in Israel that Josephus said were built by Herod to Augustus; the other two were in Caesarea Philippi and Samaria.

Recent excavations in Caesarea Maritima have uncovered the Promontory Palace of Herod with an adjacent pool about 1,000 feet (300 meters) south of the harbor. Very recently an Amphitheater built by Herod was uncovered adjacent to the north side of the palace. It was 985 feet (300 meters) long and 165 feet (50 meters) wide and may have had as many as 15,000 seats.

About 330 feet (about 100 meters) south of these structures, a later Roman theater still stands over

about fifteen miles northeast of Caesarea and is one of the best known landmarks along the entire coast of Israel—a continuing monument to the work of Herod the Great.

the theater Herod built here; the earlier Herodian remains include the foundation of the spectators' seats and the drainage system.

The reconstructed seating area of the theater reveals that it would have seated approximately 4,000 people. Luke records that "on an apppointed day" Herod Agrippa I put on his royal robes, took his seat on his throne, and gave an oration to the people (Acts 12:21-23). Josephus places this event in the theater (*Antiquities*, 19.344) and writes, as does Luke in Acts 12:23, that when Herod accepted their acclamation of him as a god, he was immediately stricken with a severely painful ailment, had to be taken from the theater, and died within five days (*Antiquities*, 19.350). This took place in A.D. 44.

The influence of Paul

Two fifth-century mosaic inscriptions of Romans 13:3 in Greek, were found in the floor of a large building (perhaps an imperial revenue office) across the street from the southern Crusader wall near the sea. They bear testimony to the influence of Paul in Caesarea in the earlier Byzantine period. The statement by Paul exhorts Christians in Rome to obey the authorities.

Further evidence of Paul's connection with Caesarea was found in 1997. It is also an inscription in a mosaic floor, which, according to the excavator, belonged to the official Roman bureau for internal security where Paul appeared before Festus (Acts 24:27; 25:1-6). The inscription reads: "I came to this office– I shall be secure."

The building complex where it was found is 161,000 square feet (15,000 square meters) in size and includes a large palace, administrative offices, a bathhouse, and courtyard. It has been described as a governmental complex, the only seat of Roman government unearthed in Israel, and one of the few ever excavated in the ancient Roman world. Since Roman rule over Palestine was centered in Caesarea, the Praetorium complex there functioned as the seat of Roman government from the beginning until the middle of the third century.

Mosaic of Romans 13:3 found at Caesarea.

Pilate Inscription found at Caesarea

In 1962 a stone was found that was originally part of a nearby temple honoring the emperor Tiberius, but had been reused in a step of the Roman theater. The stone contains a dedicatory Latin inscription stating that "Pontius Pilate Prefect of Judea, has dedicated to the people of Caesarea a temple in honor of Tiberius." This is the first and only reference to Pilate found in archaeological excavations. He was the prefect of Judea (A.D. 26-36) under whom Jesus was crucified. Tiberius was emperor from A.D. 14 to 37. The original location of the stone and the temple to which it refers are not known.

Aerial view of Caesarea, showing excavations of Roman city and walls of Crusader city.

The Harbor

At Caesarea Maritima Herod the Great constructed the first artificial harbor in the ancient world. The Herodian harbor was much larger than the later Crusader one now standing. Part of its breakwater walls can still be seen beneath the surface, and excavations on the shore have uncovered portions of the dock and many warehouses. Josephus wrote: "Abutting on the harbor were houses, also of white stone, and upon it converged the streets of the town, laid at equal distances apart."

Josephus' description

Underwater excavations have shown that Josephus' description of the design and size of the harbor is substantially accurate. He wrote: "[Herod] constructed a harbor larger than the Piraeus [the harbor of Athens] . . . the solidity of his masonry defied the sea, while its beauty was such as if no obstacle had existed . . . he had blocks of stone let down into 20 fathoms of water, most of them measuring 50 feet in length by 9 in depth and 10 in breadth [15.2 meters by 2.7 meters by 3 meters], some being even larger. Upon the submarine foundation thus laid he constructed above the surface a mole 200 feet [61 meters] broad; of which 100 were built out to break the surge, whence this portion was called the breakwater, while the remainder supported a stone wall encircling the harbor. From this wall arose, at intervals, massive towers . . . numerous inlets provided landing places for mariners putting in to harbor, while the whole circular terrace fronting these channels served as a broad promenade for disembarking passengers. The entrance to the port faced northwards because in these latitudes the north wind is the most favorable of all. At the harbor-mouth stood colossal statues, three on either side, resting on columns."

The Jewish War, 1.413-414

Below: Artist's impression of the harbor at Caesarea in the time of Jesus.

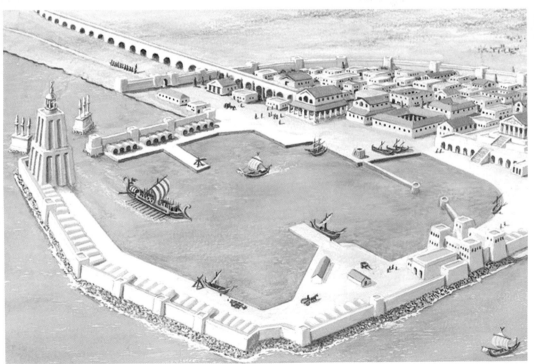

SAMARIA: IN THE CENTER OF PALESTINE

Jacob's Well

On one occasion Jesus left Judea and went to Galilee, passing through Samaria where he paused with his disciples to rest at Jacob's Well. This well was near the village of Sychar (John 4:1-6), which was located slightly northeast of modern-day Nablus (ancient Shechem). That Jacob's Well was nearby is clear from the fact that a woman from the village, after speaking to Jesus, "went away into the city" (John 4:28).

A frequently visited well is still in existence near Nablus, but there is no literary evidence confirming the identity of the well before the church historian Eusebius referred to it in the fourth century.

The well is described in the Gospel of John as being "deep" (John 4:11). Arculf, a Frankish bishop and pilgrim, who visited the modern site about A.D. 670, saw a cruciform crypt built over the well, which was probably all that was left when the upper church was destroyed, and said it was 240 feet (73 meters) deep. In 1875, Lieutenant C. R. Conder found the depth to be 70 feet (21.5 meters). It is evident that across the centuries debris had accumulated in the bottom of the well.

The water level also fluctuated. In 1687, Henry Maundrell found 15 feet (4.5 meters) of water in it; Edward Robinson found 10 to 12 feet (3 to 3.5 meters) of water in it in 1839, but in May of 1881 it was dry. It is evidently fed by underground rainwater and the level fluctuates.

During annual visits over the past thirty years, I have always found cold, refreshing water in the well. Archaeologically, it is of interest because of its geographic characteristics and location and the possibility that it could be the actual well where Jesus talked to the woman of Samaria about Jewish and Samaritan worship.

Jacob's well at Shechem.

Excavations at Samaritan temple site on Mount Gerizim. The temple complex covered a hundred acres, including living quarters for about 1,500 people.

The Samaritan temple

During their conversation, the Samaritan woman said to Jesus that her ancestors "worshiped on this mountain." She was referring to Mount Gerizim, standing on the south side of the village of Shechem. Her use of the past tense "worshiped," rather than the present tense "worship" (John 4:20), was necessitated by the fact that the Samaritan temple which had once stood on this mountain was no longer there. The temple had been built by the Samaritans around the time of Nehemiah (mid-fifth century B.C.) as a rival to the one in Jerusalem and, according to Josephus, was an exact replica. It was destroyed by the Hasmonean Jewish ruler John Hyrcanus II in 113 B.C., more than a century before the time of Jesus.

Excavations on the top of Mount Gerizim began in 1983, but only recently have the foundations of this temple been found; they measure 400 feet (122 meters) by 560 feet (171 meters). Temple walls 6 feet (1.8 meters) thick have been found, along with gates, altars, and inscriptions written in ancient Hebrew which the excavator says "indicates the Samaritans practiced Jewish customs, including prayers and sacrificial rites."

BETHANY NEAR JERUSALEM

The little village of Bethany, identified with the modern village of el-Azariyeh, is the place where Lazarus and his sisters Mary and Martha lived. It lies about 2 miles east of Jerusalem (John 11:18), on the eastern side of the Mount of Olives. Jesus visited Lazarus' family in their home here during the last week of his life. It was in this village that he raised Lazarus from the dead (John 12:1).

In the fourth century Eusebius described Bethany as "a village at the second milestone from Aelia [Jerusalem], in a steep bank of the Mount of Olives, where Christ raised

Tomb of Lazarus in Bethany.

Lazarus. The place of Lazarus is being shown even until now." This "place" is a tomb that tradition assigns to the story of Lazarus.

The original entrance to the tomb was on the east; the present entrance on the north was cut centuries later during the Muslim period. The tomb is small with a vestibule opening to the north through a narrow passage 5 feet (1.5 meters) long into the burial chamber, which is about 8 feet (2.5 meters) square. A church was built at the tomb in the fourth century but was destroyed, probably by earthquake. It was rebuilt with subsequent modifications in the following centuries. The modern church, dedicated in 1954, stands over the ruins of previous constructions. There is no way conclusively to identify the tomb as that of Lazarus.

JERUSALEM, THE HOLY CITY

Pliny the Elder spoke of Jerusalem as "the most famous city of the East, and not of Judea only," and the Babylonian Talmud exclaimed: "Whoever has not seen Jerusalem in its splendor has never seen a fine city." Jerusalem is the most important city in the history of Israel because the Temple was built there by King Solomon in the tenth century B.C. After its destruction in 586 B.C. by King Nebuchadnezzar of Babylon, it was rebuilt and rededicated under the leadership of Zerubbabel in 516 B.C.

In the New Testament era the Jewish king, Herod the Great, renovated (actually rebuilt) and greatly expanded the Temple complex. An inscription of a donor to the construction of a pavement near the Temple has been recently found below the Double Gate in the southern wall of the Temple Mount. This discovery supports Josephus' earliest date of 23/22 B.C. for the beginning of Herod's work on the Temple.

For followers of Jesus Christ, Jerusalem is Israel's most important city because Jesus was crucified, buried, and raised from the dead there (John 19-21). Information on the appearance and composition of Jerusalem at the time of Christ has increased greatly in the past thirty years as a result of increased archaeological excavation.

179

The city today

The city of Jerusalem today is about 4.25 miles (7 kilometers) square consisting of two distinct sections—the western, predominantly Jewish, section, which is about 4.2 miles (7 kilometers) north to south by 3 miles (5 kilometers) east to west; and the eastern, predominantly Arab, section, which is about 1.8 miles (3 kilometers) north to south by 1.2 miles (2 kilometers) east to west. These boundaries, however, are incessantly disputed on the basis of whether one is speaking politically, historically, ethnically, or purely emotionally. What is now called "the Old City" is the roughly 0.6 square mile (1 square kilometer) area that stretches from the Kidron Valley on the east to the Jaffa Gate on the west and from the Damascus Gate on the north to the Dung Gate on the south. This was the area known as Jerusalem in the New Testament period. It was about 250 acres (102 hectares) and was surrounded by a stone wall that was built partly in the first century, was largely destroyed in later conquests, and then completely rebuilt in the sixteenth century by the Muslim ruler Suleiman the Magnificent.

The city wall today has seven active gates in it. The New Gate, Damascus Gate, and Herod Gate are in the north wall; the Stephen Gate is in the east wall; the Dung Gate and the Zion Gate are in the south wall; and the Jaffa Gate is in the west wall. An eighth gate, called the Golden Gate, once opened into the Temple Mount area through the east wall, but it has been blocked since the ninth century when the Arabs feared that one day a conqueror would enter the city through it.

In the northern wall of the old city of Jerusalem there is a gate located below ground level on the east side of the modern Damascus Gate. The lower portions of the wall here are built with the typical Herodian-style stones used by Herod the Great, but they were probably later reused by Herod Agrippa in his construction of the northern wall. No evidence of Herod the Great's northern wall has yet been found. The rebuilt arch over the gate has been dated to the time of Hadrian in the second century.

The Temple Mount in Jerusalem from Mount Olivet.

The Temple Mount

Pinnacle of the Temple area (south-east corner).

Pinnacle and gates in south wall.

The Temple, which was the central point of importance in Jerusalem throughout its history, was located on the mount in the eastern side of the Old City beside the eastern wall, which ran along the edge of the Kidron Valley. The basically rectangular platform on the mount today represents the identical area of Herod's renovation, which doubled the size of the original temple grounds. The Muslim Dome of the Rock stands in this space today, probably on the very spot where the Jewish Temple once stood. This constitutes an area covering 465,880 square feet (41,930 square meters). Herod was able to do this renovation by extending the platform out on to the slopes surrounding the Temple to the east, south, and west. Huge retaining walls were built to support the fill upon which the platform stood. Only to the northwest did he need to shave off some of the rock, which stood higher than the platform level.

To the south a huge stone platform was constructed, resting on massive arches. The large vaulted area under the pavement is today

erroneously called "Solomon's Stables." A number of the Herodian foundation blocks on which the pillars supporting the arches were built are still visible in the vault beneath the pavement.

In the New Testament this corner of the Temple Mount is called the "pinnacle of the temple," the place where Jesus was tempted by Satan (Luke 4:9). However, the current

platform and its associated walls were not standing at that time because in A.D. 70 the Roman general Titus destroyed the entire platform area down to the Herodian foundation blocks supporting the eighty-eight pillars visible today.

Herod built two gates to provide access to the Temple Mount through the southern walls, the Double Gate and the Triple Gate (referred to collectively in Mishnah as the Hulda Gate). The Double Gate is 42 feet (13 meters) wide, slightly smaller than the 50-foot-wide (15 meter) Triple Gate. Its large

Underground arches beneath the pinnacle platform.

181

Stone paved walkway along south temple wall, 21 feet (6.5 meters) wide.

Top: South wall and gates.
Below: Jewish *Mikveh* (ritual bath). Bottom: Street beside Western Wall.

square vestibule of Herodian stone and 78-foot (24-meter) tunnel leading north to the Temple platform, which is 39 feet (12 meters) higher, are still well preserved. Since it was still being used until the Crusaders closed it and constructed a building against it, which covers the western half of the gate today, it was obviously not destroyed in the Roman conquest.

Excavations have revealed a 21-foot-wide stone pavement that Herod built in front of these gates. Monumental stairways descended 22 feet (6.7 meters) southward from the gates to a plaza. The largest of the stairways, the section in front of the Double Gates, is 215 feet (65.5 meters) wide with thirty steps made of smoothed stone paving blocks. It has been restored to much of its original beauty and may again be climbed by visitors to the Temple Mount. A passage in the Talmud refers to Gamaliel and the elders standing on top of these stairs.

Between the two gates and south of the street in front of them were found a number of pools, plastered cisterns, and *mikvaoth* (Jewish ritual baths). These were used for individual purification by large crowds of pilgrims who gathered on the plaza before entering the Temple area to

Ground Plan of Herod's Temple

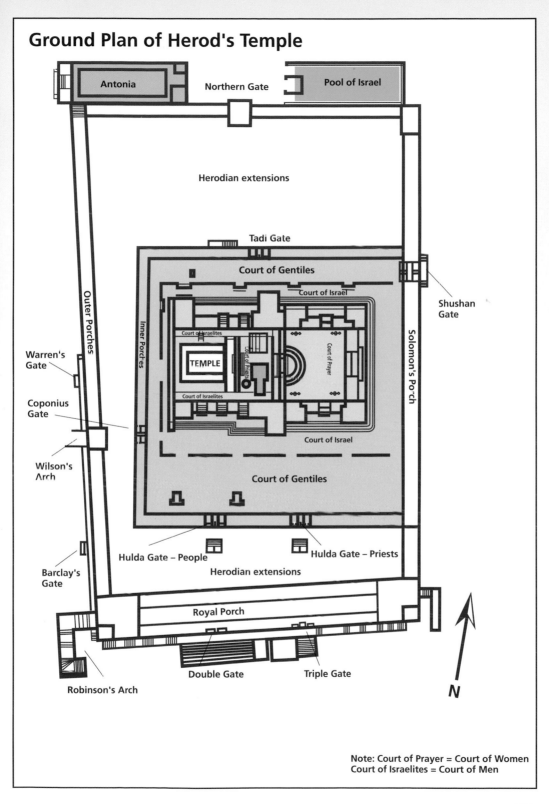

Antonia

Northern Gate

Pool of Israel

Herodian extensions

Tadi Gate

Court of Gentiles

Court of Israel

Shushan Gate

Outer Porches

Inner Porches

Court of Israelites

Warren's Gate

TEMPLE

Court of Priests

Court of Prayer

Solomon's Porch

Coponius Gate

Court of Israelites

Wilson's Arch

Court of Israel

Court of Gentiles

Barclay's Gate

Hulda Gate – People

Hulda Gate – Priests

Herodian extensions

Royal Porch

Double Gate

Triple Gate

N

Robinson's Arch

Note: Court of Prayer = Court of Women
Court of Israelites = Court of Men

The so-called "Ecce Homo Arch" in Jerusalem.

forked at this corner with the western section of it continuing northward to the Damascus Gate and the eastern section terminating at the Antonia Fortress on the northwestern corner of the mount.

Twenty-six courses of the original Herodian stone still stand in the Western Wall, sometimes known as the "Wailing Wall," seven of which are above ground and nineteen under ground. These stones, characteristic of Herod the Great's architecture, are easily identifiable by their boss, the untrimmed, raised face of the stone, which is surrounded on all four sides by a smooth, narrow border.

Josephus wrote that a priest stood at the top of the southwestern corner of the Temple and officially signaled the beginning of the Sabbath by blowing a trumpet at sunset on Friday. Here at this very

corner excavators found a trimmed stone block that had fallen from the tower above, on which were carved in Hebrew the words, "To the Place of Trumpeting to declare . . ."

The location of the Jerusalem Temple

A highly debated aspect of Herod's building program is the precise location on the mount of the Temple itself. When he rebuilt it, Herod did not relocate the Temple constructed by Zerubbabel, but archaeologists have disagreed on the precise location of the structure. Josephus affirmed that the Temple stood at the top of the mount, and therefore it has been argued that it stood adjacent to the north side of the present Muslim Dome of the Rock where the bedrock was assumed to be higher than that under the Dome.

worship. Along with others, these could have been used for the immersions in water of the 3,000 believers on the Day of Pentecost recorded in Acts 2:38-41.

Herod built a paved street along the western wall of the Temple Mount. In recent excavations portions of a Herodian street have been found at the southwestern corner of the mount. The pavement, which ran north along the western wall,

Herodian stone in Western Wall.

Jewish men at the Western Wall.

Temple Mount from the Mount of Olives.

An Israeli architect has discovered, however, that the stone floor under the small Dome of the Spirits, immediately north of the Muslim Dome of the Rock, is not actually bedrock, but is, rather, a large paving slab, and bedrock is at least 8 feet (2.5 meters) below the floor of this little monument. This means that this stone floor is not the highest point on the mount. The rock under the Dome of the Rock is actually 15 feet (4.5 meters) higher than that under the little Dome of the Spirits and is thus the only viable choice for the Temple location.

According to the tractate Middoth 2:1 in the Mishnah (a third-century compendium of Jewish regulations and beliefs), the platform of the Temple was 500 royal cubits square (861 feet, 262.5 meters). Investigations of key points around the Temple Mount have revealed that the Dome of the Rock stands on the precise 1,640-foot square area (500-meters-square) where the temple would have stood. Thus for the first time all the factors—topographical, archaeological, and historical—seem to agree on its location.

The place where Jesus stood before Pontius Pilate

Another place of archaeological interest on the Temple Mount is at

Muslim Dome of the Rock. The little Dome of the Spirits is immediately to the right of it in the picture.

its northwest corner. Herod built a fortress into the northern wall of this mount and named it Antonia in honor of Mark Antony. It has been argued that the pavement beneath the modern Notre Dame de Sion Convent on the so-called "Via Dolorosa" was the floor of this fortress and was the "pavement" on which Jesus stood before Pilate (John 19).

It has been shown, however, that the pavement is contemporaneous with the huge vaults of the Struthion Pools underneath it. The pavement above the pools could not have been built before the Roman siege in A.D. 70, if Josephus is correct, because he states that the Romans built a ramp "through" the pools to bring their siege machines

against the north wall of the Antonia Fortress. The pools, therefore, must have been open at the time, rather than covered by a stone pavement, and must have lain outside the fortress. The massive construction of the walls, arches, and ceilings seen today came later. Jesus could not have stood on a nonexistent floor.

Furthermore, excavations in 1966 revealed that the "Ecce Homo Arch," which spans the modern street called the Via Dolorosa in front of the Convent and extends inside to the chapel, rests its northern pier on bedrock rather than on the fortress pavement on which Jesus supposedly appeared before Pilate. The pier would have rested on top of the stone pavement had

185

Stone pavement beneath the Notre Dame de Sion Convent.

Stone inscription from balustrade wall around the Temple.

that pavement been standing when the arch was constructed.

It is more likely that Jesus stood before Pilate on the pavement of the Praetorium discovered by an Israeli archaeologist south of the Jaffa Gate and adjacent to the eastern side of Herod's Palace (Herod's palace, page 191).

The balustrade wall

A discovery relating to the courtyard on the north side of the Temple sheds light on Acts 21:27-40 where Paul is accused of taking Greeks into the forbidden areas of the Temple. The two inner courts, the Court of Israel and the Court of the Women, were restricted to Jewish men and women respectively. This area was surrounded by a small partition wall called the "balustrade." Outside this wall, the rest of the Temple area consisted of a huge stone platform called the Court of the Gentiles into which Gentiles could come and worship the God of all nations. This is the area Jesus had cleansed during his last week in Jerusalem, impressing upon those present the words of the prophets, "Even those I will bring to my holy mountain, and make them joyful in my house of prayer. Their burnt offerings and their sacrifices will be acceptable on my altar; for my house will be called a house of prayer for all peoples" (Isaiah 56:7; Mark 11:17). This pas-

Court of the Gentiles in Jerusalem model of the Temple.

sage was meant to declare that both Jews and Gentiles could worship at the Temple. They were, however, to respect the designated areas for each.

Josephus wrote that the Jewish section was "surrounded by a stone balustrade with an inscription prohibiting the entrance of a foreigner under threat of the penalty of death" (*Antiquities*, 15.417). The Jews were allowed by the Romans to put to death anyone—even *Roman citizens*—who crossed this boundary wall. Josephus described the wall as being three cubits (4.5 feet, 1.3 meters) high, and stated that "slabs stood at regular intervals giving warning, some in Greek, others in Latin characters, of the law of

purification, to wit that no foreigner was permitted to enter the holy place . . ." (*War*, 5.194).

Two of these stone slabs containing the inscriptions described by Josephus have been found and published. The text was republished in 1989. It reads:

NO FOREIGNER IS TO ENTER WITHIN THE FORECOURT AND THE BALUSTRADE AROUND THE SANCTUARY. WHOEVER IS CAUGHT WILL HAVE HIMSELF TO BLAME FOR HIS SUBSEQUENT DEATH.

Thus it seems that Paul was erroneously assumed to have taken Trophimus the Ephesian (a Gentile) beyond this wall into the inner Jewish courts.

Siloam Pool at south end of Mount Ophel in Jerusalem.

Sources of water in Jerusalem

Archaeological remains of water sources in Jerusalem show that the city had a number of facilities available in the New Testament period. The entire Temple Mount is honey-

Tourists walk through Hezekiah's Tunnel.

combed with thirty-seven underground chambers cut into solid rock. Some of them are passageways, but most are reservoirs that would hold ten million gallons of water. Combined with the ever-flowing Gihon Spring, they were still not adequate to meet the needs of the city, so Herod built huge public pools and cisterns to remedy the problem. The double Struthion Pool was built near the Antonia Fortress at the northwest corner of the Temple area. The Pool of the Towers (Pool of Hezekiah) was constructed north of Herod's Palace by the Jaffa Gate. The Pool of Israel (now a parking lot) was built adjacent to the northern wall of the Temple Mount. Large underground pools cut into rock have recently been found in the excavations just south of the Double Gate in the southern wall of the Temple Mount.

Pool of Siloam

Another important source of water for the inhabitants of Jerusalem was the Pool of Siloam (John 9:1-41), which was built by Hezekiah, a king of Judah in the eighth century B.C., at the southern end of a long tunnel cut through 1,749 feet (533 meters) of solid rock to bring water from the Gihon Spring to the pool inside the city walls. It was

Recently discovered large Pool of Siloam.

at this pool that Jesus healed a blind man by having him wash his eyes in its water.

Until recently, only a small portion of the original pool has been accessible, and it is considerably smaller (fifty feet long by fifteen feet wide) than it was originally, when it was probably surrounded by a colonnaded portico which must have been the one described by the Pilgrim of Bordeaux in 333 A.D. as a quadriporticus (fourfold porch). This was presumably destroyed with an associated church during the Persian invasion in the 7th century. After the site was excavated in the late nineteenth century, the people of the village of Silwan (modern spelling of Siloam) built a mosque on the northwest corner of the little pool with a minaret, which still stands above the pool. It is possible today to enter this little Siloam Pool by walking down a stone staircase beside it or entering the Hezekiah tunnel at the Gihon Spring to the north and walking through the long tunnel

until it exits at the pool.

However, excavations at the site in the past six months have uncovered the eastern portion of a large pool, fifty meters in length, (its width not yet known) which lies only about ten meters south of the little pool. This small area between them has yet to be excavated and the relation of the two pools cannot at this time be definitively stated but they are possibly a part of one complex called the Siloam Pool (like the Pool of Bethesda which had two sections). It has a series of stone steps on all four sides for entering the pool, which, being fed by fresh running water from the Gihon Spring through a small channel discovered on the north side of the pool, was probably a major facility for ritual purification before entering the temple. A stone pavement has also recently been discovered, leading from the pool up Mt. Ophel to the Temple Mount.

Pool of Bethesda

Chapter 5 of John's Gospel tells of Jesus healing an invalid at another pool: "There is in Jerusalem by the Sheep Gate a pool called in Hebrew, Beth-zatha [or Bethesda] which has five porches." It should be noted, however, that the Greek text of verse 2 is ambiguous and has been rendered differently in various translations: "there is in Jerusalem by the Sheep Gate a pool" (NRSV, NIV, GNB, REB, etc.), "At the Sheep Pool in Jerusalem there is a place [or building]" (NEB, Jerusalem Bible), and, "There is in Jerusalem by the sheep market a pool" (KJV). A gate called the Sheep Gate was built by Eliashib the high priest in the time of Nehemiah (3:1, 32; 12:39).

Excavations have revealed a twin pool with porches in the exact area of the story in John 5:1-15. This pool, which was probably fed by rainwater and underground springs, may still be seen by visitors near Jerusalem's eastern wall, about 300 feet (92 meters) west of the Stephen Gate (also known as the Lion's Gate).

At the turn of the century, the two large pools were excavated about 300 feet (92 meters) north of the Temple Mount's northern wall near the Church of Saint Anne. Cut into rock and plastered, these pools lie close to the church on its west side. The larger southern pool is estimated to be about 215 feet (67 meters) wide at its southern side and about 190 feet (58 meters) across the northern side. The east and west sides measure about 160 feet (58 meters) in length. The smaller northern pool is estimated at about 175 feet (54 meters) on its southern side, 165 feet (51 meters) on the north, and 130 feet (40 meters) on the east and west. They may have provided as much as 5,000 square yards (4,050 square meters) of water surface.

The pool was probably fed by rainwater and underground springs. The northern pool has over its southeastern corner a cistern with a vaulted chamber about 50 feet (15.5 meters) long east to west and 20 feet (16 meters) wide north to south. Water continually stands in it today, but it is only about a foot (0.3 meters) deep and stagnant. In the excavations many fragments of column bases, capitals, and drums were found. These probably belonged to the five porches (that is, porticoes or colonnaded walkways) of the pool that John mentions. There is no good reason to deny the probability that these two pools are the Sheep Pool referred to by Eusebius and the "twin pools" mentioned by the Bordeaux Pilgrim, both in the early fourth century.

Gethsemane

On the night of his arrest, Jesus is recorded as having been taken from the Garden of Gethsemane to appear before Caiaphas, the high priest (Matthew 26:57). At the foot of the Mount of Olives, and west of the Dominus Flevit Church, stands the Gethsemane Church of All Nations, which was completed in 1924. This church, built on the foundations of a prior church, marks the spot venerated since at least the fourth cen-

The Church of All Nations in Gethsemane.

tury as the Garden of Gethsemane. In front of the apse of this building there is a rock which is referred to by the Bordeaux Pilgrim in A.D. 333. Tradition holds that before his betrayal by Judas Jesus prayed on this rock. The Byzantine church, lying directly beneath the modern one, was designed so that the rock would stand in the center of the eastern end of the nave, just as it does in the modern one, which is built upon its foundations.

In A.D. 330 Eusebius identified Gethsemane as a place "at the foot of the Mount of Olives where the faithful now make their prayers diligently." Jerome, in his Latin translation of Eusebius' work in A.D. 390, alters the text to read *nunc ecclesia desuper aedificata*, "a church has now been built over it" (that is, the place where the prayers were made). It would seem, then, that the church underlying the foundations of the modern one was built between the time these two works were written. This church was destroyed, probably by the Persian invasion of A.D. 614, and was not rebuilt until a Christian presence was again felt. The Crusaders built a new one in the twelfth century, slightly to the north of the Byzantine church and partly overlapping its southern side. It was subsequently destroyed.

The Church of St. Peter of the Cockcrow (St. Peter in Gallicantu)

On the eastern slope of Mount Ophel, which is a southern extension of the mount on which the Temple stood, a flight of stairs has been found that connects the Kidron Valley with the upper section of Mount Ophel. The stairs date to the time of Jesus and run up the north side of the Church of St. Peter in Gallicantu (St. Peter of the Cockcrow). Beneath the church is a large complex of rock-hewn chambers surrounding a central room. These have rings on the walls and stone handles cut out of the walls and above the doors. The rings and stone handles could have been used to tie a person while he was

Stairs by the Church of St. Peter of the Cockcrow.

being whipped and some have therefore assumed these rooms to be a prison and the place where Jesus was kept until Caiaphas could see him.

Early Christian authors wrote about a church of St. Peter being built over the palace of Caiaphas and identified this church with that one. As early as 1888, excavations were carried out at the church, and in 1911 ruins of a fifth-century church were found beneath the modern one. The modern church was built here in 1931, and since the older church was assumed to have been the Cockcrow Church the new church was also given this name. There is, however, no clear evidence to connect this fifth-century church with the church of St. Peter mentioned in the early sources. That one must have been located north of this site, nearer the Holy Zion Church, as shown on the Madeba map, a mosaic map of Jerusalem on the floor of a church in Madeba, Jordan, which dates to about A.D. 560 in the reign of Justinian. Thus, the palace of Caiaphas could have stood on or near the present Church of the Cockcrow or farther up the hill near the Holy Zion Church.

Herod's palace

As a part of his western palace, Herod built three large towers, which he named for his friends and relatives: Hippicus, Phasael, and Mariamne. According to Josephus, Titus "left these towers as a monument to his good fortune" when he destroyed Jerusalem (*War*, 6.409-413). The lower portion of one of them, which most regard as Phasael, dates to the time of Herod and still stands intact at the modern Jaffa Gate.

Herodian foundations of a large podium have been found to the south of Phasael Tower, in the Armenian Quarter, indicating that the original palace of Herod stretched from the Citadel at the Jaffa Gate on the north, along the western modern Turkish wall, to its southern extremity where the wall turns east. This podium, on which a

Top: Phasael Tower in the Jaffa Gate.
Above: Model of Herod's palace, three towers and Lithostroton (*bema*).

stone pavement once stood, was approximately 1,100 feet (335.5 meters) long, north to south, and 200 feet (61 meters) wide, east to west. Nothing of the superstructure has been found. The pavement supported by this massive foundation is the more likely one on which Jesus stood before Pilate.

Although it has been argued that Pilate may have been staying in the Antonia Fortress when Jesus appeared before him, this now seems highly unlikely. In the first place, accommodation in the Antonia was scarcely comparable with the luxury of Herod's palace. Moreover, Philo, a contemporary of Jesus, wrote that Pilate was living in

191

Herod's palace during one of the Jewish feasts and he describes it as "the residence of the prefects." Hence Gessius Florus, who became prefect in A.D. 64, lived there just before Titus' destruction of the Temple, beginning two years later. Further evidence comes from Mark, who states in his Gospel that the soldiers "led him [Jesus] outside the palace, which is the praetorium" (Mark 15:16). The praetorium, that is, the residence of the Roman authority, must have been in the Herodian palace, and the large podium foundation discovered east of the palace must have been that on which Jesus stood before Pilate. It is called in Greek *Lithostroton* (stone pavement) and in Hebrew *Gabbatha* (elevated place) (John 19:13).

In Greek and Roman times, a tribunal platform (called a *bema* in Greek) was built in the open for the purpose of addressing the crowds. There is one still standing in Corinth, and here Paul would have stood before Gallio (Acts 18:12-14). Matthew noted in his Gospel that Pilate was seated "on the judgement seat [Greek *bema*]" (Matthew 27:19). A bema was thus apparently built by the Roman prefect on the stone pavement for the purpose of receiving his subjects. Josephus wrote that on one occasion the populace "surrounded the tribunal" (*War* 2:175) where Pilate was seated.

The crucifixion and burial of Jesus

For New Testament studies, one of the most important issues in the archaeology of Jerusalem relates to the question of the place of Jesus' crucifixion, burial, and resurrection. About a hundred yards (280 meters) north of the Old City's Damascus Gate there is a garden with a tomb commonly called both the Garden Tomb and Gordon's Tomb, because of its identification by General Charles Gordon in 1883 as the tomb of Jesus. Since then, it has long been held by the Protestant and Evangelical wings of Christianity to be the actual burial place of

In 1968 an ossified foot was discovered in Jerusalem with a spike in it belonging to a crucified man named Yehohanan. This demonstrates the method of crucifixion referred to in John 20:25, which speaks of Jesus having had nails driven into his hands.

Christ. However, although the Garden Tomb does have the aesthetic appeal of being located in a lovely garden, removed from the rush and noise of a bustling and distracting modern city, the method used by Gordon in making the initial identification of the tomb was not the result of careful scholarship. He wrote in a letter published in 1885 that when he visited the Garden Tomb and nearby "Skull Hill" he "felt convinced" that it must be the place of Christ's crucifixion, since it was north of the city, and Jesus would have been slain north of the temple altar, like the Old Testament sacrificial lambs of which he was the type. This is, of course, mere assumption, and archaeological evidence, especially tomb typology, argues decisively against this identification.

Recent study has revealed that in the time of the New Testament the city of Jerusalem was surrounded by burials. Scientific analysis of the tombs has revealed a pattern of tomb construction that changed with the

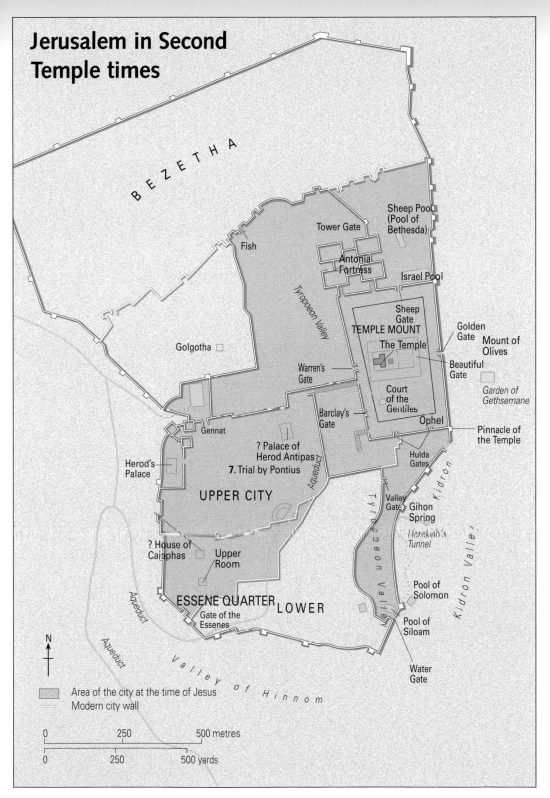

Jerusalem in Second Temple times

BEZETHA

Tower Gate

Fish

Sheep Pool (Pool of Bethesda)

Antonia Fortress

Israel Pool

Golgotha

Tyropoeon Valley

Sheep Gate

TEMPLE MOUNT

The Temple

Golden Gate

Mount of Olives

Warren's Gate

Beautiful Gate

Court of the Gentiles

Garden of Gethsemane

Barclay's Gate

Ophel

Gennat

? Palace of Herod Antipas

7. Trial by Pontius

Aqueduct

Hulda Gates

Pinnacle of the Temple

Herod's Palace

UPPER CITY

Valley Gate

Gihon Spring

Tyropoeon Valley

Hezekiah's Tunnel

Kidron

Kidron Valley

? House of Caiaphas

Upper Room

Aqueduct

ESSENE QUARTER LOWER

Gate of the Essenes

Pool of Solomon

Pool of Siloam

N

Aqueduct

Valley of Hinnom

Water Gate

Area of the city at the time of Jesus

Modern city wall

0	250	500 metres
0	250	500 yards

Rolling stone at entrance to tomb in Heshbon, Jordan.

Stephen Church on the property of the École Biblique, the French School of Archaeology. The tombs in this burial ground all date to the Iron Age and the Garden Tomb is undeniably a part of these tombs, lying only six feet (1.8 meters) from one of these major tomb complexes.

About 700 tombs from the second-Temple period—the time of Jesus—have been explored within 3 miles of the city limits of Jerusalem. Tombs from the time of Jesus characteristically were either natural or hand cut caves with small niches (called *loculi* or *kokhim*) cut into the sides of the walls in which were placed sarcophagi, small stone boxes, containing the bones of the dead person whose body had lain in the tomb long enough to decompose before the bones were gathered into the box. The entrance to the tomb was often closed by a rolling stone, like the ones still standing at the family tomb of Herod on the south side of the King David Hotel in Jerusalem, the tomb of Queen Helena in East Jerusalem,

passing of time. The Garden Tomb is built on the pattern of Iron Age II tombs (eighth to seventh centuries B.C.) and not on the pattern of tombs of the Roman period. It is cut into a rock scarp (a cliff side) and is part of two large burial complexes near the St.

The Garden Tomb in East Jerusalem.

A rolling stone outside the Tomb of the Herods, Jerusalem.

and a tomb in a cemetery west of Heshbon, Jordan. More than sixty rolling-stone tombs have been surveyed in Israel and Jordan.

The tomb inside the Church of the Holy Sepulcher is most likely the tomb of Jesus. The church, though now inside the modern city walls, has been shown by excavation to have been located outside the walls in the days of Jesus, as was characteristic of tombs at that time. This means that it cannot be excluded from consideration because of its present locality inside the current walls.

Recent excavations at the Holy Sepulcher Church have established that the area where the church is now located had been a huge limestone quarry in the seventh century B.C. This quarry was in use until the first century B.C., at which time it was filled and made a garden. It contains at least four tombs from the early Roman period. Eusebius, the fourth-century church historian, stated that emperor Hadrian, after suppressing the second Jewish Revolt in A.D. 135, built a huge

rectangular platform of earth over this quarry, on top of which he constructed a temple dedicated to the Roman god Venus.

In the lifetime of Eusebius, Queen Helena, the mother of the emperor Constantine, came to Jerusalem and was shown the site of the tomb. Eusebius wrote:

> . . . on the very spot which witnessed the Savior's sufferings . . . the Emperor now began to rear a monument to the Savior's victory over death, with rich and lavish magnificence.

This monument was the Church of the Holy Sepulcher. Jerome wrote in the fifth century:

> From the time of Hadrian to the reign of Constantine—a period of about 180 years— the spot that had witnessed the resurrection was occupied by a figure of Jupiter.

Constantine, in a letter to Macarius, the bishop of Jerusalem, referred to the discovery of the "monument of his most holy passion," which had "remained unknown [apparently the tomb itself, not the general location] for so long a series of years."

Whether the temple of Hadrian had already been destroyed is not entirely clear, but when Constantine wrote to Macarius regarding the dismantling of a building used in idolatrous worship, he may have been referring to that temple and the building of the church:

> . . . the dwelling-places of error, with the statues . . . were overthrown and utterly destroyed . . . both stone and timber . . . that sacred spot, which under Divine direction I have disencumbered as it were of the heavy weight of foul idol worship . . . a spot . . . which now appears holier still, since it has brought to light a clear assurance of our Savior's passion.

North city walls of Jerusalem

Constantine's words argue strongly that the memory of the tomb location had persevered through the intervening centuries, even though Herod Agrippa I had built a new wall on the north side of the city within about fifteen years of the death of Jesus, which placed the tomb site within the city's walls. No one in the time of Helena would have looked for the burial site inside the crowded urban walled city if there had not been a compelling reason to do so. It should be remembered that the succession of Christian bishops in Jerusalem was never interrupted during these early centuries, and even though the first fifteen Jewish Christian bishops were necessarily succeeded by Gentile Christians after the publication of Hadrian's edict expelling all Jews from Jerusalem, the memory of so sacred a place would never have been forgotten. Helena and Constantine found it convincing enough to erect a church on this site.

The tomb of Caiaphas

In 1990 workers constructing a water park in the Peace Forest about a mile south of the old city of Jerusalem accidentally uncovered

Tomb of Caiaphas in the Peace Forest, Jerusalem.

an ancient burial cave. Carved twice on one of the ossuaries in the cave was the name of Joseph, son of Caiaphas. Inside the ossuary were the bones of six people: two infants, a child between the ages of two and five, a youth aged thirteen to eighteen, an adult female and a man about sixty years old. One of the archaeologists says that we have "in all probability" found the bones of the high priest who interrogated Jesus and then delivered him to the Roman governor Pontius Pilate (Matthew 26:57-27:2).

Inscription on "Absalom's Tomb," Luke 2:25

An inscription, believed to be the first New Testament text carved in stone yet discovered, and one of the earliest New Testament quotations ever found outside the Bible, was discovered in 2003 by Emile Puech and Joe Zias in the Kidron Valley southeast of the

Kidron Valley with "Absalom's Tomb."

corner of the Temple Mount. It is on the wall of a tomb commonly (but mistakenly) called Absalom's Tomb. The text is Luke 2:25, referring to Simeon, the man who held the young Jesus is his arms when he was brought to the Temple for Mary's purification.

The ossuary of James the brother of Jesus

Another artifact that has generated widespread interest was brought to public attention in 2002 by an antiquities dealer in Jerusalem, who had in his possession an ossuary, or stone burial box, which is 20 inches long by 10 inches wide by 12 inches high (51 centimeters by 25.5 centimeters by 30.5 centimeters), and which has an inscription carved on it in Aramaic. André Lemaire, from the Sorbonne in Paris, and one of the world's leading paleographers, dated the inscription to A.D. 63 and translated it to read "James son of Joseph brother of Jesus". It was declared in *Time* magazine and *Biblical Archaeology Review* to be the "most important discovery in the history of New Testament archaeology."

This stimulated world-wide interest and leading archaeological authorities evaluated the evidence, eventually disagreeing on its authenticity, some for and others against.

The Geological Survey of Israel tested it and confirmed its authenticity as a first century ossuary that was carved out of Jerusalem limestone. But the head of the Archaeological Institute at Tel Aviv University concluded that the patina on the stone, used in dating the box, had been manufactured artificially.

Israeli police took Oded Golan, the owner of the ossuary, into custody, searched his apartment, and found a workshop containing tools, materials and half finished "antiquities." He was accused of forging ancient documents.

Debate continues over the authenticity of this burial box. But even if it is authentic, whether it is the burial box of the brother of Jesus of Nazareth cannot be proven scientifically, and will have to remain a matter of individual belief based on the nature of the evidence presented by qualified scholars in research and debate. Even if it were genuine, this stone box is not capable of proving or disproving the historical existence of Jesus of Nazareth. That is a matter of faith based on broad historical evidence supporting the authenticity of the New Testament, confirmed by the lives and testimony of those who knew him and left their witness for the world in literary and oral tradition.

The James ossuary.

HEROD THE GREAT: A MAGNIFICENT BUILDER

Matthew 2:1 states: "Jesus was born in Bethlehem of Judea in the days of Herod the king . . ." From archaeological excavations and the writings of Josephus, a large amount of evidence pertinent to this king has been revealed; some has already been mentioned here. He is known to have been involved in building projects at twenty sites within his kingdom and thirteen outside its borders.

These activities included the construction of villages, cities, palaces, fortresses, ports, squares, colonnaded streets, theaters, stadia, hippodromes, gymnasia, public baths, monuments, agricultural and urban water systems, formal gardens, vaulted warehouses, water reservoirs, pagan sanctuaries, and the renovation of the Temple in Jerusalem. Whether Herod himself was directly involved in the architectural planning and execution of these projects is still being debated among archaeologists, but his influence upon them, directly or indirectly, is unmistakable.

Cave of Machpelah in Hebron

Herod built a monumental wall around the Cave of Macpelah in Hebron where Abraham, Isaac, Jacob, and their wives Sarah, Rebekah, and Leah were buried, but not Rachel, whose tomb is in Bethlehem. The beautifully dressed "Herodian" stone is laid with a smooth surface half way up the wall, at which point slight alternating indentations produce the effect of pilasters reaching to the top. This design is identical to the design Herod used on the enclosure wall of the Temple Mount in Jerusalem.

The desert palaces/fortresses of Herod the Great

In the deserts of Judea, Herod built a number of palaces that also functioned as fortresses. Their locations were probably

The Cave of Machpelah in Hebron.

Top: Herodium—distant view with pool in foreground. Below: Inside mound on Herodium.

chosen, among other reasons, to provide him with luxurious living-quarters when he was traveling outside Jerusalem and to give him safe fortresses in times of political and military danger. Three of these palace/fortresses, Herodium, Jericho, and Masada, have been excavated and reveal evidence of considerable beauty, reflecting in their design Herod's love for Roman architecture, acquired while living in Rome.

Herodium, south of Bethlehem
On a hill at Herodium, about 3 miles southeast of Bethlehem, Herod built a desert palace/fortress that was the third largest in the entire Roman world. The palace was sur-

Herodian Jericho.

rounded by two concentric circular walls with four towers. Inside the walls Herod had living-quarters, a courtyard that functioned as a garden, a triclinium (dining hall) that was later converted into a synagogue by Jewish Zealots, and a full Roman bath with hot, cold, and warm rooms. To supply the necessary water, four large underground cisterns were built in addition to the one above ground, which may be seen in the top of the tall eastern tower.

At the foot of the hill Herod built a huge lower palace covering 45 acres (18.4 hectares) which included the residence, a huge causeway, a monumental building, and a magnificent garden containing a huge colonnaded pool with a circular island in the middle. The colonnade has been partially restored on the western and southern sides of the pool. According to Josephus, when Herod died, he was buried at Herodium with lavish ceremony. Archaeological excavation has not yet discovered his burial place, but it is thought to lie somewhere in the vicinity of an elaborate building south of this pool. Excavations have revealed part of the palatial administrative complex north of the

palace on the north side of the modern road. It was used by Herod's staff and contained baths for use by the servants.

Jericho: another desert palace of Herod

Although Herod was buried in Herodium, he died in Jericho where he had built another of his desert palaces. Excavations in Herodian Jericho, several miles to the south of Old Testament Jericho and southeast of the modern city, have revealed three areas of construction in which Herod the Great had a part.

Herod rebuilt the older Hasmonean palace in the northwest sector of the Herodian site on a smaller scale, probably as a villa. Beside it, on the east, is a large swimming pool, more than 100 feet (30 meters) long, sixty feet (18 meters) wide, and twelve feet (3.6 meters) deep. It was divided in the center by an 18-foot- (5.4-meter-) wide partition of earth which was only 6 feet (1.8 meters) high. Herod had Aristobulus III, his seventeen-year-old brother-in-law and rival, drowned one night in this pool (Josephus, *War* 1.437). In this general area the Hasmoneans had several residential quar-

Masada.

ters for themselves and guests. In these houses six ritual baths have been found, the earliest yet discovered in the Holy Land, along with other pools and even stone bath tubs.

A second area of construction by Herod is located on the south bank of the little valley called the Wadi Kelt. A huge sunken garden, 360 feet (110 meters) long, and a large swimming pool, 130 feet (40 meters) by 300 feet (91.5 meters), were discovered here. South of the southeastern corner of the sunken garden Herod built a mound on which he put a 50-foot by 66-foot square (15 meters by 20 meters) building, containing a round hall measuring 52 feet (16 meters) in diameter and built of Roman concrete. The building may have been another villa, a pavilion, a reception hall, or even an elaborate, elevated Roman bath.

The third and latest area of Herod's building program in Jericho lay on the northern bank of the Wadi Kelt. Here Herod built an impressive palace with a large reception hall or triclinium, 95 by 62 feet (29 meters by 19 meters), adorned with mosaic floors.

Adjacent to the reception hall, on its east side, Herod built one of his two open courtyards. Ionic in style, it was 62 feet (19 meters) by 61 feet (18.5 meters) in diameter with a northern semicircular apse almost 30 feet (9 meters) in diameter. Adjoining the courtyard on the east was a large full Roman bath consisting of five rooms with a well-preserved circular room similar to the central pavilion in another of his palaces built on the northern slopes of Masada.

Masada by the Dead Sea
Masada is a 1,300-foot- (396.5-meter-) high rock butte located on the west side of the Dead Sea about 30 miles south of the northern shore. Its history was written by Josephus, the first-century Jewish historian, who vividly described the deaths here of 960 patriotic Jewish men, women, and children, who, during the first Jewish revolt against

Opposite: Aerial photograph of the fortress of Masada near the Dead Sea, showing clearly the northern palace and structure on top.

Northern Palace of Masada, third level down.

Rome, came under siege by the Roman general Flavius Silva in the spring of A.D. 73 and committed suicide rather than surrender. Josephus was the only source for the history of the site until Yigael Yadin, a preeminent archaeologist, military commander, and later deputy prime minister of Israel, excavated the site from 1963 to 1965. His book, *Masada*, confirmed in broad outlines the account of Josephus . . . that is until now.

Three articles in the journal *Biblical Archeology Review* (24:6, November/December 1998) by eminent Jewish archaeologists have challenged many of the details given in Josephus' account and seemingly corroborated by Yadin's work. The articles include the following questions: Did the Jews really commit mass suicide? Did the Masada commander really make the speech encouraging suicide? Did Yadin really find the lots used to select the ten men who killed the others? Were there really 960 rebels? What happened to the bodies of so many people? Did Yadin really find some of these bodies, as he claimed? These scholars have

not only challenged Yadin's conclusions, they have even accused him of dishonesty.

One of the more significant charges relates to the description Yadin gave in his report of "about twenty-five skeletons scattered in disorder about the floor" in a cave on the south end of Masada. On 7 July 1969, these bones, presumably of the Jewish defenders of Masada, were buried with full military honors in a funeral attended by Yadin, future prime minister Menachem Begin, and other dignitaries. Yoram Tsafrir, who directed the cave excavations for Yadin, said, however, that he saw only ten to fifteen skeletons, that only five appear in the excavation photo of the cave, and only one skeleton was intact and undisturbed. Dr. Nieu Haas of Hebrew University, to whom Yadin turned over the bones, cataloged only 206 bones and observed that since an adult skeleton has 220 bones, if Yadin actually found 25 skeletons, 5,300 bones (96 per cent) are missing!

Furthermore, Joseph Zias, in an article entitled "Whose Bones?" states that the bones of pigs were found with the skeletons

Masada.

and that Yadin admitted this both to him in the early 1980s and in 1982 to a *Jerusalem Post* reporter. Pigs were used by Romans as sacrificial offerings for the dead, and according to the first century B.C. Roman philosopher Cicero, "Only when a pig had been sacrificed was a grave legally a grave." Since the bones of non-kosher animals would not be found in a Jewish burial, further research was done in caves in Judea, which led to the conclusion that this cave in Masada was a small cemetery for Roman soldiers and perhaps their women (a well-preserved three-month-old fetus was found among the bones). It was later disturbed by hyenas, which carried off most of the bones to their dens. Tooth marks and mutilations have been found on many of the bones.

A related question concerns the failure of Yadin to find the bones of the 960 defenders of Masada. Zias suggests the possibility that they were buried near the Western Palace. It is possible, however, that the thousands of Jews who were forced by the Romans to build the siege ramp for them were also made either to bury their own dead somewhere on the top of Masada or in the valley beneath. That many bones could not easily disappear.

Zias writes:

All in all we must conclude that the picture Yadin draws of the skeletal remains at Masada is highly exaggerated in an apparent attempt to dramatize his finds by having them corroborate Josephus' description of the Jewish rebels' last stand.

Another scholar feels that the failure to find the bones is irrelevant, asking, "Were the bodies from Jerusalem ever found?"

Others argue that a passage in Josephus' *The Jewish Wars* (7.8.3) was altered relatively soon after it was written, either accidentally or intentionally, by people who wanted to obscure the location of this mass suicide and burial. The original Greek text, as well as early translations into Latin and Syriac, also omit a crucial part of this verse—the part that makes it appear that the burials took place at the Northern Palace rather

Ottoman gateway, Damascus

than at the Western Palace where the Roman ramp was built. As it now reads, part of the verse makes no sense, contradicting the geographical description given in the rest of the verse, which requires a burial near or under the Western Palace.

Meshel's article argues that Masada was not just a place of refuge for Jewish rebels hiding in the desert but represented a familiar scenario of the time, a kind of Jewish mini-state, functioning during the two revolts against Rome. David had similarly fled to the desert about 1000 B.C. to escape the wrath of King Saul and may have lived here. One of his desert strongholds is called *mesadot* (1 Samuel 22:4; 23:14) which Meshel thinks may have been Masada. The Hasmoneans also fled to the Judean deserts when overthrown by Herod the Great in 37 B.C., and the rebels during the Bar-Kokhba revolt (A.D. 132–135) did the same, being defeated finally at Bethar, west of Bethlehem. Perhaps the events that hap-

pened at Masada during the years of the first revolt and destruction of Jerusalem were part of what Jesus prophesied when he said:

> So when you see the abomination that causes desolation spoken about through the prophet Daniel standing in the Holy Place (let the reader understand the allusion), that will be the time for those in Y'hudah [Judea] to escape to the hills (Matthew 24:15-16).

At the present time many archaeological sites are being reexamined and the original excavators' views challenged. Included in the general furor are Qumran, Jericho, Megiddo, Hazor, and Jerusalem. Masada is one more name on a long list. This may be an inevitable consequence of the ongoing quest of archaeologists' spades, but the symbolism of Masada makes these latest conclusions especially disappointing. Perhaps it needs to be reemphasized that archaeology is not an exact science, and much of what is set forth in a final archaeological report of n excavation should be reported not as irrefutable fact, but as educated, conscientiously researched, and carefully documented conclusions that in the last analysis are, nevertheless, still opinions. Opinions change; facts and truth do not.

SYRIA: DAMASCUS AND THE CONVERSION OF PAUL

Paul was converted to Christ on the road to Damascus in Syria. In New Testament times the city was located in the southeastern section of modern Damascus, and its ancient streets are still discernable in the modern street plan. The street called "Straight Street" where Paul went immediately after his conversion (Acts 9:11) probably lies beneath the modern street. It was a fifty-feet-wide (15-meter) colonnaded street and was the *cardo maximus*, that is, the main street of the city. Some of its columns have been excavated while others stand amid the modern day shops. Remains of a theater, a monumental Roman arch, and perhaps a palace have been found along this street.

Part of the city's Roman wall has been found about a 1,000 feet (305 meters) south of the East Gate, beneath a small chapel built by Greek Catholics under the present Ottoman gateway (opposite). A gate from the Roman period once stood beneath the chapel built into the wall that tradition associates with Paul's escape, when he was "let down in a basket through a window in the wall" (2 Corinthians 11:32-33; Acts 9:25).

7

ANATOLIA AND THE BIBLE

ANATOLIA AND THE BIBLE

Most of the land area that today comprises the modern country of Turkey was earlier called Anatolia and, before that, Asia Minor. It stretches approximately 1,000 air miles west-east with Troy on its western limits and "Mount Ararat" on its eastern edge (there is no biblical basis for accepting the peak popularly labeled Mount Ararat as authentic, see page 44). Within Old Testament times Anatolia was the homeland of the Hittites. For the New Testament it was the region through which some of Paul's missionary journeys led. It was also the location of the seven churches of the Revelation.

PRE-HITTITE ANATOLIA

Less archaeological attention has been paid to Anatolia than to some other parts of the Near East. What excavation has been done shows that the area was initially comparable to, or even more advanced than, much of the Near East. The Neolithic site of Çatal Hüyük in south central Anatolia, for example, boasted well-planned architecture, elaborate wall paintings, dozens of decorated shrines, and both male and female statues. Even in size, it was at least three times larger than Neolithic Jericho in Palestine, and ten times the size of Jarmo in Mesopotamia.

There is clear evidence of early contact with the outside world. By the sixth millennium, in the east, pottery dating to the Halaf

Left: The walls of Troy VI. Although Troy is a place of enduring interest in both literature and archaeology, it has no biblical significance. Its major distinction is as the site of the events surrounding the mythical battle between the Greeks and Trojans in the epics usually attributed to the blind Greek poet Homer. Archaeologically, it is important, because although it is a small site, about 656 feet (200 meters) from one end to the other, its forty-six separate occupation levels and nine settlements (designated Troy I to Troy IX) illuminate the gradual development of northwestern Anatolian civilization from 3000 B.C. to A.D. 400. The area around Troy, known as the Troad, is an area of rich farmland and forest strategically located at an intersection of routes that linked Europe and Asia throughout history. It is near the shortest crossing of the Hellespont or Dardanelles. It is important to biblical study because of its nearness (13 miles [21 kilometers]) to Alexandrian Troas, the embarkation point of the apostle Paul from Asia Minor to Greece.

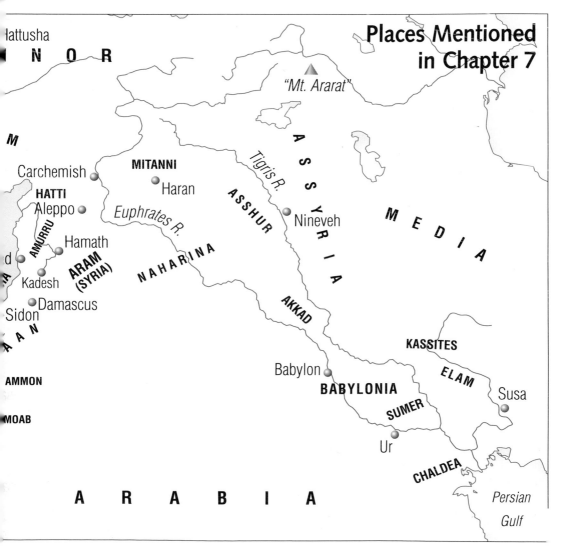

Places Mentioned in Chapter 7

Hattusha

N   O   R

"Mt. Ararat"

M

Carchemish

MITANNI

Haran

HATTI

Aleppo

Euphrates R.

Tigris R.

ASSHUR

A S S Y R I A

Nineveh

M E D I A

AMURRU

Hamath

ARAM (SYRIA)

NAHARINA

d

Kadesh

Damascus

Sidon

A A N

AKKAD

KASSITES

AMMON

Babylon

BABYLONIA

ELAM

Susa

MOAB

SUMER

Ur

CHALDEA

Persian Gulf

A   R   A   B   I   A

and Ubaid periods of Mesopotamia began to appear. In the west, the lower levels of Troy (third millennium) contained megarons (buildings featuring a rectangular hall and an open porch on one end) that later became characteristic of temples in the Greek world.

THE HITTITES

The origin of the Hittites is not yet fully understood. A people speaking an Indo-European language, they apparently entered Anatolia from Europe in the beginning of the second millennium, but some would say earlier. In time they imposed their rule over the indigenous population. The following summary provides examples of how, as today, the history of one country is intertwined with that of its neighbors.

The Hittite "Old Kingdom" dates from about 1650 to 1400 B.C. Of the several kings known from this period, Hattushili I is credited with founding the capital at Hattusha. He advanced into Syria where he defeated Aleppo, the first time the Hittites claimed territory outside Anatolia (Hatti) proper. The next king (Murshili I) went even farther afield, sending an expeditionary force down the Euphrates where it sacked Babylon, ending the First Dynasty of Babylon founded by Hammurapi. A period of internal trouble soon followed and, as Syria was lost to the rising power of Mitanni, parts of Anatolia fell from Hittite control. When Telepinu took the throne, he did not reclaim the territories but, importantly, he issued an edict on succession, and rules of conduct for kings and nobles, reforms which seem to have been observed until the last days of the Empire period. Toward the end of the Hittite Old Kingdom Thutmose III (see pages 79–82) of Egypt marched into Syria and pushed Mitanni back east of the Euphrates.

The Hittite Empire, or New Kingdom period, is dated from about 1400–1180 B.C. Its opening years saw a swirl of marching armies and short-lived alliances as the Hittites, Mitanni, and Egypt vied for

The rock-sanctuary of Yazilikiya is located a mile or so from Hattusha. A temple fronted a limestone outcropping on which the rock faces of two open-air "galleries" were covered with several dozen gods and goddesses carved in bas-relief. This relief, from the smaller gallery, is 5.4 feet (1.67 meters) high. "Hittite hieroglyphs" identify the two figures as the god Sharruma and King Tudhaliya IV. Sharruma, son of the storm god, wears a short tunic and tall horned crown. He embraces the king, who carries a curved staff and is dressed in a robe and cap used for religious ceremonies.

control of Syria. When Shuppiluliuma I led a successful surprise attack, the Mitannians were crushed and Hittite control of Syria stretched from the Mediterranean to the Euphrates River. Sons of Shuppiluliuma were installed as governors in key Syrian cities. When Shuppiluliuma advanced toward Damas-cus, he intruded into territory claimed by Egypt but at that time Egypt was too internally preoccupied to respond (see pages 82–83). One fascinating episode during Egypt's internal turmoil came when a queen (probably the widow of Tutankhamon) asked Shuppiluliuma to send a son for her to marry!

Hattusha. Exterior view of the arched Lion Gate and adjoining Upper City wall. This gate is one of five constructed when the Upper City was added to Hattusha during the latter part of the New Kingdom period. The gateway, 10 feet (3 meters) wide at ground level, is named after the high-relief sculpture on its door jambs. Another sculptured gate is called the King's Gate (where a god is depicted as a warrior and protector of the city). A third decorated gate is known as the Sphinx Gate.

A son was sent, but he was murdered by a faction in Egypt opposed to such a union.

Empire continued past the reign of Shuppiluliuma, but difficulties arose and intensified when Egypt entered her nineteenth dynasty and again began pressing for control of Syria. The armies of Muwatalli of Hatti and Ramses II of Egypt fought one of the more famous battles of antiquity at Kadesh. Ramses II rode into a trap and was fortunate to escape with his life, but the subsequent Egyptian account of the battle boasts of victory.

Some years later Ramses II signed a parity treaty (a treaty in which each party sees the other as an equal) with Hattushili III, then the Hittite king; both countries seemed worried over an emerging Assyria. Hattushili III also signed a treaty with the Kassites in southern Mesopotamia, undoubtedly in the hope that this alliance would further keep the Assyrians in check. Some two dozen treaties between the Hittite king, the "Great King," and subject kings were also found in the archives at Hattusha.

As the twelfth century began, Anatolia was caught up in the upheavals that rocked the eastern Mediterranean. Hattusha was burned to the ground. For the next five centuries, an afterglow, termed either Neo-Hittite or Syro-Hittite, existed in the southeastern portion of the old empire as people who had been acculturated tried to maintain aspects of the Hittite way of life. In the ninth century Assyrian forces began marching west into Syria, or "Greater Hatti," as they called it. Greater Hatti was finally snuffed out by Tiglath-pileser III during his campaigns of 734 to 732 B.C. into Syria and Israel (see page 52).

213

Hattusha

The modern Turkish town of Boghazkale (formerly called Boghazköy) sits beside the ruins of Hattusha, and its name is sometimes used in reference to the Hittite capital. During the Empire period Hattusha is said to have been the largest and most strongly fortified city in the Near East. As much a fortress as a city, it spread out on both sides of a rocky gorge, and a double wall encircled the 300 plus acres (123 hectares) of the upper and lower city. Brick battlements sat atop megalithic-sized stones, and gateways protected by two sets of doors and flanked by massive towers allowed access to the city. Several tunnels cut through the defensive ramparts served as sally ports in the event of attack. There were several temples within the city; the largest, 138 feet by 210 feet (42 meters by 64 meters), was surrounded by rows of storerooms. The royal palace perched on a rocky citadel.

When excavation of the site began early in the twentieth century, clay tablets were immediately found, and over 10,000 tablets and fragments have been recovered thus far. These tablets, in a cuneiform script that had been adapted to write Hittite (and several other languages), provide rich insights into the whole fabric of Hittite life. References to foreign kings, places, and events help to place the Hittites firmly within the history of the ancient Near East.

The Hittites and the Old Testament

Hittites are mentioned nearly four dozen times in the Old Testament, but as recently as the mid-nineteenth century some scholars insisted they must be an imaginary people since there was no record of them except in the Bible. Clues to their existence began to be recognized, however, and before the end of that century no doubt remained that the Hittites had indeed existed. Today the history of these "imaginary" people can be expanded far beyond the sketch above.

Hundreds of books and articles now deal with Hittite history, religion, art, literature, law, and more.

The recovery of the Hittites was seen as one of the early archaeological "triumphs" over those who would question the reliability of the Bible. At the same time, the recovery provides another example of how archaeology can sometimes present problems not previously envisioned. Hittites are mentioned several times within the Patriarchal period, the most well-known instance being in Genesis 23 where Abraham purchased a cave from

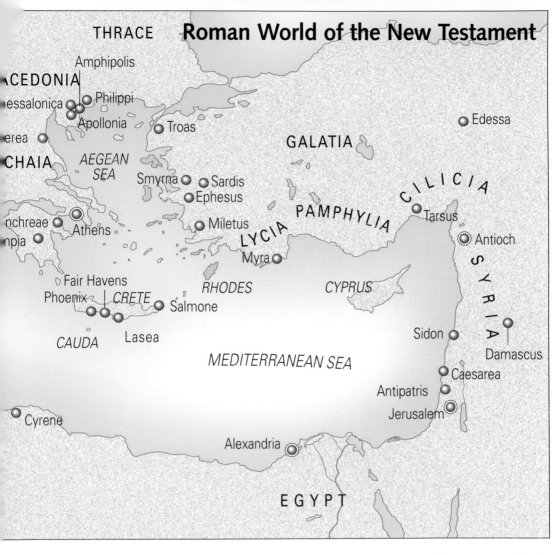

Ephron the Hittite. But evidence that any group that could be identified with the Hittites existed in Palestine prior to 1200 B.C. is tenuous at best. How, then, could Abraham and other patriarchs living in the first half of the second millennium have interacted with Hittites living in southern Palestine?

Various options have been proposed to account for this apparent discrepancy but the simplest solution is that put forth by a leading Hittitologist, Harry A. Hoffner Jr.: Hittite and Hethite are written identically in consonantal Hebrew and the pre-monarchal

references are to Hethites, one of the Semitic speaking sub-groups mentioned as populating Palestine in the second millennium B.C. This reading can be found in scholarly literature and the margin notes of some current Bible translations. On the other hand, when Hittites are mentioned in monarchal times, that reading can stand. They, like Uriah the Hittite who was married to Bathsheba (2 Samuel 11), were Neo-Hittites, people from Greater Hatti who clung to aspects of Hittite culture long after the collapse of the Hittite empire in 1180 B.C.

Patmos.

TOWARD THE
NEW TESTAMENT

The Phrygians, who, according to tradition, migrated to Asia Minor from Thrace in the early twelfth century B.C., replaced the Hittites as the controlling power in central Asia Minor. Gordion became the capital city of Phrygia. In Homer's *Iliad* (2.862) the Phrygians are closely associated with the Trojans. Phrygian control was broken by the Cimmerian invasion from the steppes of Russia, and Midas, the last Phrygian king, committed suicide during this invasion (693 B.C.). After this invasion Lydia emerged as the dominant Anatolian power with its capital at Sardis. Cyrus, the king of Persia, overthrew the Lydian Croesus in 546 B.C., but Persia was not to remain supreme, and Alexander the Great eventually led the Macedonians in the conquest of Asia Minor in 334 B.C., securing his control of Asia by "cutting the Gordian knot."

After the death of Alexander, who had not appointed a successor, his seven generals competed among themselves for control of the Mediterranean world. Four survived the struggle for power and created their own empires in the huge area ruled by Alexander. Seleucus I Nicator, one of these Greek-speaking generals, took control of much of Alexander's empire and established the Seleucid dynasty, which ruled Syria and adjacent areas. As many as ten cities in his new empire were named Seleucia, including the one in Syria, which is mentioned in Acts 13:4, and others in the Anatolian districts of Phyrgia, Pisidia, Pamphylia, and Caria. Although Seleucus probably considered Seleucia in Syria as his primary city, choosing it as his burial place, Antioch-on-the-Orontes eventually became the capital of the Seleucid empire after his death, largely because the intersection of the major land routes that connected the Euphrates, Asia Minor, and central and southern Syria ran through it. These routes, combined with the accessibility of the Levant (Palestine/Israel/Syria) to Rome via the Mediterranean Sea, facilitated the conquest of the area by the Roman empire in the New Testament period.

ANATOLIA AND THE NEW TESTAMENT

Patmos

Archaeological remains in Asia Minor relating to the New Testament center primarily around the lives of the apostles John and Paul. John received his revelation on the island of Patmos, which is 8 miles long and 5 miles wide and lies 65 miles west of Ephesus. Skala, the small modern port of Patmos, is one of the finest anchorages in the Aegean Sea. The modern town of Patmos clusters around an eleventh-century monastery located on Ayios Elias, an 800-foot (244-meter) summit that dominates the southern half of the island. Tradition has it that John received his revelation here, in a cave behind the monastery.

The nature of John's exile on Patmos is not revealed. Whether he was under imperial or proconsular ban is not recorded. Early church history attributes his presence here to a persecution of the church that resulted in John's condemnation to exile on the island. The text of Revelation merely states that he was "on the island called Patmos, because of the word of God" (1:9). This does not necessarily imply a penal sentence; the earliest evidence for that interpretation is Clement of Alexandria in the late second century. Nevertheless, some form of judicial exile remains the best hypothesis for the separation of John from the churches in Asia and his presence on the island.

Some have thought that he might have been exiled here to work in mines, but no archaeological evidence of ancient mining has been found. Iron-bearing rocks have been discovered, however, and there is a record of mining in modern times, so the supposition is not improbable.

Patmos.

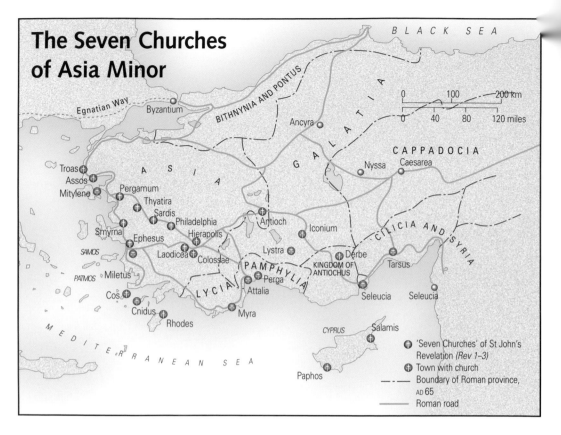

The Seven Churches
of Asia Minor

THE SEVEN CHURCHES OF ASIA

The seven churches to which the book of Revelation is addressed were all located in the Roman province of Asia, in western Asia Minor, which is modern-day Turkey. The main routes of communication in this area have remained the same through the centuries, being dictated by natural topography. The main road ran clockwise up the coast from Ephesus to Smyrna and Pergamum, and from there through the valleys to Thyatira, Sardis, Philadelphia, and Laodicea, thus connecting the cities with one another on what functioned as an ancient postal route. It is no accident that the letters in Revelation 1 to 3 are arranged in this same sequence. Beginning with Ephesus, they form a geographical semicircle, extending northward, turning to the east, and continuing southward to Laodicea.

Undoubtedly Ephesus, the largest and most important city of the province, situated on a commercial harbor and functioning as a distribution point for a wide area, circulated goods and correspondence to the other cities. Ephesus was the mother church, from which Paul evangelized the entire province of Asia over a two-year period. These other cities in the group must have, in turn, been postal centers for further dissemination of information to still other cities farther inland. Paul asked the church in Colosse to be certain that the Laodicean church read its letter and vice versa (Colossians 4:15). The book of Revelation was clearly meant to be circulated to at least the seven churches to which it was addressed, and if the number seven is apocalyptically symbolic, it may have been intended for the entire province.

Ephesus

Ephesus, a city of about 200,000 people, was called "a most illustrious city" in an inscription found there, and the first-century geographer Strabo called it the greatest emporium in the province of Asia. The city contained a fine harbor, which eventually silted up because engineers narrowed the entrance in a counter-productive effort to prevent that very problem. Much of it remains in that condition today, but underwater investigations are under way in the twenty-three-foot (7-meter-) deep lagoon to establish the harbor's original shape. Its commerce, trade guilds, and banking capacities made it a city of preeminent importance.

Ephesus was uniquely laid out to relate to the two hills, Mount Koressos and Mount Pion, around which it was built. The main thoroughfare of Ephesus was composed of several sections. The section called Curetes Street began at the Magnesian Gate in the east and proceeded westward to the lower marketplace, where it turned northward, becoming "The Marble Road." This portion of the street then ran along the full length of the eastern side of the marketplace to the theater. At the theater it became Stadion Street and continued northward. A 36-foot- (11-meter-) wide colonnaded street was built from the theater to the harbor, almost 2,000 feet (610 meters) to the west. It was named the Arcadian Way for the emperor Arcadius, who commissioned it at the end of the fourth century. This may, however, actually be an embellishment of an already-existing street that stood here in the time of John, because, first, a Hellenistic gate has been found on the axis of this street at the harbor end, and, secondly, a street from the harbor to the theater must certainly have been one of the first building projects of the city.

It is not difficult to imagine the impressions one must have received while walking through this city and observing its religious institutions. Foremost would have been the overwhelming beauty of the temple of the Ephesian Artemis, one of the "Seven Wonders of the Ancient World." Today there is virtually nothing left of the famed structure except portions of the foundations constructed by Croesus, recently discovered sections of the north and south faces of Croesus' building, and part of the great altar on the west side of the temple.

Ephesus: the Marble Road with the restored facade of the Library of Celsus, left background.

Mazaeus-Mithridates Gates, near possible site of lecture hall of Tyrranus.

The marketplace

When John was in the city, it had two centers of activity—a civic forum on the hill to the east and a commercial marketplace near the harbor. The commercial agora or market was 360 feet (110 meters) square, surrounded by shops and double-aisled stoas or porches. It was renovated by both Augustus and Nero, and some of the shops still remain intact on its south side. On the east side is an elevated doubled-aisled stoa or porch with Doric colonnades of the time of Nero, 5.5 feet (1.6 meters) high, with steps on the northern and southern ends. Walking along this stoa provided an excellent view of both the road on the east and the lower market on the west.

Considerable archaeological work is being done in this lower commercial marketplace, including the restoration of an eastern gate and, along the south perimeter, the uncovering and reconstruction of shops that were used by local merchants. Paul, and Priscilla, and Aquila (Acts 18:2-3), who were leather-workers who made tents and other products of leather, probably worked in these kinds of shops in the market areas of cities they visited. The apostle John may also have worked here. The southeast gate of the market, called the Mazaeus and Mithridates Gate,

is identified as having been built by these two men in 4 or 3 B.C., by inscriptions in both Greek and Latin above the arches.

Lecture hall of Tyrannus

Adjacent to the Mazaeus and Mithridates Gates, on the east, an auditorium or lecture hall has been identified that is mentioned in a first-century A.D. inscription found nearby. It is of interest because Luke states that Paul reasoned daily in Ephesus in the lecture hall of Tyrannus (Acts 19:9), and this structure may have been that lecture hall. Little, if any, of the actual structure has yet been found. However, portions of a Hellenistic

circular platform, which was destroyed when the auditorium was constructed, have been found.

The agora

There was also a state agora in the upper eastern part of Ephesus, measuring 525 feet (160 meters) in length. It lay at the southern foot of Mount Pion. It was bordered on the north by a 65-foot- (19-meter-) wide basilica, which was a building used for civic purposes. The structure stood several steps above the open square to the south and was bordered by colonnaded aisles. It contained rather unique Ionian bull's-head capitals on its colonnades. A bronze dedicatory inscription, in Greek and Latin, includes the names of Augustus and Tiberius, along with those of Artemis and the People, thus dating it to the Early Imperial period. Meetings of the law courts probably took place here, just across the street from the town hall in which state affairs were conducted.

The town hall

The religious and political center of the city was the town hall (*prytaneion*). Various banquets, ceremonies, and receptions were held there, in addition to meetings for the purpose of conducting political business. This building was the office of the "town clerk," the

"Lecture Hall of Tyrannus" in Ephesus.

Town hall—office of the town clerk of Ephesus.

head of the municipality of Ephesus. When Paul was in Ephesus, the town clerk went from the town hall to the theater adjacent to its north side to placate the mob gathered there in loud protest at the work of Paul (Acts 19:35-41). Several inscriptions found in the city refer to this office.

The theater in Ephesus
The theater is still standing across the street from the commercial marketplace. Originally built in Hellenistic times as a Greek theater, it was modified into a Roman theater and enlarged under both Claudius (A.D. 41–54) and Nero (A.D.

54–68) about the time Paul was in the city. The first two storeys of the Roman stage were built in Nero's reign. The cavea, or auditorium, would seat 24,000 on three levels of twenty-two rows each, reaching a height of almost 100 feet (30 meters). The stage wall was enlarged to three storeys in height by the time the apostle John was there.

The mob's protest against Paul was economically based, motivated by the loss of income experienced by the silversmiths, who, as a result of Paul's teaching against idolatry, were selling fewer silver images of Artemis (the Roman Diana). Two of her beautifully sculpted statues, which were excavated in the town hall, are housed in the museum in nearby Seljuk. These statues of Artemis reveal an emphasis on fertility, portraying on their chests either multiple breasts or eggs. The larger statue, twice life size, was sculpted in the reign of Domitian (81–96), during the time John was

The great theater in Ephesus, with a striking view to the site of the ancient harbor.

A residential area in Ephesus.

in Ephesus. A Greek and Latin inscription found in the theater tells how a Roman official provided a silver image of this goddess and other statues, which, as was customary, were displayed in the theater when civic meetings were held there.

The stadium

Remains of a stadium have been found north of the theater, identified by an inscription as having been rebuilt in the reign of Nero. A circular area at its eastern end was designated for gladiatorial fights and the baiting of animals. This is of interest in the study of the life of Paul because he stated in 1 Corinthians 15:32, which was written from this city, that "humanly speaking I fought with beasts at Ephesus." It is not likely that Paul literally fought animals in this arena, first, because Paul was a Roman citizen and could not be forced to engage in such activity, which was usually reserved for slaves and

captives. (He used the privileges provided by his citizenship under arrest in both Philippi, Acts 16:37, and Caesarea Maritima, Acts 25:11.) And, secondly, if he was illegally or mistakenly put in this stadium and "fought beasts" he surely would have mentioned his miraculous delivery from death in 2 Corinthians 11, and Luke would have referred to it in Acts. Perhaps Paul meant by his comment that the "beasts" with whom he struggled in Ephesus were of a "human nature."

It is noteworthy that among Paul's "friends" in Ephesus, there were political figures of wealth and power, called "asiarchs" by Luke. Strabo wrote in the first century that Ephesus was "as well peopled as any other city in Asia by people of means; and always some of its men hold the chief places in the province, being called *asiarchs*." Asiarch inscriptions have been found in more than forty cities throughout Asia. The recent monumental publication of the repertorium of

inscriptions from Ephesus containing 3,500 (both those known previously and new ones) has brought the number of asiarchs mentioned in Ephesus to 106, including both men and women.

The fact that Paul could be the friend of such Roman officials indicates that the Roman Empire at this time was not hostile to the Christian faith. It may also imply that the wealthy and educated people of Ephesus were not opposed to Paul. John may not have been exiled later by imperial decree of Rome but by some proconsul in Asia over a local issue.

Private houses

Some of the most recent discoveries in Ephesus are in the housing complex on the south side of Curetes Street, the main thoroughfare, where both upper and lower economic classes of society lived, the apartment housing for the lower classes being located adjacent to the large impressive

Interior of a wealthy person's house in Ephesus.

On Curetes Street, first floor shops opened on to a colonnaded paved street with apartments built above them. The sidewalk between the shops and stone pavement was beautifully inlaid in mosaic patterns. A staircase is still preserved with entrances to the apartments along the side. If the apostle John stayed in Ephesus itself, he probably lived in a unit of this kind, unless he was wealthy or had wealthy friends; or he may have lived out in the nearby countryside in a farmhouse. Early church records give us no knowledge of his residence.

The apartments were multi-storied units with a single apartment per floor. Normally they had no running water, so that access to public latrines across the street was necessary. These small apartments had few windows and very little light. For a church group meeting in such cramped conditions, in a room lit by oil lamps which emit fumes, a situation like the one described in Troas, just north of Ephesus (Acts 20), was almost inevitable. Eutyches, while listening to Paul speak, fell out the window and was picked up dead on the street below. It is

villas of the wealthy. Since the church could not legally own property in the first century, it had no church buildings. Christians met house to house and conducted their worship in small apartments and in the larger homes of well-to-do members, as indicated in the last chapter of Paul's letter to the church in Rome.

The interiors of some of these large villas testify to the considerable wealth of the city and provide space enough in their *atria* (courtyards) for Christians to assemble for worship and study in what may be called house churches. Paul's friends among the wealthy and influential asiarchs may have lived in such accommodation.

View of the odeion, Ephesus.

The apostle John at Ephesus

According to the fourth century author Eusebius, the apostle John was exiled to the island of Patmos from Ephesus during the reign of the emperor Domitian (81–96), returned to Ephesus under the Emperor Nerva (96–98), and died there under Trajan (98–117). The Church of St. John, on a hill northeast of the city, is not earlier than the fourth century, though there are second-century legends that place the burial of John under the apse of this building. Several temples dedicated to emperors during the period of John's residence in Ephesus have been found. A temple of Domitian stood adjacent to the state agora, on its west side. It contained a colossal cult statue of Domitian, which would have been 16 feet (4.8 meters) high sitting, and 23 feet (7 meters) high standing. Thus some of the buildings at Ephesus that date to this time would coincide with the presence of John. The Book of Revelation is set against the background of provincial Asia at this time.

Worship of the Roman emperor through an imperial cult had been authorized for the provinces of Asia and Bithynia in 29 B.C. under Augustus. Probably in the reign of Domitian, some time in the late first century, Pergamum, Smyrna, and Ephesus, three cities that were seats of emperor worship, became officially designated "temple-keepers." This title was used in the theater by the town clerk at Ephesus (Acts 19:35) when he said: "the city of Ephesus is the guardian [temple-warden] of the temple of

Large statue of Artemis in Seljuk Museum.

Temple-Warden inscription in Ephesus theater. Ephesus is mentioned as Temple-Warden three times in this inscription on a monumental stone in the upper section of the theater. The inscription is well preserved and can easily be read: "Ephesus, the first and greatest metropolis of Asia and three times Temple-Warden . . ."

significant that in this connection Luke records that: "There were many lights in the upper chamber where we were gathered." Perhaps the lack of ventilation was responsible for this young man's choice of a window for a seat. It is also possible that on this occasion this particular group may have been meeting in a rented hall, since Paul's presence may have necessitated a larger place.

the great Artemis". Some other cities, along with Pergamum, Smyrna, and Ephesus, built two such temples and were designated as "Twice Temple-Wardens."

A brothel, identified by inscriptions at the entrance, which was located at the main intersection of the city (Curetes Street and the Marble Road), was constructed at the time John was in Ephesus. A Christian lady named Scholastica renovated the structure around A.D. 400 and made it into a bathhouse. A large public latrine was discovered there. It contained non-partitioned seats and used large amounts of water brought in from a Roman aqueduct through underground clay pipes.

A number of other civic structures utilized the water supply of Ephesus. One of these was the huge harbor gymnasium and bath constructed on the east side of the harbor north of the Arcadian Way. The bath was built largely in the reign of Emperor Domitian and was completed a few years later under Emperor Hadrian.

Due to its recent impressive reconstruction south of the lower agora, the library of Celsus is one of the most prominent civic structures in Ephesus today (see page 219). Celsus was consul in A.D. 92, while John was there, and later he became proconsul of Asia. The library stood adjacent to the major southern gates entering the market area but was also sandwiched between the brothel on the east and the temple of Serapis on the west. Such a location would be unthinkable in modern society, but it should be remembered that sacred prostitution was a part of the religion of ancient Roman society, and social prostitution was an acceptable part of the pagan culture. It was an impressive building, located in full view of the street intersection as it led to the courtyard and into the Mazeus and Mithridates Gates. According to Greek and Latin inscriptions on the wings of the front steps, the library was constructed between A.D. 110 and 135 by the son of Celsus, in

Temple-Warden inscription (foreground) in Ephesus theater.

honor of his father. It was multi-storied and contained storage for manuscripts on different levels.

The book of Revelation and the Ephesian theater

One of the most fascinating studies now being made in connection with Ephesus and the book of Revelation involves the Ephesian theater, the largest in the ancient Greek world. Discussions revolve around the question of how Revelation is put together. Why did John choose to present his vision on Patmos to the Greek and Roman world of his day

the way he did? His book is not like the ordinary genre of apocalyptic literature in several ways. On the one hand, it does not utilize such essential apocalyptic themes as pseudonymous authorship, secrecy, and historical periodization, while on the other hand, it employs prophecy and a use of the Old Testament not found in other apocalyptic literature of the period. So it is rather unique in the ancient world.

It has been argued that, to present his Patmos vision, John adapted the genre of Greek tragedy, choosing this approach because this

Symbols indicating the nearby brothel at the main intersection of Ephesus (Curetes Street and Marble Road).

The theater in Aspendos. Roman theaters were built with no more than five openings onto the stage from the back wall, as can be seen in the one still well preserved in Aspendos on the southern coast of Turkey.

Theater stage at Ephesus.

medium was very familiar to the Christians in Ephesus, and the other seven churches in Asia, and because he was not able to express his extraordinary visual experience in ordinary prose. He needed a dramatic medium and the timeless poetic forms of Greek tragedy were well suited to capture his cosmic visions of another world. He wanted to stun his audience with the power of his images and visions, but because of Roman persecution, he had no hope of ever producing on stage the drama he had seen. So perhaps he adapted the format of Greek tragedy—making innovative adaptations in the process——and wrote Revelation as though the dramatic revelation he received were being acted out on the stage of this theater.

Although most of the stage is now missing from the Ephesian theater, enough of it has been preserved to allow archaeologists to determine that Ephesus had not only the largest theater in the ancient world, but was also the only one to have seven openings on to its stage. It is suggested that John's constant use of the number seven in Revelation was in order to accomodate this stage in presenting his vision. It is further suggested that the use in Revelation of poetical stanzas in frequent responses to a speaker may reflect the customary role of choruses, which were situated in the orchestra below the stage. Some studies have suggested that the Gospel of Mark may also have been written on this same pattern of Greek tragedy, though there is no evident connection to a particular theater.

227

Smyrna

Smyrna is the second city of the seven churches of Asia. Overlooking the beautiful Gulf of Izmir, it was situated about 35 miles north of Ephesus on the main road to Pergamum. The city was probably the birthplace of the Greek poet Homer. Unfortunately, almost nothing of the New Testament city is still standing. We are therefore dependant upon literary descriptions for our knowledge of its structures. Strabo, the first-century geographer, called it "the most beautiful of all" the cities along the coast, describing it as having streets paved with stone and as much as possible laid out in straight lines. Excavations have revealed a 33-foot- (10-meter-) wide well-paved street, running east-west, which may have been a part of the Sacred Way. For the benefit of pedestrians, it had a roof over the pavement along the side.

Smyrna contained a gymnasium near the harbor, a stadium on the west, a theater on the northwest slope of Mount Pagos, a commercial agora near the docks, a harbor that could be closed, a state agora on the hill above the city, and a library.

A provincial temple of Tiberius was erected here, the city having been selected from eleven competing cities for the honor of housing the Imperial Cult. Thus it was first given the title *neokoros*, "Temple-Warden," under the emperor Tiberius. In the second century, the city was referred to as the "second neocorate of the Augusti," establishing that it had received the honor again under the emperor Hadrian, just after the death of the apostle John.

Nothing remains of the theater or the stadium, and the commercial Forum has not been identified. The state Forum, however, the only part of the city that has been excavated, is well preserved. It contained a rectangular piazza, 425 feet by at least 250 feet (130 meters by 76 meters), bordered on two sides, and perhaps three, by two-storied triple porticoes (colonnaded porches). The north side was enclosed by a huge basilica, which also had two storeys. It had a rostrum

State Forum in Izmir (Smyrna).

(public speaker's platform) at its west end. Beneath it ran a magnificent vaulted basement, the arched ceilings of which supported the floor above. The area was also covered with inscriptions of various periods.

Pergamum

Pergamum, the next city mentioned in Revelation, was beautifully situated 16 miles from the Aegean Sea, where it was served by the port city of Elaea. The city sat on a precipitous mountain of rock, 1,165 feet (355 meters) above sea level, looking southward over the broad fertile valley of the Caicus River. The acropolis stronghold was thus impregnable except from the south, and it was on this southern slope that the city was eventually built in an upper and middle section. The population of the city in the Roman period is estimated at 100,000 to 200,000, similar to that of both Ephesus and Smyrna.

The city's structures that are visible today are largely from either the tremendous original building program of Eumenes II,

the ruler of Pergamum in the second century B.C., or the renovations by the emperors Trajan and Hadrian in the second century A.D.

The upper city contained facilities that would have been frequented by city officials, military personnel, educators, and worshipers. Here were located two palaces, residences of officers, and the barracks and arsenals of the military, the foundations of which can still be seen.

Here, too, were the doric temple of Athena with its large precinct, built by Eumenes II, and the Trajaneum, a Corinthian temple built by Hadrian in honor of the emperor Trajan very near the time of the death of the apostle John. The discovery of colossal heads of both emperors indicates that they were both worshiped here. A statue of Hadrian, found in the excavations of Pergamum, is in the museum at Bergama (modern Pergamum). Both of these temples are beautifully reconstructed in a model of the city that is displayed in the Pergamon Museum in Berlin.

Altar of Zeus in Pergamum.

The 10,000-seat theater in Pergamum.

Altar of Zeus

The most imposing structure on the mountain is the altar of Zeus, built by Eumenes II, though little remains today of its original magnificence. The altar dominated the southern end of the upper city where there was a magnificent view of the valley below. It was a large marble structure, almost square in shape, 112 feet by 118 feet (34 meters by 36 meters). A magnificent partial reconstruction of this altar is also exhibited in the museum in Berlin.

Most of the huge frieze is still preserved on the sides of this reconstructed altar. It is 365 feet long by 7.5 feet high (34 meters by 2.2 meters) and was constructed of 118 panels. It depicts a battle between gods and giants, probably symbolizing the victory of the people of Pergamum over the Galatians. Ekrem Akurgal, the eminent Turkish archaeologist, calls it "the most significant artistic achievement of the Hellenistic age."

The opinion of many scholars is that the altar was dedicated to Zeus and Athena Nike (goddess of victory) and may have been the object of the reference to Pergamum in Revelation 2:13 as the place "where Satan's throne is." The assumption is that this huge and impressive pagan altar may indeed have been that "throne of Satan."

However, the book of Revelation was evidently written in the context of emperor worship (the Imperial Cult), and it is more likely that Pergamum's temple of Augustus, the first provincial temple built to a Roman emperor in Asia Minor, was the "throne of Satan" in that verse. That temple of Augustus has not yet been identified in the excavations, but some coins minted in Pergamum portray the temple on one side and the head of Augustus on the other.

Library

In the second century B.C., Eumenes II built his world-renowned library against the eastern side of the north porch of the Athena temple precinct. Portions of the library are still standing, although the southern wall has disappeared. This library, and the one in Alexandria, Egypt, were the two greatest in

The Sacred Way leading to the Asklepeion, Pergamum.

the world at that time. Dio Cassius wrote in the late second century that the volumes of the Pergamum library were "of the greatest number and excellence," and Plutarch in the early second century referred to 200,000 volumes in its collection. The invention of parchment was attributed to the city of Pergamum. Parchment is specially treated animal skin on which ancient scrolls were written, and the Greek and Latin word, *pergamena*, translated into English as "parchment," derives from the city's name.

The theater

An impressive theater with 10,000 seats was built on the mountainside overlooking the Caicus Valley. It was erected in the third century B.C., was renovated in the Roman period, and was functioning when Revelation was written. An 800-foot- (244-meter-) long terrace resembling a street ran north in front of the theater and led to the adjacent temple of Dionysus. Religion was never out of sight for the ancients, it was an ever-present, all-pervasive influence on their thinking and conduct. In his sermon on Mars Hill in Athens, the apostle Paul stated that the Athenians were "in every way" very religious, an observation prompted by his "passing along and observing" their "objects of worship" and "altars" in the market place (Acts 17:22-23).

The Asklepeion

Most of the buildings now visible in the lower part of Pergamum were constructed in the second century A.D. very soon after John wrote about the city. They include an amphitheater, which would seat 50,000, and a theater slightly south of it, which would hold 30,000 spectators. Farther west, at the end of a 2,700-feet- (823-meter-) long Corinthian colonnaded street, lay the Asklepeion, which was 60 feet (18 meters) wide, including the colonnaded areas on each side. Dedicated to Asklepios Soter, the god of healing, the facility was a medical clinic of the ancient world, where medicine was practiced in the context of pagan idolatry and superstition.

The Asklepeion of Pergamum represented

The Asklepeion in Pergamum.

the cutting-edge of medical technology in the New Testament period, although it had been founded much earlier. Under Hadrian, shortly after the time of John, the building was developed and was so magnificent that it was included in some lists of the seven wonders of the ancient world.

The Asklepeion of Pergamum ranked equally with other well-known centers of Asklepios, such as the one on the island of Cos, off the southwestern coast of Asia Minor, and the ones in Greece at Epidauros and Corinth, all of which are partially preserved. Some of the votive offerings to this pagan god that were used in these medical facilities have been excavated and may be seen by special permission in a private room of the museum in Corinth. These include ceramic models of human body parts. A model corresponding to the afflicted part of the sick person's body was brought to the temple with an appropriate offering in the belief that Asklepeios would heal that organ or limb. There was no perceived incompatibility between science and religion in the ancient world, or, for that matter, between religion and any activity of everyday life. That is a comparatively modern phenomenon.

Thyatira

The next city on the postal route, and the next one in the order presented in Revelation, is Thyatira, just east of Pergamum. The modern Turkish village is alive with activity, limiting excavation possibilities to a few vacant sites, such as vacant lots or the yards of various homes.

Archaeologically, Thyatira has remained untouched except for a brief period of work from 1968 to 1971. It was a city with numerous trade-guilds, especially those of the textile industry. Evidently the guild of dyers was especially prosperous. Women of Thyatira today work in a number of these industries, as they did in New Testament times when Lydia, a seller of purple dye and a resident of this city, was converted by Paul in Philippi (Acts 16:14).

The best purple dye was obtained from the murex shellfish, which were available along much of the eastern Mediterranean seaboard. Phoenicians harvested the shells for the dye, which eventually also became an important part of the textile industry in Asia Minor. Since purple was the color of royalty, this dye was very expensive, and we may assume that Lydia, whose trading ventures had taken her as far as Philippi, was a wealthy woman.

Sardis

Sardis, the fifth of the seven cities addressed in the book of Revelation, had a population in the first century estimated at 120,000. The city was located in the Hermus Valley, the broadest and most fertile of all the river-basins of Asia Minor, and lay to the west of its acropolis, which stood on a projecting spur of Mount Tmolus. The Pactolus River, famed for its gold, flowed beside the temple of Artemis. According to early literary sources, a tragic earthquake hit the area in A.D. 17, and Sardis was one of the most severely hit cities. Although impressive

Byzantine-level remains of a gymnasium and adjoining synagogue have been partially reconstructed, the imperial Roman city of New Testament times is largely unexcavated.

Synagogue and gymnasium-bathhouse
The remains of the synagogue are post-fourth century. Beneath the synagogue, however, there are Hellenistic and Roman levels that date back to the time of the apostle John. The beautifully reconstructed Byzantine period gymnasium-bath in the northern part of the city was built upon remains of an earlier structure, the western section of which was probably built in the last half of the first century in the time of John, or shortly thereafter in the first half of the second century.

A colonnaded, approximately 50-foot- (15-meter-) wide main avenue (the Marble Road) was built from the Pactolus River eastward for 4,600 feet (1,402 meters), running adjacent to the south side of the gymnasium area. The avenue was probably begun under Tiberius and finished under Claudius, and so

Synagogue and gymnasium-bathhouse in Sardis.

The temple of Artemis, Sardis.

would have been there in the time of the apostle John.

The avenue was paved with marble blocks and had a raised pedestrian sidewalk along its southern side. The colonnade bordering the early Roman street was probably 16 feet (4.8 meters) wide. This street ran very near the ancient Persian Imperial Road from Susa in Persia to Sardis. A north-south street intersected the Marble Road at the southeast corner of the bath-gymnasium complex, providing the axis for the east-west division of the city. Sardis was not laid out on the typical grid system of ancient Roman roads.

The temple and houses

The temple of Artemis was one of the most impressive structures in ancient Sardis. It was probably begun in the third century B.C. and went through three building phases, the last covering the century and a half after the A.D. 17 earthquake. The 328-foot- (100-meter-) long temple was surrounded by Hellenistic columns of Ionic design, some of which survived the earthquake and were used in the post A.D. 17 Roman reconstruction following the earthquake and a later flood.

Substantial evidence for residential housing in Roman Sardis has been recently found on the south side of the Marble Road, immediately south of the bath-gymnasium. Excavation reports describe them as modestly constructed terrace houses with small courtyards; they resemble the *Hanghausern* (slope houses) in Ephesus, discussed above. The architecture represented in this temple and these houses is typical of the architecture John would have seen all over Asia in both civic and religious buildings.

Philadelphia

The New Testament city of Philadelphia, the sixth on the ancient postal route, lies beneath the modern city of Alasehir and has never been excavated. Alasehir has a small population because it is still subject to constant earthquakes as it has been since the first century. According to the first-century geographer Strabo, the entire Meander

Laodicea

Laodicea, the last of the seven cities on the semi-circular route, was situated almost 100 miles due east of Ephesus, at the eastern end of the Lycus Valley. It was destroyed by earthquakes in the reigns of Augustus Caesar (27 B.C.–A.D. 14), Tiberius Caesar (A.D. 14–37), and Nero (A.D. 54–68). The city had become prosperous enough to rebuild itself following the A.D. 60 quake, and the book of Revelation depicts the church in Laodicea as saying, "I am rich; I have acquired wealth and do not need a thing" (Revelation 3:17).

Laodicea had not been excavated until 2003 and its ancient remains have to be interpreted largely from coins and inscriptions. Only a few traces of the city wall and its gates are still visible, and a monumental street has been uncovered. Portions of a Greek and Roman theater are preserved, along with a small Roman *odeion* (recital hall), which lies still unexcavated beside the road. About 15 feet (4.5 meters) of a water tower still stand, along with several miles of an aqueduct.

Revelation's letter to the Laodiceans (3:16) comments on the conduct of the city saying,

Limestone pools near Laodicea.

Valley was prone to seismic activity. As recently as 1969 Alasehir was near the epicenter of an earthquake.

Ruins of Laodicea.

"Cleopatra's Gate" at Tarsus.

"Because you are lukewarm, and neither cold nor hot, I will vomit you out of my mouth" (NKJV). This figure of speech may have been prompted by the fact that Laodicea was located only six miles from Hierapolis, a famous resort city that stood on a limestone hill with putrid warm springs whose water was channeled into the city. The water there was excellent for swimming but unsatisfactory for drinking. The Laodiceans would have been familiar with the natural response of spewing the water of nearby Hierapolis out of one's mouth after tasting it.

Hierapolis contains a number of impressive ruins, although little of it can be dated to the New Testament period. It was destroyed by the earthquakes that hit Laodicea in the reigns of Tiberius in A.D. 17 and Nero in A.D. 60. Rebuilding started immediately and continued into the Flavian period, beginning in A.D. 69. The city was considerably enlarged under the emperor Domitian (A.D. 81–96) in the time when Revelation was written.

CITIES OF TURKEY IN THE ITINERARY OF THE APOSTLE PAUL

Tarsus

The city of Tarsus lay on the Cydnus River about 10 miles north of the southeastern coast of Turkey (ancient Asia Minor) in the Roman province of ancient Cilicia. It is clear from Acts 32:27-28, which states that Paul was "born a citizen" in Tarsus, that Paul's father was a Roman citizen. Paul spent his early years in this city and described himself as a "citizen of no ordinary city" (Acts 21:39).

Along with Alexandria and Athens, in the time of Paul Tarsus was one of the three most important educational centers of the Mediterranean world, providing Paul with an educational environment in which to experience the Hellenizing effects of the Diaspora. His later writings are saturated with Greco-Roman images, which play an important role in his communication and interaction with his Jewish-Gentile environment.

An important international highway, which connected the west coast of Asia Minor to Syria-Palestine and points east, ran through Tarsus, passing to the north of the city through the narrow Gates of Issus in the Taurus Mountains. Julius Caesar visited Tarsus in 47 B.C., as did Mark Antony and Cleopatra six years later.

Tarsus has had only a brief excavation, and nothing significant was found from the Roman period. Material from the excavation is housed at Adana, about 25 miles east of Tarsus. Occasional discoveries by local workmen are displayed in a small museum in Tarsus. St. Paul's Well, a spring in the center of the city, and a gate at the entrance to the city, known both as St. Paul's Gate and Cleopatra's Gate, have no historical or archaeological verification. Roman Tarsus still lies buried perhaps 20 feet (6 meters) beneath the surface of the modern city.

Antioch of Syria

Next to Jerusalem, the Greco-Roman city, Antioch of Syria, played a larger part in the history of the early church than any other single city. It was the focal point of Christianity as it spread beyond the borders of Palestine and into the Diaspora. The apostle Paul headquartered his work in this city, the population of which was probably about 300,000 in the first century A.D. It was here that the term "Christian" was first used for the disciples of Jesus (Acts 11:26).

Antioch lay between the Orontes River on the east and Mount Silpius on the west, an area of approximately 1 by 2 miles. It was surrounded by a wall rebuilt in New Testament times by the emperor Tiberius. Antioch was bustling with activity and excitement during a time of rebuilding when Paul first arrived there about A.D. 43, the year when the city established its Olympic Games. It was a huge cosmopolitan city, where barriers of religion, race, and nationality were easily crossed, a perfect base of operations for a new religion that had begun in the religion of ancient Israel and had been internationalized by Jesus of Nazareth.

Antioch had a large and wealthy Jewish population in the first century. Christian refugees from Jerusalem, Cyprus, and Cyrene came there and quickly interacted with the Jews as well as preaching to God-fearing Gentiles, whom Luke simply calls Greeks (Acts 11:19-21), stating that "a large number who believed turned to the Lord" (Acts 11:21).

There are few archaeological remains in the city from the time of Paul. From ancient literary sources we learn that many important buildings were constructed by the Romans for the citizens of Antioch. Beginning in 47 B.C., Julius Caesar built an aqueduct to provide water for residences on the side of Mount Silpius. Some evidence has been found both of these private residences and also of small bathhouses, the construction of which was facilitated by the building of the aqueduct. At the foot of the mountain Caesar constructed a theater in the monumental center of town and an amphitheater near the southern gate. Somewhere, undoubtedly near the town center, he built a basilica for use by the cult of Rome; it is perhaps the oldest in the East. It bore his name and housed a statue of himself. He rebuilt the Pantheon in Antioch, which was in a state of deterioration, and built (or reconstructed) a theater on the slope of Mount Silpius.

A colonnaded street cut Antioch in half, running north to south the full length of the city. Josephus wrote:

> And for the Antiochenes, who inhabit the greatest city in Syria, which has a street running through it lengthwise, he adorned this street with colonnades on either side and paved the open part of the road with polished stone.
>
> *Antiquities* 16.148

Antioch—distant view from above the city.

The emperor Tiberius appears to have built bathhouses in the city, erected *tetrapyla* (four-columned structures) at each main intersection of the city's streets, expanded the theater, and completed and improved the southern section of the city. In Antioch, however, it is not possible to differentiate the building program of Augustus from that of Tiberius. Augustus visited Antioch twice and commissioned his architect Marcus Agrippa to conduct an extensive building program in the city, funded by the considerable treasure Augustus had found in Egypt after the defeat of the Egyptian queen Cleopatra and Mark Antony, the Roman general, at Actium on the western coast of Greece in 31 B.C. Several temples were built by Augustus as well as some other projects that may have been started by him and later attributed to Tiberius.

Antioch was hit by earthquakes often. Two of these occurred in the period with which we are concerned. The first happened on 9 April A.D. 37, during the reign of Caligula (A.D. 37–41), who rebuilt the devastated city. The second earthquake occurred in the reign of Claudius (A.D. 41–54) and damaged other cities in Asia Minor, including Ephesus and Smyrna.

Cyprus

Paul and his traveling companions, Barnabas and John Mark, began their first missionary journey by leaving Antioch of Syria and sailing to the island of Cyprus, probably selecting Cyprus as the place for their first missionary journey because it was Barnabas' home. (See Acts 4:36 where he is called "a Levite, of Cyprian birth".) They went to Salamis, a city 5 miles from the modern city of Famagusta, and preached there in the "synagogues of the Jews" (Acts 13:5).

Above: Theater in Salamis, Cyprus, with gymnasium and *palestra* behind. Below: Paphos harbor.

Remains of a Roman theater dating to the end of the first century B.C. may still be seen in Salamis near the gymnasium, whose palestra (exercising area), restored by Augustus Caesar, has been excavated and is surrounded by marble columns with Corinthian capitals.

Paul and Barnabas left Salamis and went through the entire island to the west coast town of Paphos (Acts 13:6) which had an excellent harbor. Here Paul converted the Roman proconsul Sergius Paulus to Christ. The family of this Roman official had large estates in the area of Pisidian Antioch and Paul's decision to go there next may have been prompted by this official who wanted him to speak to his family (see page 243).

Above: Forum at Perga. Below: Horseshoe gate entering forum at Perga from south.

Perga, where Paul entered Asia Minor on his First Journey

Paul, Barnabas, and John Mark traveled from Paphos on the island of Cyprus to Perga, a port city up the Cestrus River from the southern coast of Asia Minor (Acts 13:13). In Paul's time, according to the first century geographer Strabo, Perga was about 7 miles from the coast: "Then one comes to the Cestrus River [modern Aksu]; and sailing 60 stadia up this river, one comes to Perga" (*Geography* 14.4.2). This clearly shows that sailing up the river was not unusual and implies a landing facility near the city. Whether they landed first at the harbor of Attalia or went directly to Perga, where John Mark left Paul and Barnabas and returned to Jerusalem, is unclear. There is no record of Paul preaching here at this time, but he did

Forum at Perga.

"speak the word in Perga" at the end of this first missionary journey, when he returned to the city on his way to the harbor at Attalia (Acts 14:25).

Perga today is a 151-acre (62-hectare) site with impressive archaeological remains from the time of Paul that are surpassed only by Ephesus and Athens. Recent work has identified a large Roman forum or market place. The city walls and towers, built in the third century B.C., were standing at the time of Paul's visit and are well preserved. In the south wall, there was a gate, shaped like a horseshoe, and this is the most impressive archaeological structure in Perga.

Paul would have entered the city from the south through its twin circular Hellenistic gates to a colonnaded street running north to a gymnasium with an exercise ground (*palestra*), which had been built and dedicated to the Roman emperor Claudius shortly before Paul arrived. A number of Roman baths existed in the city, and foundations of a temple, probably Hellenistic in date, have been discovered about half a mile south of the city, near the end of the main street. The deity to which it was built is not known. A Greco-Roman type of theater, which would have seated about 14,000 spectators, has been partially excavated, and a well-preserved stadium is still standing outside the wall of the city.

Attalia, the port city for Pamphylia

When Paul left Asia Minor at the end of his first journey, he sailed from Attalia (modern Antalya) (Acts 14:25), a major harbor on the southern coast, which provided excellent shelter from the prevailing westerly winds. Attalia was a part of the plain of Pamphylia, and from here Roman roads led northwestward to Asia and Galatia, westward along the coast of Lycia, eastward through Pamphylia to Tarsus and Antioch of Syria, as well as northeastward to Lycaonia. From such a major intersection Paul would have had no difficulty finding a coast-hopping vessel to Antioch of Syria.

The harbor at Antalya.

Today little remains from the first century except the large cylindrical mausoleum, which stands on a square base and overlooks the harbor. One of the best local museums in Turkey is located in Attalia, where much of the excavated statuary from Perga is housed. A well-preserved arched gate from the time of Hadrian (A.D. 117–138) leading from the harbor to the city may mark the site of the gate of Paul's time, but this is not certain.

Pisidian Antioch

In addition to Antioch of Syria, discussed above, Paul entered another city by that name on both his first and second missionary journeys in Asia Minor (Acts 13:14; 14:21). It was located in the southern section of Galatia called Pisidia, and is thus referred to as Antioch of Pisidia (Acts 13:14). Acts states that on this journey Paul taught in the cities of Antioch, Iconium, Lystra, and Derbe. No significant archaeological discoveries have been found in the last three cities, but recent excavations at the site of Antioch, on the outskirts of the modern town of Yalvac, have produced impressive remains.

Antioch had been founded by the third century B.C., and was designated as a Roman colony in 25 B.C. by the emperor Augustus. Significant construction took place between 15 B.C. and A.D. 30, not long before Paul arrived some time between A.D. 47 and 48.

This building activity included a temple to Augustus, parts of which have now been excavated. Portions have been found of a Latin inscription that was attached to the temple shortly before the death of Augustus. This tells of the construction done by the emperor and it was thus in existence when Paul and Barnabas were in the city. Known as the *"Res Gestae Divi Augusti,"* the inscription is of considerable importance for studying the history of that time. Some fragments are now located in the yard of the museum in Yalvac. A copy of the *Res Gestae* has also been found from a temple in Ancyra (Ankara), and one is known to have been in the temple of the Vestal Virgins in Rome, carved on bronze tablets outside Augustus' mausoleum. It was also reproduced on the stone walls of many temples throughout Asia Minor.

City walls and towers have been found extending almost 10,000 feet (3,050 meters) and encompassing an area of about 115 acres (47 hectares). Portions of the wall date

Excavations of Temple of Augustus at Antioch.

Photo used by permission of HolylandPhotos.org.

to the Roman period, while other sections were built in the earlier Hellenistic period and the later Byzantine period. Some city streets, a bathhouse, a nymphaeum, and a fourth century church dedicated to Paul have been discovered. Foundations of a triple arched monumental gate are still standing.

Excavators also discovered a theater that had been constructed as a Greek theater in the Hellenistic period and expanded by the Romans. Significant sections of the stone *cavea* (semi-circular seating area) are still preserved; it would have seated about 5,000 spectators on twenty-six rows of seats. It was standing when Paul and Barnabas were there.

One of the most interesting discoveries in Antioch may provide background to the visit of Paul to this city. A Latin inscription carved into a stone fragment that is now in the yard of the museum in Yalvac has the name Sergius Paulus on it. As we have seen, Acts records that before coming to Antioch, Paul converted this man, who was a proconsul on the island of Cyprus (Acts 13:7-12). This proconsul had the same name as Paul (Acts 13:9), interestingly, and the first time that Saul is given the name Paul in Acts is in the account of Sergius Paulus' conversion (Acts 13:9).

It has been erroneously argued that Paul took his new name as a result of his encounter with Sergius Paulus, and with his permission, as a sign of good will. Luke, however, does not state that Paul changed his name in Cyprus, but simply that Saul "was also called Paul." Since this is the first time that the name Paul appears, and since it continues to be used from this point forward, it is to be assumed that Paul himself used his Roman name in his work among Gentiles. The use of his Hebrew name would have been natural while working among Jews in Palestine, but less appropriate now that he was preaching predominately to non-Jews. Paul now assumed the position of leadership on the journey and from this point on

Sergius Paulus inscription from Yalvac museum.

Photo used by permission of HolylandPhotos.org.

Luke refers to "Paul and his company," not "Barnabas and his company" (Acts 13:13) and to "Paul and Barnabas" (Acts 13:43, 46, 50; 15:2, 22, 35) as often as to "Barnabas and Paul" (Acts 14:12, 14; 15:12, 25).

Miletus

On the return portion of his third missionary journey, Paul set out from Macedonia after Passover in a hurry to reach Jerusalem by Pentecost, which took place fifty days later (Acts 20:16). For undisclosed reasons it took five days to sail from Macedonia to Troas, and he had to spend seven days there in order to worship with the church on the Lord's Day (Acts 20:6-7). When Paul left Troas for Jerusalem, he bypassed Ephesus, realizing that if he stopped there he would be detained further by his many friends. He stopped instead at Miletus just to the south. From here he sent for the elders of the church in Ephesus, 28 miles away, to come meet with him in Miletus where he gave them a farewell address (Acts 20:17ff).

Today Miletus sits 6 miles inland, but in Paul's time it lay on the coast. It has suffered

the same problem of silting harbors and extension of shorelines through sedimentation experienced by Ephesus and all the cities along the coast.

Forum area in Miletus.

Miletus Theater.

A theater still standing in Miletus contains some of the best-preserved hallways among ancient theaters. Portions of several buildings in the large city still stand, including the base of an impressive monument that Paul would have seen as he sailed into the harbor. The outline of the harbor can still be seen, though it is now silted up several miles inland, and the lions that guarded it are still now partially visible in the sediment.

Among the most impressive remains of ancient Miletus is the marketplace, the foundations of which remain in the city. Its monumental gate was dismantled and transported in sections by the German excavators to the Pergamon Museum in Berlin where it was reassembled and can be viewed today. Paul would certainly have walked through this massive gate.

Miletus Gate in Pergamon Museum in Berlin.

8

GREECE
AND THE BIBLE

GREECE AND THE BIBLE

Since the time of Alexander the Great in the fourth century B.C., Greece has been a country of major historical and archaeological importance. In New Testament times it was divided into two sections: Achaia in the south and Macedonia in the north. Several of its cities were visited by the apostle Paul and his traveling companions as they spread the gospel to the non-Jewish world. Between Asia and Europe, about midway across the Aegean Sea, lay the island of Samothrace.

SAMOTHRACE

On his second missionary journey Paul was divinely led to Troas on the west coast of Turkey where he received a heavenly call to go to Macedonia and preach the gospel. Paul and his companions sailed toward Macedonia in the straightest possible route, which Luke calls a "direct voyage" (Acts 16:11), stopping only for the night at the island of Samothrace, and then continuing on to Neapolis, the harbor city of Philippi. Whether they went ashore that night is not stated, but Paul did not remain at Samothrace even one day to preach to the island's inhabitants. There was no Jewish synagogue on the island, and Paul was answering the heavenly call to go to Macedonia (Acts 16:9-11), which did not include stopping on the island to preach at the Sanctuary of the Great Gods. The nighttime activities of the cult at this internationally known sanctuary were open to anyone who wished to attend, unlike the Eleusinian Mysteries, which were only open to participants. On Samothrace Paul could have attended and observed. In the fourth century B.C. Philip and Olympias, the mother and father of Alexander the Great, met here while attending and perhaps during the actual celebration of one of these festivals.

The apostle probably arrived in Samothrace in the fall of A.D. 49 during the reign of the emperor Claudius (A.D. 41–54). An inscription on a well-preserved stele mentioning Claudius was found there in excavations in 1986.

Samothrace is a pleasant island with lots of farmland and scrubby hills but few trees; it consists of 69 square miles of lovely coastlines, but has no natural harbors. It is unlikely that the modern harbor on the western tip of the island at Kamariotissa was used by ships in Paul's time. Remains of an old harbor mole may still be seen on the north coast near the ruins of the ancient sanctuary, and Paul's boat probably dropped anchor in this vicinity.

The Sanctuary of the Great Gods, lying to the west of the ancient city, was entered through a propylon of Thracian marble opening to a beautiful terrace view northward to the sea and overlooking the rotunda of Queen Arsinoe. This rotunda, 65 feet (20 meters) across, is the largest circular building presently known in Greek architecture

Circular rotunda of Queen Arsinoe on Samothrace.

and was an imposing structure dedicated to the Great Gods of the Samothracian Mysteries. Its foundations are still impressive to behold. Several of the sanctuary's structures are partially preserved and may be seen by today's visitor. They were all standing and in full operation in Paul's time.

ACHAIA IN THE SOUTH

During the time of Paul's visit, the two major cities of Achaia were Athens and Corinth.

The harbor of Athens in Piraeus

Athens was accessible from the south by sea through the port of Piraeus, which continues to function as its harbor in modern times. Although it was destroyed in 86 B.C., it was

restored and functioning when Paul was in Athens.

Athens, the heart of Greek culture

Paul escaped to Athens from Berea, farther to the north, where the Jews were stirring up the crowds against them, waiting for Silas and Timothy to join him.

The acropolis

The acropolis was a huge rock hill on which stood the Parthenon, which was a temple of Athena, the Greek goddess of wisdom, and a major center of idol worship. A significant portion of the structure remains today, though much of it was destroyed during the Crimean War. Paul referred to this pagan idolatry when he spoke to the Stoics on Mars

Harbor of Piraeus.

Athens

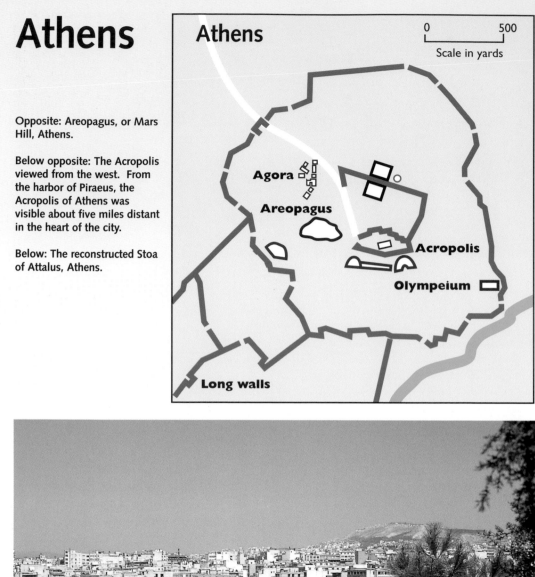

Athens

Agora

Areopagus

Acropolis

Olympeium

Long walls

0 — 500
Scale in yards

Opposite: Areopagus, or Mars Hill, Athens.

Below opposite: The Acropolis viewed from the west. From the harbor of Piraeus, the Acropolis of Athens was visible about five miles distant in the heart of the city.

Below: The reconstructed Stoa of Attalus, Athens.

Inset: Parthenon reproduction in Nashville, Tennessee.

The eastern commercial agora, Athens, with the Tower of the Winds in the distance.

Left: panoramic view of the Acropolis, Athens.

Below: Overall view of the westen agora or market place of Athens, from Mars Hill.

Below left: The Acropolis, with the Parthenon just appearing; on the right Mars Hill, or the Areopagus, from the western agora.

Inscription on temple of Roma and Augustus in Athens.

Hill adjacent to the Acropolis and said: "We ought not to think that the Deity is like gold, or silver, or stone, a representation by the art and imagination of man" (Acts 17:29).

Other temples stood on the summit of the Acropolis, including the Erechtheion and the temple of Athena Nike. Less well known, but more significant for Paul and his "new religion," was the Ionic circular columned temple of Roma and Augustus, only a few yards east of the Parthenon. This temple was built soon after the inauguration of the emperor Augustus in 27 B.C. in honor of him and the goddess Roma and represents the importance of emperor worship in the Mediterranean world, during the time of the New Testament. Remains of the temple include a circular stone inscription with the name of Augustus (Greek—Sebastos) on it.

The marketplace
Acts 17:17 states that Paul argued daily with the Jews and religious Greeks in the marketplace (called an agora by Greeks and a forum by Romans). These discussions took place not in the well-known agora of the Classical period but in the eastern portion of the large market area adjacent to the north side of the Acropolis. This Roman marketplace was endowed by Julius Caesar and completed by Augustus in the last decade of the first century B.C.

The Areopagus
In the midst of his discussions in the agora, Paul was arrested and taken before the Areopagus Council of Athens on Mars Hill

(Acts 17:19). Paul had been speaking about "foreign divinities" (Acts 17:18) and therefore fell under the jurisdiction of the Areopagus, which had surveillance over the introduction of foreign divinities into Athens. The council derived its name, Areopagus (which means Mars Hill in

Tower of the Winds in Roman forum, Athens. The best-preserved ancient monument in Greece is located in the agora. This combined water-clock, sundial, and weather-vane served as a public timepiece for the city. Paul would have checked the time of day from this clock.

Acrocorinth, the huge hill that overlooked Corinth, with ruins of the ancient city in the foreground.

Latin), from the hill on which it met, adjacent to the west side of the Acropolis. The hill is still a prominent landmark.

Paul began his speech to the Areopagites by referring to an altar he had seen containing an inscription that read "to an unknown god" (Acts 17:23). Altars with this inscription are mentioned by early authors. Apollonius of Tyana wrote in the first century that Athens was a place "where altars are set up in honor even of unknown gods." Pausanias, who visited Athens in the mid-second century, described his trip from the harbor to the city in these words: "The temple of Athene Skiras is also here, and one of Zeus further off, and *altars of the 'Unknown gods' . . .*" At Olympia, he described the altar of Olympian Zeus and wrote that "near it is an altar of the unknown gods . . ."

Corinth, where Roman culture prevailed

Corinth is a city of even greater importance than Athens for New Testament studies. It is located about 50 miles south of Athens on the Peloponnese, the large peninsula south of the mainland. While Athens had a population of about 25,000 in the New Testament period, Corinth's population has been estimated at approximately 150,000, plus slaves. It had walls extending 6 miles around the city.

The Temple of Aphrodite

Paul wrote to the church in Corinth that "because of the prevalent fornications in Corinth, each man should have his own wife and each wife her own husband" (1 Corinthians 7:2). A temple of Aphrodite, the Greek goddess of "love," was located on the Acrocorinth, a huge hill beside Corinth. According to Strabo, the first-century geographer, just prior to the time of Paul, this temple "owned a thousand temple-slaves, prostitutes, whom both men and women had dedicated to the goddess." Because of these, he maintained, "The city was crowded with people and grew rich." Excavations of the Acrocorinth have found evidence of the temple's foundations, and determined its size to have been no larger than 33 feet by 52 feet

The "Erastus inscription" in Corinth.

(10 meters by 16 meters). Although the thousand prostitutes Strabo mentioned could not have functioned in this small, isolated temple, which was difficult to access, they certainly could have in the populous city below. The accuracy of Paul's observation about Corinth's well-known reputation for immorality is supported by the ancient use of the term "Corinthianize" for being immoral (much as the term "Sodomize" is used today) and by the traditional association of Aphrodite with immorality.

Inscriptions

Corinth is also important for the large number of inscriptions that have been excavated there, 104 of which date from 44 B.C. to the early second century A.D. Of these, 101 are in Latin and 3 are in Greek.

The speaker's platform

One of the paving stones excavated beside the northeast corner of the city's 14,000-seat theater contained part of an abbreviated Latin inscription that reads, "Erastus in return for his aedileship laid [the pavement]

Bema in Corinth. The remaining portion of the stone structure is in the heart of the marketplace in the row of central shops.

at his own expense." He was the treasurer for the city. In Paul's letter to the Romans (16:23), which was written from Corinth, he said, "Erastus, the city treasurer greets you." The name is an uncommon one in Corinth and is not otherwise found in the literature and inscriptions of the city. This is undoubtedly the same Erastus who later remained in Corinth when Paul was taken to Rome (2 Timothy 4:20). He was also in Ephesus with Paul on his third journey (Acts 19:22).

Another important discovery that relates to the New Testament is the tribunal, the speaker's platform, from which official proclamations were read and where citizens might appear before appropriate civic officials. According to Acts 18:12-17, Paul stood here before Gallio.

The *bema* was identified by several pieces of an inscription found nearby and dated to the period between A.D. 25 and 50, just prior to Paul's arrival in the city. The beginning of Gallio's reign as proconsul is dated to A.D. 51 by fragments of a stone inscription found in the city of Delphi across the Corinthian Gulf. Since Paul stayed in Corinth eighteen

months (Acts 18:11), and arrived there at the time of the emperor Claudius' expulsion of Jews from Rome (Acts 18:2) in 49, this establishes the year 51 as the date of his leaving Corinth after appearing before Gallio in the summer of A.D. 51. (See also page 20 in chapter 1.)

MACEDONIA IN THE NORTH

Neapolis, the major harbor in Macedonia

Archaeological remains of the New Testament period have been found to the north of Achaia, in the region of Macedonia, at the harbor city of Neapolis where the apostle Paul first entered Europe from Asia (Acts 16:11). There is little in the city from this period except some remains of the ancient harbor and, in the yard of the museum, some milestones that stood beside the Egnatian Way, the international highway that passed through Neapolis. Paul undoubtedly traveled this road from Neapolis to Philippi (Acts 16:12).

Neapolis harbor.

Above: Krenides Stream, Philippi, possible site of
Lydia's conversion.
Below: Floor of octagonal church in Philippi.

Philippi, where Paul founded the first church in Europe

Acts 16:1-15 records Paul's conversion in
Philippi of a woman named Lydia, a god-
fearing Gentile who was worshiping "outside the gate beside the river."

The scene of Lydia's conversion
The exact location of Lydia's conversion is
not known but might have occurred in one
of three locations. One possibility is beside
the Gangites River. Another possible site is
by the Krenides Stream west of Philippi
and near the Krenides Gate in the city wall.
If so, this gate may be the one mentioned in
Acts 16:13. This stream, which still flows
with abundant, cold water, is about half a
mile from the forum and is referred to
locally as "the River of Lydia." A small excavation has revealed part of the pavement of
a road that ran westward toward the
stream and some inscribed Roman burial
monuments.

The Roman forum in Philippi, to which Paul and Silas were dragged before magistrates.

The third possibility for the location of Lydia's conversion is the Neapolis Gate, the eastern gate of the city, a portion of which has been excavated next to the theater on the south side of the modern road. A stream bed may still be seen immediately outside the gate. A fourth-century church was excavated beside this stream in 1956, and recently an octagonal church with mosaic floors was found on the south side of the road just inside the Neapolis Gate. The church, which was dedicated to Paul, was reached through a gate from the nearby Egnatian Way, on which Paul was traveling when he entered the city a few days before his encounter with Lydia. The location of these churches near the eastern gate may indicate an early recollection that Paul converted Lydia near here.

Arrest and imprisonment

Portions of this stone-paved road have been excavated in Philippi adjacent to the north side of the Roman forum, the marketplace in the heart of the city, to which Paul and Silas were dragged by the owners of the slave-girl. There they were set before magistrates, who ordered them to be beaten and then thrown into prison, for disturbing the city (Acts 16:19-24). Just as Paul was later accused before Gallio at the tribunal in Corinth (Acts 18:12), so he was in Philippi. Paving-stones from the time of Paul still stand in this forum and portions of a tribunal (called a bema in Greek) have been excavated in the north side of the forum. This would have been the place where Paul and Silas stood before the magistrates of the city.

A theater, built about the time the city was founded and remodeled into a Roman theater in the second century A.D., was standing when Paul was in the city. The current seats in the theater are not original but were restored in 1957 to 1959 for modern use.

Vitruvius, an early Roman architect and a contemporary of Jesus, wrote that prisons were normally built near the forum of an ancient city. It is, however, not clear from the archaeological remains whether the stone crypt that has been considered the prison of Paul since the fifth century could have been big enough to have constituted a larger complex with an inner prison as ....

The remains of a stone crypt at Philippi, which, since the fifth century, has been considered the prison of Paul, stand on the north side of the forum on a hill above the Egnatian Way.

16:24. Paul and Silas were divinely released when the doors of this prison were opened by an earthquake, their Roman citizenship became known, and they were admonished by the Roman authorities to leave the city (Acts 16:37-38).

Amphipolis and Apollonia

Since it was their missionary method to stop in cities that had Jewish synagogues and preach the gospel "to the Jew first and also to the Greek" (Romans 1:16), when Paul and Silas left Philippi, they bypassed Amphipolis and Apollonia. According to Otto Meinardus, a leading Greek archaeologist, there was no synagogue in Amphipolis or Apollonia at this time. Luke may refer to such a strategy by Paul when he says: "They came to Thessalonica, *where there was a synagogue of the Jews*" (Acts 17:1); the natural inference is that Amphipolis and Apollonia had none. No archaeological evidence of a Jewish popula-

tion in either of these cities has been found, although extensive work has been done at Amphipolis, showing it to have been a large and prosperous capital city of the first district of Macedonia.

Excavation has revealed that a wall extended four and one half miles around the city of Amphipolis. A gymnasium, which is really a typical palestra (exercising area) has been partially excavated and its identification confirmed by seven inscriptions.

One lengthy inscription from 21 B.C., found outside the north entrance of the gymnasium, contains an *Ephebic Law* (that is, a Law for Youth), which provides detailed instruction about athletic activities and equipment in the gymnasium as well as references to the city's road system, factories, a theater, and an agora. This confirms the impression of Amphipolis as a major city. Neither the agora nor the theater have been found. Nothing of significance has yet been found at Appollonia.

Top: The author at the wall around Amphipolis. Bottom: Excavations of a gymnasium in Amphipolis.

Excavations of the Roman forum area in Thessalonica, modern Salonika.

Thessalonica, where there was a synagogue of the Jews

The city of Thessalonica is beautifully situated in a natural amphitheater at the head of the Thermaic Gulf. Little is to be seen here from the time of Paul because this second largest city in Greece still functions busily over the buried remains of Roman Thessalonica. Systematic excavations were done here for the Greek Archaeological Service during which a typical rectangular forum with a paved open court and small theater were uncovered.

Berea

Two of the politarch inscriptions are housed in the museum in Thessalonica and another in the museum of Berea, a town Paul visited after leaving Thessalonica (Acts 17:10). The museum and its courtyard in Berea contain a large number of excellent statues, inscriptions, and funerary altars, one of which is a

Opposite: Politarch inscription in Thessalonica. Archaeology has made a positive contribution to a problem that has centered around Thessalonica for many years. Critics of the New Testament asserted that Luke was mistaken in his use of the term *politarkes* ("politarch") for the officials before whom Paul's followers were taken in this city (Acts 17:6). However, an inscription from an arch containing this term was found in the excavations at Thessalonica, and eventually a list of thirty-two inscriptions that contain this term was published, nineteen of which come from Thessalonica. Three of these date to the first century A.D.

ΦΙΛΙΠΠΟΠ
ΓΕΟΠΠΕΡΑΣΑ
ΜΕΝΟΝΕΝΚΑΤΣ
ΣΕΒΑΣΤΟΦΕΙ
ΚΑΙΕΘΗΒΑΡΧΩΝ
ΓΕΠΟΙΕΠΟΙΕΝ
ΤΟΑΥΤΟΣΕΙΚΑΙ
ΠΟΛΕΙΤΑΡΧΗΑΙΣ
ΥΙΟΠΠΑΡΕΙΠΙΑΝΣ
ΦΙΛΙΠΠΟΣΚΑΡ
ΥΙΕΡΕΟΣΚΑΙΑ
ΓΟΝΟΘΕΥΤΗΣ
ΛΑΜΠΡΑΣΘΕΣ
ΣΑΛΟΝΙΠΚΑΤΟΝ
ΚΗΤΡΟΠΟΛΕΩ
ΚΑΙΠΚΟΛΩΝΕΙ
ΑΣΚΑΙΕΤΡΑΚΙΣ
ΝΕΩΚΟΡΟΥ
ΚΑΙΕΥΓΟΝΟΝ
ΜΑΡΕΙΠΙΑΝΣ

Above: Yard of the museum in Berea, which Paul visited after Thessalonica.

Below: The theater in Nicopolis.

stone monument containing an inscription with the name Berea in the center of the top line.

Nicopolis

Years after Paul's release from his first Roman imprisonment, he journeyed to the eastern Mediterranean, left Titus on Crete (Titus 1:5), went to Colosse and visited Philemon as planned (Philemon 22), and then eventually made his way to Macedonia, leaving Timothy at Ephesus (1 Timothy 1:3). During this time Paul wrote 1 Timothy and Titus. Macedonia seems to be the most likely setting for the composition of these two Pastoral Epistles (1 Timothy 1:3), best fitting the historical and geographical setting.

Paul then traveled south to spend the winter on the west coast of Epirus, the southwestern sector of modern Greece. He had stated in his letter to Titus, written from Macedonia, that he intended "to spend the winter there [not here] in Nicopolis" and urged Titus to do his best to join him there (Titus 3:12).

Among the archaeological remains in this city are a small Roman theater, portions of a bathhouse, and fragmentary portions of a stadium.

Perhaps the most important artifact at Nicopolis, located on a hill north of the ancient city, is a monument built by the Roman emperor Augustus Caesar celebrating his victory over Mark Antony and Cleopatra in 31 B.C. Many stones of the monument lie around the southern edge of the hill. They contain portions of a Latin inscription commemorating the victory and dedicating the newly founded city to the Roman god Neptune.

9

ITALY
AND THE BIBLE

ITALY AND THE BIBLE

When Paul made his appeal to Caesar before the Roman governor Festus in Caesarea Maritima (Acts 25:11-12), he was placed under Roman guard and taken by ship to Italy. Along the way the ship stopped at an occasional port. Not all of these ports have archaeological remains from Paul's time.

PAUL'S VOYAGE TO ROME

The boat docked at Myra on the southern coast of Turkey where Paul and those with him disembarked (Acts 27:1, 5), after which the ship continued its journey up the coast toward Adramyttium. The coastline at Myra, which is only 50 miles south of Attalia, is impressive. Myra is located on a natural inlet that runs deep into the peninsula to a harbor whose northern section is now silted like most harbors along the coasts of Turkey. The best-preserved archaeological structure in Myra is the Roman theater.

Traveling by ship in the first century

In Myra, Paul and his companions boarded a grain ship from Alexandria. This ship was typical of those that brought huge cargos of grain from Egypt to Rome (Acts 27:4-6). It was probably a three-masted ship, though most vessels had only two. Archaeology has provided some evidence of ancient boats of this time, and this is helpful in putting Paul's voyage in its proper context. Although excavators have not yet identified an Alexandrian grain ship among the numerous shipwrecks discovered in the Mediterranean world, Lucian, a second century A.D. Greek writer and traveler, wrote about an

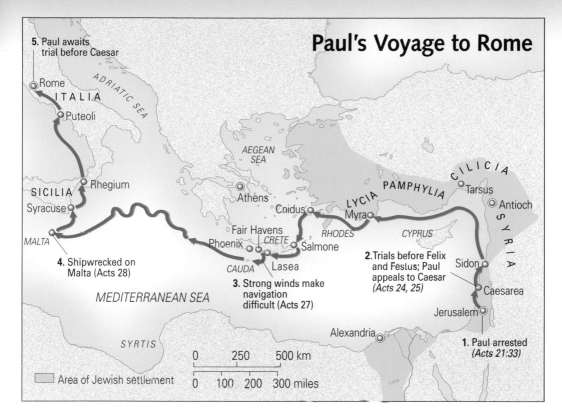

Paul's Voyage to Rome

5. Paul awaits trial before Caesar

Rome
ITALIA
Puteoli

ADRIATIC SEA

AEGEAN SEA

CILICIA

PAMPHYLIA

Tarsus

Antioch

Rhegium

SICILIA

Athens

LYCIA

Syracuse

Cnidus

Myra

SYRIA

MALTA

Fair Havens
Phoenix   CRETE
Salmone

RHODES

CYPRUS

4. Shipwrecked on Malta (Acts 28)

CAUDA   Lasea

2. Trials before Felix and Festus; Paul appeals to Caesar (Acts 24, 25)

Sidon

3. Strong winds make navigation difficult (Acts 27)

Caesarea

MEDITERRANEAN SEA

Jerusalem

Alexandria

SYRTIS

1. Paul arrested (Acts 21:33)

0   250   500 km

Area of Jewish settlement

0   100   200   300 miles

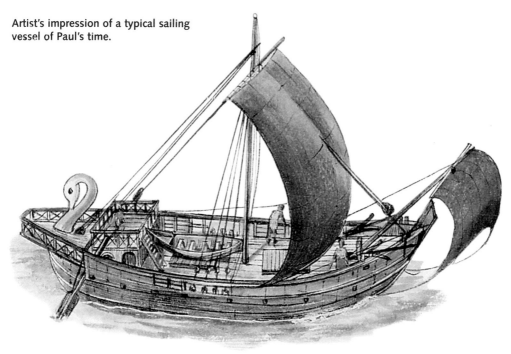

Artist's impression of a typical sailing vessel of Paul's time.

Church at Milqui on Malta. Acts records that while Paul was shipwrecked on the island of Malta he visited Publius. Archaeological remains of a Roman house have been discovered at Milqui, beneath a little stone church named St. Paul's Church, and some archaeologists think it could be the place Paul visited.

Alexandrian grain ship named the *Isis*, which followed a similar route to Paul's ship. He said it was 174 feet (53 meters) in length, 45 feet (14 meters) wide, and had a "crew like an army."

A ship almost this same size, which had a frame larger than that of any known Roman vessel yet discovered, was excavated off the coast of Caesarea. Josephus, the first-century Jewish historian, wrote about sailing for Rome from Judea in a huge boat that carried about 600 people. It foundered in the Sea of Adria along the west coast of Italy, and the passengers had to swim all night in the open sea (as Paul once did, 2 Corinthians 11:25). About eighty were rescued by a vessel from Cyrene that took them to Puteoli, a nearby city on the Italian coast. The total number of people on board Paul's new vessel was most likely 276 (Acts 27:37), although some ancient manuscripts of Acts give the number as only 76.

Paul's ship left Myra and sailed between the islands of Rhodes and Cnidus, where it turned south because of the winds, sailed past Salmone on the eastern end of the island of Crete (Acts 27:7) and on down the leeward east coast, which is protected from the wind. It then turned westward along the southern coast of Crete, where it docked at the port of Fair Havens (Acts 27:8, 12), near the city of Lasea. Since it was the end of the Mediterranean sailing season, which closes from November to February, the crew, seeking a more desirable harbor for the winter, persuaded the Roman centurion not to stay there but to sail a bit farther, to Phoenix, near the west end of the island (Acts 27:11-12).

Smith's Bay, Malta, possible site of Paul's shipwreck.

Shipwrecked on Malta

Before the ship reached Phoenix it lost the protection of the shore and suddenly encountered the tempestuous winds of a "northeaster" (Acts 27:14), a gale coming from the northeast, which blew them south-westward for two weeks to the island of

Mistra Bay is unlikely to be the shipwreck site.

Malta (Acts 27:27ff), just south of Sicily off the toe of the boot of Italy. Malta had been part of the Roman province of Sicily before Augustus put it under its own procurator, who appointed the leading local official of the island to be "the chief man." This title is found in Greek and Latin inscriptions and was accurately used in Acts of Publius, the Roman official on Malta (Acts 28:7).

The place of Paul's shipwreck
The exact spot of the wreck is not known. A current attempt to place it at St. Thomas Bay on the south side of the island has no real support in archaeology or geography. This effort at identification is stated to be on the basis of a discovery of four anchors in the bay and the assertion that this correlates with the mention of four anchors used on Paul's boat (Acts 27:29), but this is totally insufficient grounds for such a conclusion.

After exploring possible sites of the wreck, the author suggests two places that appear to him to be more likely candidates. One is the

271

Remains of Roman Puteoli market area, near the coast of Italy.

beautiful area named Mistra Bay on the north side of the island (see page 271). Luke says in Acts that the northeasterly winds blew the ship southwestward to the island, and they could have blown it into this small bay; the western shoreline, however, seems to be too far inside the bay to fit the story.

Smith's Bay, a little farther north on the same shore, which has been the traditional site for the landing of Paul's ship, seems the most likely choice. The geographical features of the area fit the circumstances described in Acts. The bay opens toward the northeast, and the wind blowing toward the southwest would force the ship's bow into the rocks here.

The approaches to Smith's Bay generally fit well with the soundings reported in Acts 27:28. St. Paul's Island, a small island on the north side of the bay, has a monumental stone statue of Paul standing on its crest, reflective of the tradition of the shipwreck in the bay. Some have argued that the shipwreck never actually happened and that the story is a fabrication. An archaeological team is currently searching for the shipwreck, the discovery of which would silence such agnostic rumor.

The language spoken on Malta was a Phoenician dialect of the Semitic family of languages and so Paul could probably have spoken with the islanders in his native tongue, Aramaic, which was also Semitic. Semitic inscriptions have been found on the island, one of them in Hebrew. The culture was Punic and Punic inscriptions are preserved from the island.

Puteoli, the harbor for Rome

When the sailing season opened again in February or early March, Paul's company boarded an Egyptian vessel from Alexandria, which had spent the three months of the closed sailing season on Malta, and sailed north for Rome, putting in at the harbor in Puteoli (Acts 28:11-13). The normal means of approaching Rome by sea at this time was to sail into Puteoli (modern Pozzuoli), which had a small harbor on the northwestern end of the huge Bay of Naples, and put the passengers ashore. The cargo was then carried on by sea farther north to the port in Ostia. Puteoli had served as the major seaport for Rome until Claudius built the harbor at Ostia, which was closer to Rome. Some remains of the Roman city have been found near the coast, but much of it lies underneath the modern city and has not been excavated.

THE APPIAN WAY

As Paul and his companions continued their journey to Rome from Puteoli, they would have traveled north on suburban roads to Capua where they would intersect the Via Appia (Appian Way), a major national highway that ran from Rome south to Capua and then southeast to Brundisium (Brindisi) on the eastern coast.

Roman highways were normally 13 to 15 feet (4 to 4.5 meters) wide and covered with large polygonal blocks of hard stone. Near Rome the road was covered with basalt stones (formed from volcanic lava), as were the streets in Pompeii and Herculaneum, with no essential difference in their construction in these various places. Running along either side of the Appian Way were slightly raised footpaths, covered with gravel. Most of the Appian Way has been covered with asphalt today, but a section in Rome has been left untouched so that it may be seen as it was when Paul traveled on it.

Paul's imprisonments and death

In the "two whole years" (Acts 28:30) that Paul spent in house arrest during his first imprisonment in Rome, he probably wrote the four "prison letters" (Philemon, Colossians, Ephesians, and Philippians); all of these mention his incarceration. The second letter to Timothy was also written from prison (2 Timothy 4:6-8), but unlike the four prison letters, which anticipate Paul's release, 2 Timothy anticipates his

Part of the Appian Way, near Rome.

Rome

Rome was built on seven hills along the east bank of the Tiber River. The heart of the city was the area between the Palatine and Esquiline Hills, occupied by the Roman forum and the Imperial Fora. This forum had been reconstructed by Julius Caesar. It was the chief marketplace and civic center for the city; here people gathered to conduct commercial, political, and religious affairs. By the first century B.C. the Palatine had become the choicest residential area in Rome, where notables such as Cicero, Mark Antony, and Augustus Caesar lived. In A.D. 52, only five years prior to Paul's arrival, the emperor Caligula completed a new aqueduct in the central area of the city.

View of the Roman forum with the Colosseum beyond.

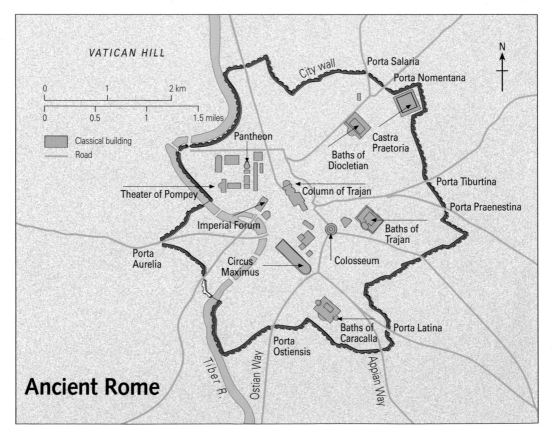

Top: Detail of *Menorah.*

Left: Arch of Titus.

Below left: Close-up of the menorah in the Arch of Titus. Under the Arch of Titus one can see a carving depicting the army carrying away the menorah or lampstand from the Jerusalem temple, adding archaeological credibility to the literary history of the war.

At the west end of the forum was built the Milliarium Aureum (the Golden Milestone) from which were measured the distances to the main cities of the empire. As he entered Rome, Paul would have seen this and many other inscribed milestones marking the distance from Rome. North of the Golden Milestone stood the Umbilicus Romae, which marked the center, not only of Rome, but also of the Roman world.

Ancient arches are found in the forum and throughout the city. In A.D. 70, only a few years after Paul's final return to Rome one of these arches was built by the Roman Senate in honor of Titus' conquest of Jerusalem. It stood in a prominent position on the south end of the forum, and the road into the forum passed under its arch. Titus, son of the Roman emperor Vespasian, became emperor himself in A.D. 79 upon the death of his father.

Left: Colosseum of Vespasian, Titus, and Domitian (exterior view).

The Colosseum

The Colosseum, so named because of the colossal statue of Nero that stood nearby, was on the south side of the Roman forum, and was the most imposing building in ancient Rome, as it is today, but it was not standing when Paul came to Rome. It was begun by the emperor Vespasian (A.D. 69–79) and completed by his sons, the emperors Titus (79–81) and Domitian (81–96). Thus it was standing in the lifetime of the apostle John. The Colosseum measured 617 feet by 512 feet (188 meters by 156 meters) and would seat about 45,000 people. The arena (floor) was 289 feet by 180 feet (88 meters by 55 meters).

A supreme example of the best in Roman architecture, the exterior of the building is still breathtaking. The outer wall rests on eighty piers connected by barrel-vaults made of stone. Three concentric rows of piers on the first three levels provided two

The Circus Maximus, Rome.

parallel passageways, which encircled the building. The external facing on each pier utilized the three basic patterns of Greek architecture in the form of columns with bases and capitals in the Doric, Ionic, and Corinthian orders on the first, second, and third storeys respectively (about 120 feet [36.5 meters] high). A fourth level, added in the early

third century and bringing the height to 157 feet (48 meters), consisted of a plain wall with alternating square Corinthian pilasters and open windows. Some Christians later died in this arena, but most were killed in the Circus Maximus, a short distance west of the Colosseum between the Palatine and Aventine Hills.

The Pantheon in Rome. The Pantheon, a temple to the Roman gods that is still standing in its architectural splendor, was among the many impressive buildings, such as temples and bathhouses, that were built surrounding the central area of Rome.

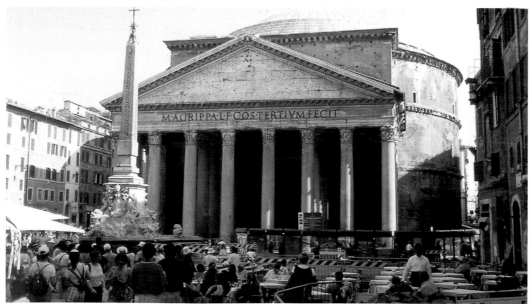

The Mammertine prison, Rome.

death and thus requires a different historical context—his beheading in Rome about A.D. 67 or 68.

Associated with the Roman Forum were two buildings that figured prominently in Paul's final imprisonment (2 Timothy 4:6-8). One of these was the Basilica Julia, where Paul may have heard his death sentence. It was built by Julius Caesar on the western side of the forum.

The second building connected with Paul's imprisonment was the Mammertine Prison, which still stands near the Roman forum at the foot of the Capitoline Hill near the Temple of Concord. Paul probably spent the last days of his life in this prison. A church was constructed there in the sixteenth century and called San Pietro in Carcere, preserving a tradition that Peter was imprisoned there. It is possible that both Peter and Paul were incarcerated in this two-level prison.

According to tradition, Paul was eventually beheaded at Aquae Salviae (modern Tre Fontane) near the third milestone on the Via Ostiense (Ostian Way). A memorial chapel was built at the Aquae Salviae in the fifth century, above which stands the present church of St. Paul at Tre Fontane.

The Church of St. Paul Outside the Walls is located about a mile from the Gate of St. Paul on the Via Ostiense. No significant

Entrance to the Mammertine prison.

Mammertine prison interior.

excavation has been done there, but tradition associates this church with the life of Paul. The site is thought by some to be the location of an earlier church commissioned by Constantine in the fourth century to replace an oratory (private chapel) that had been built over the place where Lucina, a Roman matron, had buried Paul in her vineyard. When the present church was constructed, a marble slab was observed under the altar

Church of St. Paul Outside the Wall.

A stretch of the Ostian Way outside Rome, with shrines and mausolea built beside it.

that read *PAULO APOSTOLO MART[YRI]* in script characteristic of the time of Constantine.

The beautiful building reminds visitors of the words of Paul in his final letter:

> For I am already on the point of being sacrificed; the time of my departure has come. I have fought the good fight, I have finished the race, I have kept the faith. Henceforth there is laid for me the crown of righteousness, which the Lord, the righteous judge, will award to me on that Day, and not only to me but to all who have loved his appearing.
>
> 2 Timothy 4:6-8.

This prompted the respectful and admiring words of Clement of Rome written near the end of the first century:

> Through jealousy and strife Paul showed the way to the prize of endurance; seven times he was in bonds, he was exiled, he was stoned, he was a herald both in the East and in the West, he gained the noble fame of his faith, he taught righteousness to all the world, and when he had reached the limits of the West he gave his testimony before the rulers, and thus passed from the world and was taken up into the Holy Place—the greatest example of endurance.
>
> 1 Clement 5.5-7

RECOMMENDED READING

Averbeck, Richard E., Mark W. Chavalas, and David B. Weisberg, eds. *Life and Culture in the Ancient Near East*, CDL Press, 2003. Nearly two dozen scholars focus on aspects of daily life ranging from biblical and Mesopotamian law, through farming economy in Iron Age Israel, to games people played.

Chavalas, Mark W., and K. Lawson Younger, Jr., eds. *Mesopotamia and the Bible*, Baker Books, 2002. An international group of scholars explore the points of connection between the Bible and its ancient Near Eastern context, specifically Mesopotamia and surrounding areas.

Currid, John D. *Doing Archaeology in the Land of the Bible*, Baker Books, 1999. A brief introduction to the history and methods of archaeological excavation.

Dowley, Tim ed. *Discovering the Bible*, Marshall Pickering/Eerdmans, 1986. This book explores the results of archaeological finds before 1986 which illuminate the backgrounds to the Bible.

Finegan, Jack. *The Archaeology of the New Testament*, Vol. I, Princeton, 1969; Vol. 2, Westview, 1981. A scholarly, authoritative treatment of archaeology and the New Testament.

Hoerth, Alfred J. *Archaeology and the Old Testament*, Baker Books, 1998. A survey of the way archaeology illuminates the history of the Old Testament and the world in which it existed.

Hoerth, Alfred J., Gerald L. Mattingly, and Edwin M. Yamauchi, eds. *Peoples of the Old Testament World*, Baker Books, 1994. A group of leading scholars examine how various ancient powers interacted with the people of the Old Testament.

Hoffmeier, James K. *Israel in Egypt*, Oxford University Press, 1997. An Egyptologist, equally at home in biblical scholarship, responds to those who would question the biblical tradition concerning Israel's sojourn in and exodus from Egypt.

King, Philip J., and Lawrence E. Stager. *Life in Biblical Israel*, Westminster John Knox Press, 2001. A richly illustrated and very readable collaboration between a biblical scholar and an archaeologist as they examine all aspects of life in ancient Israel.

Kitchen, Kenneth A. *On the Reliability of the Old Testament*, Eerdmans, 2003. One of the world's leading Egyptologists expansively marshals Near Eastern evidences which support the historicity of the Old Testament.

McRay, John. *Archaeology and the New Testament*, Baker, 1991. A rather thorough discussion of the archaeological sites in the Mediterranean world that relate to the New Testament.

McRay, John. *Paul: His Life and Teaching*, Baker Book House, 2003. The first half of the book covers the journeys of Paul, exploring the archaeological sites of the cities he visited.

Price, Randall. *The Stones Cry Out*, Harvest House Publishers, 1997. A discussion of what archaeology reveals about the truth of the Bible.

Rast, Walter E. *Through the Ages in Palestinian Archeology*, Trinity Press International, 1992. A semipopular synthesis of the history and archaeology of ancient Palestine, comprehensive, authoritative, and clearly written.

Shanks, Hershel. ed. English edition. *Recent Archaeology in the Land of Israel*, Biblical Archaeology Society, 1984. A collection of leading scholars reporting on all the major areas and periods of Israel's culture and history; a summary of important discoveries since the founding of the state of Israel in 1948.

Shanks, Hershel. *Jerusalem: An Archaeological Biography*, Random House, 1995. The story of Jerusalem is told in its archaeological setting with a wonderful collection of photos celebrating the city's trimillennium as Israel's capital. The book, written by the editor of *Biblical Archaeology Review*, makes Jerusalem as accessible to the layman as to the scholar.

Yamauchi, Edwin M. *Persia and the Bible*, Baker Books, 1990. This noted historian has provided the most complete book available on Persian history as it relates to both the Old and the New Testaments.

Yamauchi, Edwin, M. *Africa and the Bible*, Baker Books, 2004. A scholarly, but readable, look at the role Africa played in biblical history, as well as an examination of current Afrocentric biblical interpretation.

INDEX

A

Abraham 18–19, 32, 37, 40, 76–7, 101, 106
Absalom's Tomb 198
Abu Simbel 85
Achaia 249
Acropolis 249–50
Adad–nirari III 52
agora 220
Ahab 48–9, 54, 120
Ahasuerus 145
Ahaz 52
Ai 108
Akhenaten 82, 84, 107
Albright, William Foxwell 15
Alexander the Great 65, 125, 216
Alexandria 92
alphabet 112
altars 122, 230
Amarna 77, 82, 83
Amarna Letters 107–8
Amenhotep II 80, 82, 109
Amenhotep III 82, 86, 107
Amenhotep IV 82
Amorites 102
Amphipolis 260–61
amulets 124
Anatolia 210–45
annunciation 158
Antalya 242
Antioch on the Orontes 216
Antioch in Pisidia 242–4
Antioch of Syria 237–8
Antiochus IV 127
Antipater 127
Aphrodite 255–6
Apollonia 260–61

Appian Way 273, 278
Ararat, Mount 44, 210
archaeology 10–17
Areopagus 254
Artaxerxes I 132, 145–7
Artaxerxes III 92
Artemis 222, 225
Asklepion 231–2
Aspendos 227
Assurbanipal 60–61
Assurnasipal 48
Assyrian empire 48–61, 120, 122
Athens 249–55
Attalia 241–2
Avaris 82, 83

B

Babel 46
Babylon 61, 63, 124, 134
  fall 65
  hanging gardens 64
  sacked by Hittites 212
Bagatti, Bellarmino 158
Barnabas 240
Baruch 123
Behistun Relief 14, 137
Belshazzar 65, 134
Berea 262–5
Beth Shan 17
Bethany 178–9
Bethesda Pool 189
Bethlehem 155–8
Bethsaida 167
biblical archaeology 11–12
boats 163, 269
Boghazkale 214

Botta, Paul 14
brickmaking 81
Burckhardt, Johan Ludwig 14
Byblos 90

C

Caearea Philippi 170–71
Caesarea Maritima 172–6
Caiaphas 196
Cambyses II 91, 135
Cana 169
Canaanite religion 109
Capernaum 160–64
Carchemish 61, 91
Carmel 49
ceramic typology 15
Chaldean empire 61–5
chariots 19, 53
Chorazin 164
chronology
  Jesus 26
    New Testament 26–9
    Old Testament 17–25
    Paul 27–9
city gates see gates (city)
city states 100, 101
city walls 101, 196
Claudius 28
Cleopatra VII 93
Clermont, Charles 15
coinage 125
Colosseum 276–7
Conder, C. R. 15
Constantine 196
coregency 74
Corinth 192, 255–7
courtyards 102
creation story 42
cuneiform script 14, 32, 47, 64, 108
Cyprus 238–9
Cyrus Cylinder 135
Cyrus II (the Great) 65, 124, 134–5

D

Damascus 206, 207
Dan 102–4, 119–20, 121

Daniel 61, 65, 134
Darius the Great 91, 132, 136–8
dating 15, 19
David 90, 113–16
Dead Sea Scrolls 150–55
Der el-Bahri 86
de Saulcy, F. 15
divorce 40
Dome of the Rock 181, 185

E

Ecbatana 131
Eden 42–4
Edfu 93
Edom 90
Egypt 68–94
    beaten at Carchemish 61
    breaks away from Assyria 60
    divided 83
    and Palestine 79, 109, 119, 125
    and Persian empire 91–2, 146
    and Roman empire 93
Ekrem Akurgal 230
Elephantine papyri 92
Eliezer 106
Enumah Elish 42
Ephesus 218–27
Esarhaddon 59–61
Esau 106
Essenes 150
Esther 145
Eusebius of Caesarea 12
Evil-Merodach 64
excavations 16–18
    sites in Palestine 13
Exodus 81–2, 83
Ezekiel 62
Ezra 146

F

fertility religion 109
Festus 29
flood 44, 46
food 105–6

G

Galilee, Sea of 160
Gallio 28–9
gates (city) 101, 103
    Damascus 206
    Dan 103
    Ephesus 220
    Hattusha 213
    Jericho 108
    Jerusalem 180
    Miletus 245
    Persepolis 142
Gergesa 165–7
Gerizim, Mount 178
Gethsemane 189–90
Gezer 90, 116, 118
Gibeah 113
Gilgamesh Epic 44–6
Giocchino de Alcubierre, Rocco 12
Giza 72–3
Goliath 113
Gordion 216
Gordon, Charles 192
Greece 248–65

H

Haas, Nieu 204
Habiru 107
Hadad 90
Hagar 106
Hammurapi 46, 47, 62, 212
hanging gardens 64
Haran 42
Hasmonean kingdom 127
Hatshepsut 79, 86
Hattusha 212, 213, 214
Hattushili I 212
Hazor 17, 27, 108, 118
Hebron 199
Helena 12, 156, 195
Herakleopolis 74
Herculaneum 12
Herod Agrippa 171
Herod Antipas 164
Herod the Great 127, 176, 199–202

    palaces 191, 201–2
    rebuilds Temple 179, 181
Herodium 200–201
Hezekiah 58–9, 120, 121
    tunnel 121–2, 187
Hierapolis 236
high places 100
Hittites 83, 212–15
Hoshea 52–3, 90
houses
    Ephesus 223–4
    Palestine 111, 161–2
        patriarchal 101–2
    Ur 39, 41
Hyksos 77–8, 79
Hyrcanus, John 127

I

idolatry 96
Iran 130
Iraq 32
Isaac 101
Ishmael 106
Ishtar Gate 63, 64
Israel, divided from Judah 119
Italy 268–81

J

Jacob 101, 106, 107
Jacob's Well 177–8
Jehoahaz 52
Jehoiachin 64–5
Jehoiakim 61
Jehu 49–50, 54
Jericho 96–7, 104, 107–8
    Herod's palace 201–2
Jeroboam 90
Jerusalem 114–15, 179–98
    Bethesda Pool 189
    capital of Judah 120
    Dome of the Rock 181, 185
    fall (586 B.C.) 62
    Garden Tomb 192
    Herod's palace 191
    Hezekiah's tunnel 121–2, 187
    praetorium 192

Sheep Pool 189
Siloam Pool 187–8
size 124
Temple Mount 180–82
walls 196
Jesus
    birth 156
    chronology 26
    crucifixion and burial 192–6
    hometown 158
    miracles 165, 167, 169
John 29, 217
    in Ephesus 225
John; *see also* Revelation
John Mark 240
Joseph 19, 78–9
Josephus 176, 204, 205, 270
Joshua 107–8
Josiah 91
Judah
    attacked by Egypt 90
    divided from Israel 119–23
    fall (586 B.C.) 62
    invasion by Sennacherib 58
judges 109–112

K

Kadesh 213
Karkar 49
Karnak 80, 88
Kenyon, Kathleen 108
Khorsabad 14, 53, 56–7
Kidron Valley 197–8
Kitchener, H. H. 15

L

Lachish 58, 59, 122
    Letters 123
Laodicea 235–6
La Vega, Francesco 12
law codes 46
Layard, Austen 14
Lazarus 179
Lemaire, André 198
libraries 219, 230–31
Libyans 90
Luxor 86

Lydia (Anatolia) 216
Lydia (convert) 232, 258–9

M

Macedonia 216, 248, 257–65
Machpelah, Cave of 199
Malta 270–72
Mammertine prison 278–9
Manasseh 60
Marathon 136–7
Marisa 126–7
Mark Antony 93
Martorellu, Giacopo 12
Mary 158
Masada 202–7
Medes 134
Megiddo 79, 100, 116, 118
Memphis 74
Merenptah 83, 90
    Stele 85, 112
Merodach-baladan 58–9
Mesopotamia 32–65
Miletus 244–5
Milqui 270
Mitanni 212
Moabite Stone 120, 121
monotheism 82
Mordecai 145
Moses 79–82, 107
Murshili I 212

N

Nabonidus 65
Nabopolassar 61
Napata 91
Neapolis 257
Nebuchadnezzar 61–2, 91, 122
    illness 64
    palace in Babylon 64
Necho 91
Nefer 75
Nefertiti 84
Nehemiah 146
New Testament, chronology 26–9
Nicopolis 264, 265
Nimrud 48

Nineveh 14, 55, 59, 60
    falls to Chaldeans 61
Noah 44
nomads 101
Nubia 91
Nuzi texts 46, 106–7

O

Old Testament, chronology 17–25
Omri 120
Ophel, Mount 190
Osorkon IV 90
ossuaries 198
Ostian Way 280

P

Palestine 96–147, 150–207
    excavation sites 14
    in exile 123–4
    invaded by Egypt 79
Pantheon 277
Paphos 239
parchment 231
Parthenon 251
Parthians 65
Pasargadae 131, 136
Patmos 216, 217
patriarchal age 101–7
Paul 173, 207
    chronology 27–9
    in Ephesus 220, 221, 223
    imprisoned in Rome 278
    journey to Rome 268–73
    missionary journeys 236–45, 248
    in Philippi 232, 258–60
Pekah 52
Perga 240–41
Pergamum 229–32
Persepolis 7, 132–4, 138, 139, 141–3
Persian empire 65, 124–5, 130–47
    and Egypt 91, 146
Peter's house 161–2
Petrie, Flinders 15

pharaohs 19
Phasael Tower 191
Philadelphia 234–5
Philippi 258–60
Philistines 83, 112
Phoenicians 115
Phrygians 216
Pi-Ramses 83
Pilate 173
Piraeus 249
Pompeii 12
pottery 15
Psamtik I 91
Ptolemy I 92, 125
Puteoli 272–3
pyramids 71, 72–3, 76–7

Q

Qumran 150–55

R

Ramses I 83
Ramses II 83, 86, 109–112, 213
Ramses III 83
Ramses XI 83
Rawlinson, Henry 14
Redford, Donald 82–3
Revelation 217–18, 226–7
Robinson, Edward 14
Rome 274–9
    Colosseum 276–7
    and Egypt 93
    empire 26–9
    Mammertine prison 278–9
    Pantheon 277
Rosetta Stone 14, 94

S

Sais 91
Sakkara 75
Samaria 53, 120, 177–8
Samaritans 124
Samothrace 248–9
Sarah 76, 106
Sardis 134, 233–4

Sargon II 53, 120
satrapies 137
Saul 112
Schliemann, Heinrich 11
Scythopolis 17
Sea Peoples 83, 112
seals 32, 36
Seetzen, Ulrich 14
Seleucia 216
Seleucids 65, 127, 216
Seleucus I Nicator 216
Sennacherib 54, 58, 59
Sepphoris 168–9
Septuagint 92
Seti I 83, 109
Setnakht 83
Shalmaneser III 48–52
Shalmaneser V 53
Shechem 120, 177–8
Sheep Pool 189
Shiloh 116
Shishak 19, 88–9, 90, 119
Shuppiluliuma I 212
Siamun 90
Siloam Pool 187–8
Sinuhe 101, 105–6
slings 113
Smenkhkare 83
Smith, Eli 14
Smith's Bay 272
Smyrna 228–9
Solomon 90, 116–18
Sparta 146
sphinx 71, 72
sports 82
Susa 132, 133
synagogues 161
Syria 52, 207

T

tablets (writing) 14, 36, 42, 45,
    46, 47, 64, 108
Taharqa 58, 90
Tanis 83
Tarsus 236–7
Taylor Prism 58
Telepinu 212
Tell Beit Mirsim 15

Tell Gezer 10
Tell Hesi 15
tells 16
Temple (Jerusalem) 116–18,
    136
    destroyed (586 B.C.) 62
    rebuilt by Herod 179, 181
Temple Mount 180–82
temples
    Asia Minor 230, 234, 243
    Egypt 86–9
    Greece 255–6
theaters 221, 226–7, 230–31,
    239, 245, 264
Thebes 74, 79, 83, 86, 90
Thessalonica 262
Thiele, Edwin R. 19
Thutmose III 79–82, 107, 212
Thutmose IV 82
Thyatira 232–3
Tiberias 164–5
Tiberius 238
Tiglath–pileser III 52, 53, 120,
    213
Tirzah 120
Titus, Arch of 275
tombs
    Egypt 75, 76
    Palestine 102, 104, 126–7,
        179, 194–8
    Persia 136, 139
Troas 248
Troy 211
Tsafrir, Yoram 204
Tutankhamum 83, 84

U

Ur 36, 37–44
Urartu 44

W

walls (city) 101, 196
Warren, Charles 15
weapons 50, 80, 105
Weber, Karl 12
Woolley, Leonard 44

writing 36, 65, 112, 231; *see also* cuneiform script

X

Xerxes 91, 132, 138–44

Y

Yadin, Yigael 17, 204
Yazilikiya 212

Z

Zedekiah 62
Zias, Joseph 204–5
ziggurats 39, 46